BANKSY
THE BRISTOL LEGACY

BANKSY
THE BRISTOL LEGACY

Edited by **PAUL GOUGH**

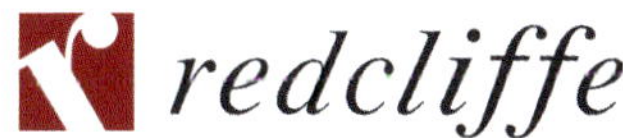

First published in 2012 by Redcliffe Press Ltd., 81g Pembroke Road, Bristol BS8 3EA

www.redcliffepress.co.uk
info@redcliffepress.co.uk
t: 0117 9737207

Follow us on twitter: @RedcliffePress

ISBN 978-1-906593-96-4

Main texts printed in Interstate ExtraLight 10.5

British Library Cataloguing-in-Publication Data
A catalogue record for this book is available from the British Library

Designed by Mark Cavanagh and printed by HSW Print, Tonypandy, Rhondda

Contents

Contents continued

Acknowledgements

A book like this draws upon the expertise and enthusiasm of a great many people. First and foremost I would like to acknowledge Dr Alice Barnaby, Katy Bauer, Maria Bowers, Kate Brindley, Eugene Byrne, Tim Corum, Dr Anna Farthing, John Hudson, Andrew Kelly, David Lee, Andrew Mearman, Anthony Plumridge, Dr Steve Poole, Phil Walker and John Webster.

I am grateful to the great many artists, writers, journalists and experts who met me during the development of this project, sharing their thinking, lending images, and corresponding with me as the book grew and changed shape, amongst them Paul Barnett, Jono Boyle (Motorboy), Felix Braun, Chris Chalkley, Julian Claxton, Nicola Donovan, Sam Downie, Julie Finch, Harry Gough, John Hallett, Paul Hassan, Julian Perry, Dr John Manley, Shawn Sobers, Stic, Paul at 'King of Paint', Dee Smart, Janet Wilkinson, and Wilf Whitty.

The editor and publishers wish to thank the Pest Control Office for consent to reproduce Banksy images in this book, and extend their gratitude to Simon Galloway and colleagues at the *Bristol Evening Post* for allowing access to their picture archive. David Emeney at Bristol Record office was a great help in supplying images from the 2009 exhibition. Thanks also to photographer Stephen Morris for allowing me to use photographs from his book of graffiti images published by Redcliffe Press.

As ever, I am deeply indebted to Clara Hudson for her logistical genius and ability to source the most obscure image, and I pay homage to the venerable John Sansom whose faith in this project never wavered and whose enthusiasm rarely waned, even if we sometimes differed in our views on Banksy as *agent provocateur*, polemicist and artist.

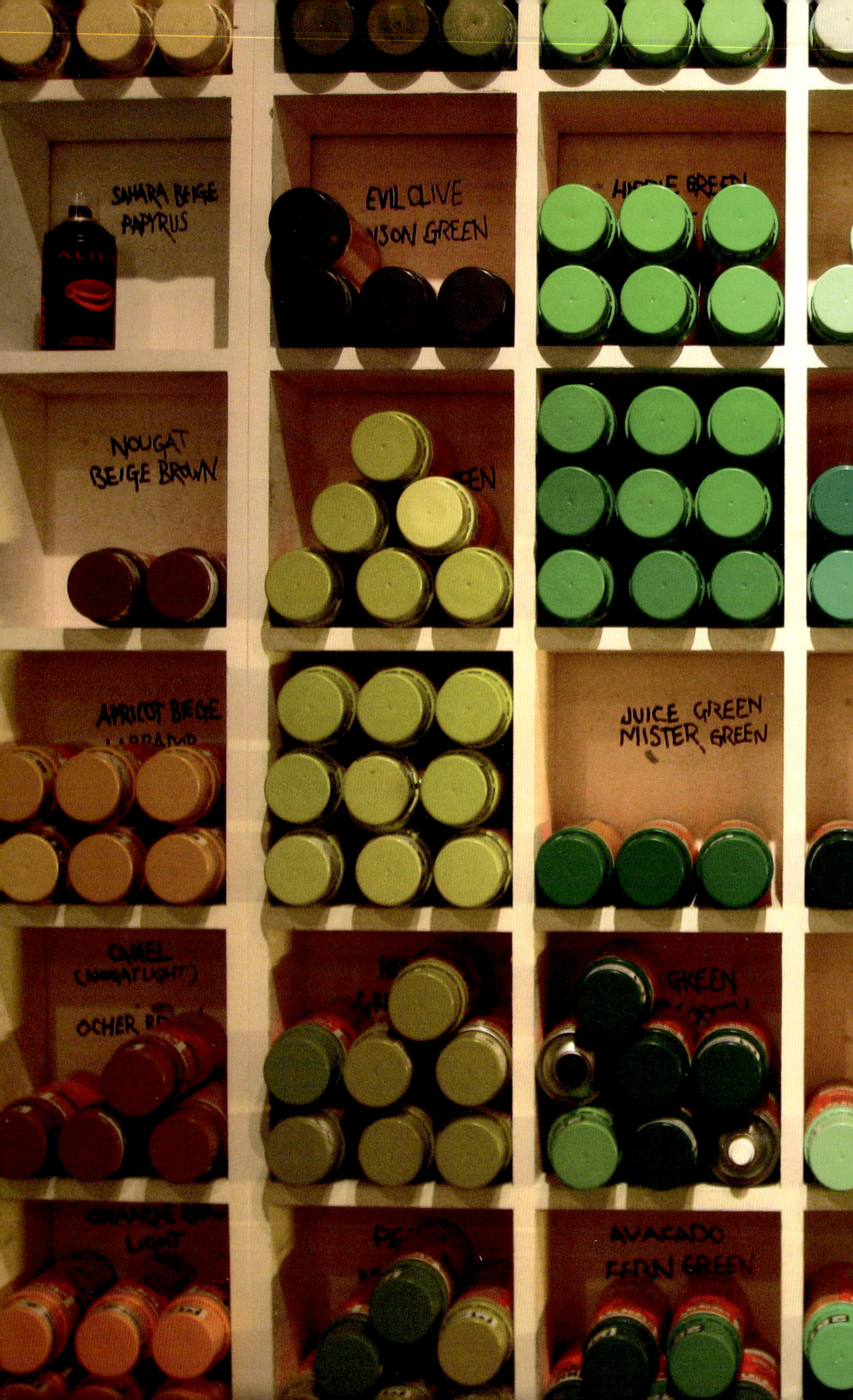

SAHARA BEIGE
PAPYRUS
EVIL OLIVE
...SON GREEN
HIPPIE GREEN
CALY
NOUGAT
BEIGE BROWN
EEN
APRICOT BEIGE
JUICE GREEN
MISTER GREEN
TUR
CAMEL
(NOUGAT LIGHT)
OCHER B
GREEN
SE
ME
ORANGE B
LIGHT
PE
AVACADO
FERN GREEN
M

Introduction
Banksy: Painter, Prankster, Polemicist
Paul Gough

Everyone asks the same two questions: 'Have you actually met Banksy?' and 'Does he know you are writing this book?' Answer to the first: 'Possibly; but how would I know?'; answer to the second: 'Probably, but why do you think it's important?' These and other frequently asked questions – and my cryptic responses – reveal several things about us and Banksy: first, our continuing fascination with this most secretive of public artists; secondly, a begrudging respect at times bordering on genuine affection for his role as a spokesman on contemporary matters; and thirdly, the British fascination with the 'whodunnit', who exactly is this person about whom so much is apparently known but who chooses anonymity and absence over visibility and instant recognition. Banksy's absence throws down a blatant challenge to our cult of instant celebrity. His is the missing face from the weekly glossy gossip mags; a global 'name' who simply refuses to reveal himself; the empty seat on the ubiquitous chat show.[1]

By choosing to be notoriously reclusive, Banksy has become a celebrity figure inside both the DIY activist communities and in mainstream popular culture.[2] Far from alienating him from the British public, his closely guarded identity appears to have endeared him to many who have become tired of the self-regarding, hi-visibility of many 'celebrities' whether they be TV cooks, overpaid footballers, or peripheral royals. However, despite the many who revere the humorous and subversive nature of his artwork, there are as many others who regard it as simply criminal; those law enforcement figures who view any illegal painting in public spaces as little more than wilful vandalism; other street painters who see his work as little more than a sequence of stunts (and who believe street art should stay in the street not in neat frames on the gallery wall), and others who regard Banksy as a clownish one-liner, a prankster with attitude and a spray can. In his public statements Banksy cleverly toys with these disparate views, threatening on the one hand that 'A wall is a very big weapon. It's one of the nastiest things you can hit someone with'[3] while raising Calvino-esque poetic aspirations on the other:

> *Imagine a city where graffiti wasn't illegal, a city where everybody could draw whatever they liked. Where every street was awash with a million colours and little phrases. Where standing at a bus stop was never boring. A city that felt like a party where everyone was invited, not just the estate agents and barons of big business. Imagine a city like that and stop leaning against the wall – it's wet.[4]*

This book offers a platform to a variety of views, to voices of dissent questioning some of the aesthetics and ethics behind his work, to those who revere his contribution to the culture of our over-furnished cities. Above all, this book sets out to locate the Banksy phenomenon within a wider socio-economic-cultural context in the aftermath of the 2009 exhibition in Bristol, aptly named 'Banksy versus Bristol Museum'. It was not difficult to garner strong views. Everyone, it seems, has a Banksy story: a recollection, an anecdote, an opinion about one of his artworks, or more than likely a 'queue' story.

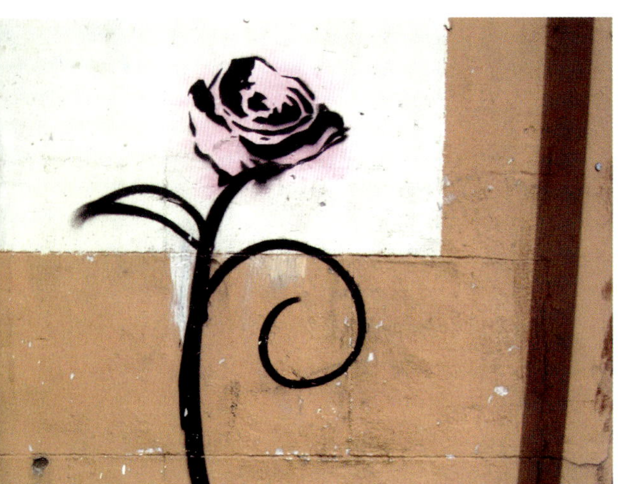

Seeing Banksy or anonymous street art is a daily occurrence in Bristol. This 'Rose' stencil, by an unknown artist, is in the Hotwell Road, Bristol. [photograph: Harry Gough October 2011]

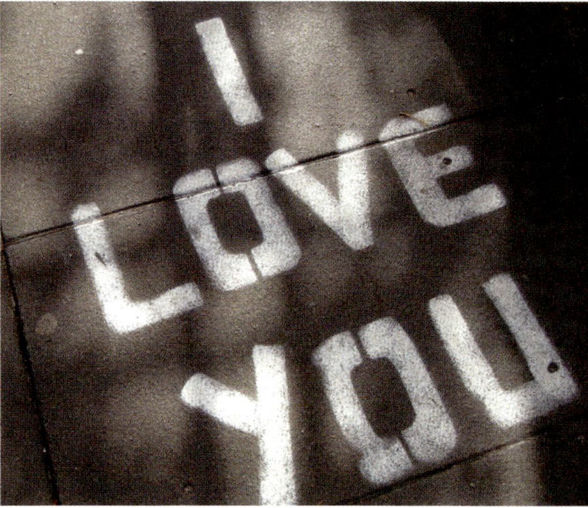

I love you: another example of a random stencil in central Bristol, Gaol Ferry Bridge, Bristol [photograph: Harry Gough October 2011]

During the making of this book I heard a great many such stories, freely and generously re-told, often richly embellished, and resonating in ways that one would never expect to hear about 'conventional' pieces of art in a gallery. Many of these personal narratives (indeed some of the contributions in this book) were offered by people who had heard of the project and wanted, in some way, to be part of it. One woman volunteered this tale:

The Banksy work at the bottom of Park Street is a source of fascination for my five year old son and we pass it on the way to school and on the way back. He has multiple questions mainly starting with the word 'why.....?' and relating to each of the characters painted. It has really tested me to continue to find age-appropriate answers to the questions of fidelity. We've been through a few stages that have covered.... 'he's hiding'.... 'he's angry'.... and our latest (and so far satisfactory) interpretation is 'whether it is okay to be naked in someone else's house?' My little one has so far agreed that it isn't necessarily a good idea. It has made me think ahead about how we deal with questions of relationships and answer honestly but in an appropriate way and how the questions I'll need to answer in the next 4-5 years will be much more testing. My observation is that public art has the

Others who offered their thoughts had queued in the interminable lines outside the gallery; others had failed in their attempt to see the show, thinking there would be plenty of time but eventually realizing there wasn't. Instead they had to resort to the hundreds of newspaper reviews, the thousands of pictures taken by visitors and shared on *Flickr* or other social networking sites, and of course there is the rather brilliant 'official trailer' on *YouTube*, which concludes with a PG Certificate and the warning 'Contains scenes of a childish nature some adults may find disappointing'.[6]

As both a teaser for the show and the nearest we may have to an artist-sanctioned synopsis of the event it seems wholly authentic, except perhaps for one very short sequence (two seconds long, 54 seconds in) which captures at close quarters the figure of Sir Nicholas Serota, Director of the Tate, striding up the steep hill of Park Street ostensibly *en route* to the Banksy show. Sandwiched between footage of a hooded figure spray-painting through a stencil, Serota seems to be answering the question 'What d'you think of Banksy', to which an overdubbed voice answers 'he's frighteningly amazing'. Shot within inches of the Director's face the words might actually be 'frightening and amazing'. Whatever the words, they're patently not Serota's.

By contrast every word in this book is authentic; most authors happy to reveal themselves and to share their reflections of the show and its aftermath. The aim of this book was not to reveal the identity of the artist, nor to uncover how the show was created, although some of the contributors hint at both. Its aim was to try to evaluate the legacy of the show, to ask if there was an estimable impact, a lingering influence on Bristol, on its culture, on the museums, and whether this could be evaluated in economic terms.

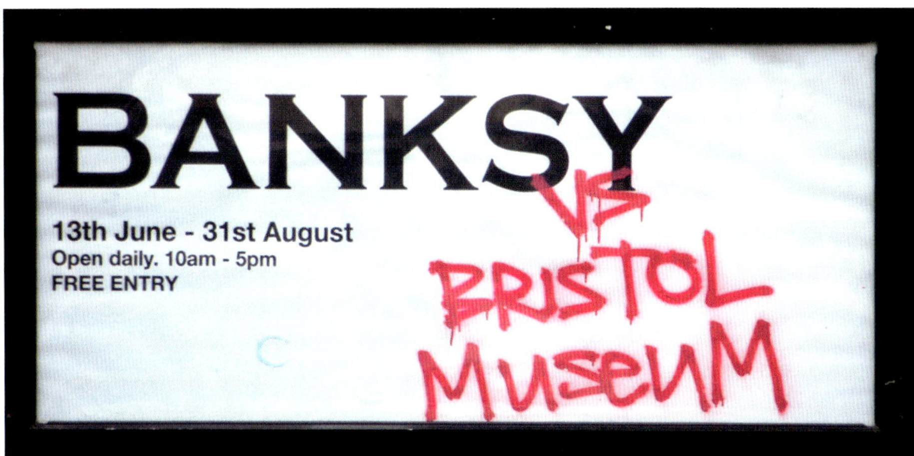

The Queen's Road poster for the ground-breaking Banksy exhibition.
[photograph: Dr John Manley]

Clearly, the first port of call had to be the museum itself. Not the most settled of workplaces on the eve of the show, it had been blighted by a 'staff-management dispute' for some time that year as the then Director was leading a programme of re-structuring and staff 'downsizing' to meet wider budget constraints and realignment of the service.[7] As others relate elsewhere in this book, the show caught its own staff by surprise, many were delighted, a few though were actually unpleasantly surprised, feeling that their integrity as curators had been compromised by 'intruders' having the freedom of their collections. I recall walking past the museum on the Thursday evening before the unveiling and peering into the rather scruffily masked plate windows, taped over with sheets of paper, the doors labelled with A4 notices 'Closed For Essential Maintenance Work'.

We now know that the weeks leading up to those frantic few days of installation had been fraught indeed. Significantly, it started with a cold call from the artist himself. The curators who picked it up and ran with the idea were running quite a risk; after all in mid-2009 Banksy was still an outlaw to many in the council. The waste and cleaning department had been irritated by the popular vote to preserve the Banksy painting of the naked man opposite the Council House.[8] After all, although Banksy clearly had a deep affection for the museum recollected from his many childhood visits, in 1998 he had commented tongue in cheek that:

> *As far as I can tell the only thing worth looking at in most museums of art is all the schoolgirls on daytrips with the art departments.*[9]

The curators had to conduct clandestine mobile phone conversations in quiet corners of normally crowded museum offices, a relationship of trust had to be established, and negotiations conducted using code-words and pseudonyms. Surprise was paramount. Anonymity had to be assured at all times. Fewer than six staff across the whole of the city council knew about the Banksy project and they agonised over whether it was some horrible hoax that would ricochet badly.

It might surprise many to learn that a contractual agreement was actually drawn up between Banksy, his crew and the City Council. Graffiti artists don't normally 'do' contracts. Civil servants don't do much without them. However, without some form of contract Banksy couldn't dictate his own terms and the museum would run the risk of being badly exposed should something go wrong. It can still be viewed online – all 14 pages of it – redacted (blacked out) in many places, and accompanied by numerous emails one of which begs the artist to 'stay schtum' as the museum and their lawyers clamber up the 'mountain of work' that faced them.[10]

Given the eventual success of the show it's now hard to remember the actualities of the time. The stakes were high on both sides. Not only had the cultural chiefs closed their flagship building for over 48 hours without being able to tell their own staff why, but they had allowed what some might regard as a motley crew of hooded youth and 'urban guerillas' the freedom to roam at will amongst galleries of rather expensive paintings, rooms full of historic artefacts, and the largest collection of Chinese ceramicware in Europe. And, of course, they had no idea what to expect when the doors were opened to the public. In the end the top team at the museum – Paul Barnett, Kate Brindley, Tim Corum and Phil Walker – pulled it off and their story is told in this book.

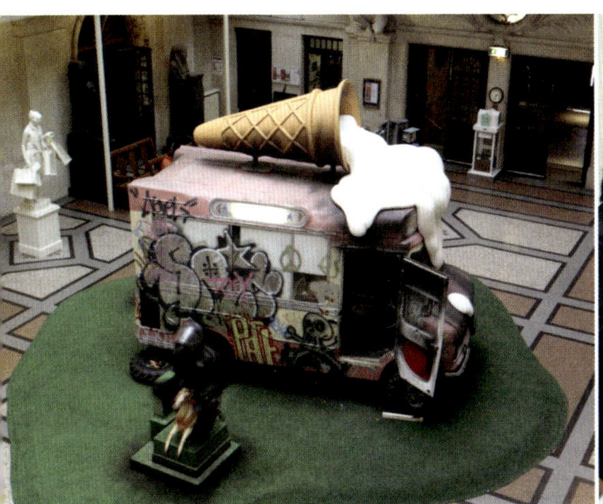

The sight that greeted unsuspecting museum staff arriving for work on the opening day. The choice of ice-cream van was not random or a mere whimsy. In a BBC Radio 4 documentary on ice-cream vans (30 July 2011) Banksy, his voice heavily disguised, recalled with affection 'the classic Bedford, gloopy tiny little row of headlights shining out from a droopy bonnet; yeah, it was made for selling ice-cream right? Because it looked like one.' Adding, with characteristic edge, 'it was a childhood thing gone wrong, really; slight loss of innocence, the broken shards of a burnt-out husk of Britain – but still with a soft centre.' (photograph: Bristol Museum & Art Gallery)

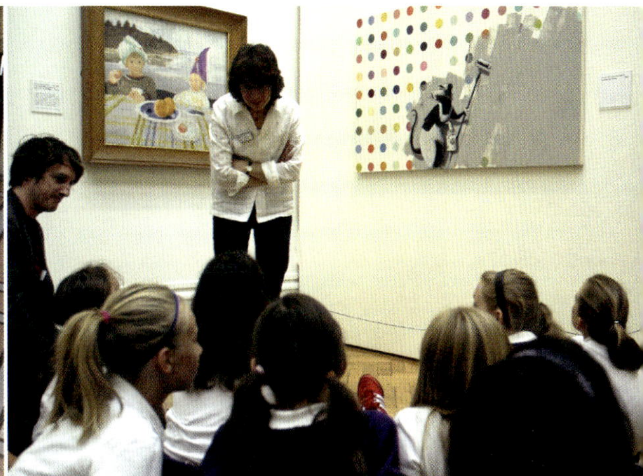

Banksy Defaced Hirst, 2009. Children on a school visit are introduced to Banksy's work at Bristol Art Gallery. [photograph: Nadia Nasser]

They don't, however, tell the full detail of the story and neither should we expect to have it revealed. Anonymity is essential to the Banksy myth. Still, it would have been fascinating to know how he and his crew managed to drag and assemble an ice-cream van into the lobby of the museum, or how they actually placed the orange-suited Guantanamo Bay figure in the middle of the flimsy balsa-wood box aeroplane that hovers over the main entrance. The 'How Did He Do That?' questions were never answered, nor did I really expect them to be. The curators had entered into a pact with Banksy and his crew which they did not want to compromise, not least because they might want to work with him and his team again, but primarily because they respected him and his team of fabricators, decorators, animatronic-ists, and installation professionals. A 'reveal' was not going to happen: that was the deal. That deal, however, didn't stop national newspapers (allegedly initiated by *The Daily Mail*) from filing repeated Freedom of Information requests asking to see copies of any written correspondence, data, or transcripts of phone calls between the artist and the museum. Under pressure as a publicly funded body to release something, the museum eventually reproduced a heavily redacted copy of the contract and an extensive sequence of email exchanges. Fascinating as these are they don't reveal much, but they made a striking headline for the national press and pacified those in authority who feared that the council, the museum and the collection had been violated by the hoody and his crew.[11]

Although some contributors suggest in this book that they know the 'true' identity of Banksy (indeed that 'fact' can be found within a few seconds on *Wikipedia*) the general public seems to have actually lost interest. By comparison, there is an increasing interest in how a large city like Bristol relates to Banksy, how he and his breed of artists *speak* for the city, and somehow represent a dimension of the city that is often difficult to quantify – its 'spirit of innovation, creativity and unorthodoxy'[12] or what the UK *Rough Guide* describes as an unusual blend of 'new technologies, the arts and a vibrant youth culture [that] have helped to make this one of Britain's most cutting edge cities.'[13]

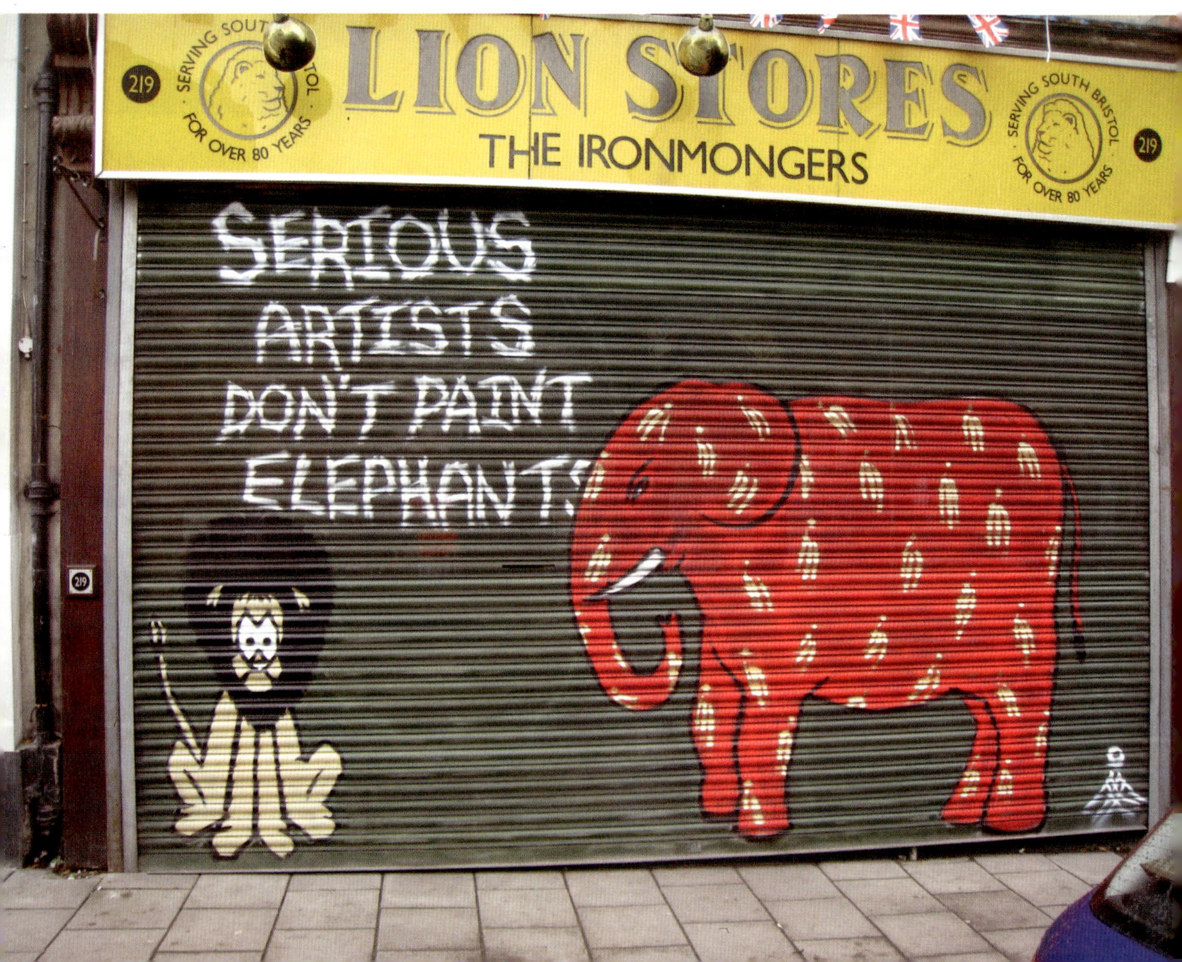

Cities however can easily forget. And as several contributors to this book loudly argue, Bristol has done its fair share of strategic forgetting. So, this book attempts to recall, remember and remonstrate with the easy amnesia that characterizes urban memory. It does so by asking several questions: what was the impact of the Banksy show in 2009 on the city of Bristol, on its earnings at the time and afterwards, on the businesses that benefited directly and indirectly from such a blockbuster show; what have been the mid- to long-term effects on the cultural sector in the city-region; what, if any, the impact on museum policies, direction-of-travel and its relationship to the community of artists that produce street art; what opportunities were missed (or taken) in re-positioning the city authorities and their relationship to its cultural players. The book suggests that there have been both some predictable and some unforeseen consequences to the show: in the more predictable column we might include the major street art show of 2011 – 'See No Evil' – and the annual UPFest (Urban Paint Festival) which have now become part of the Bristol *zeitgeist*; less predictable is the interest in issues of heritage and preservation, the move to recognise Banksy and his ilk as the creators of venerable *objets d'art* that must be looked after and valued as cultural markers. That could not have happened without the show in 2009, nor would the gathering of feisty street artists in Bristol museum during 2010 as part of a Research Council-funded project called 'Design Against Crime', which brought together a couple of dozen artists, gallery curators, Council community liaison officers, and academics like me squirrelled away in a corner taking notes and trying to understand the peculiar vernacular of tagging, buffing, and 'green walls'.[14]

The gathering suggested how amenable (at least on the surface) the city of Bristol has become in the past five years to hosting street art, regarding it not as a curse on its architecture but an aesthetic gift to the public.[15] It now takes the form of a 'street dialogue' in which the urban scene has become the subject and background of 'an infinite flow of coded messages and interferences'.[16] Artists such as Stic and Motorboy gave convincing and committed presentations, arguing that local authorities would actually save considerable sums of money if they courted urban painters, collaborating with them and with property owners to create dedicated spaces for their graffiti. Across the UK most councils had a reputation for being negative and hostile to street art, harassing and arresting perpetrators, painting over their work. The uniform grey of municipal censorship was described by one artist as 'the greatest act of minimalist painting in the world.'

A fellow street artist's commentary on Banksy's notorious decoration of an elephant for his 2006 exhibition in Los Angeles; the animal, called Tai, was covered in pink and gold paint and placed in a mocked-up house to represent how world poverty is widely ignored. This comment was painted at the Bristol UPFest, June 2011. [photograph: Harry Gough]

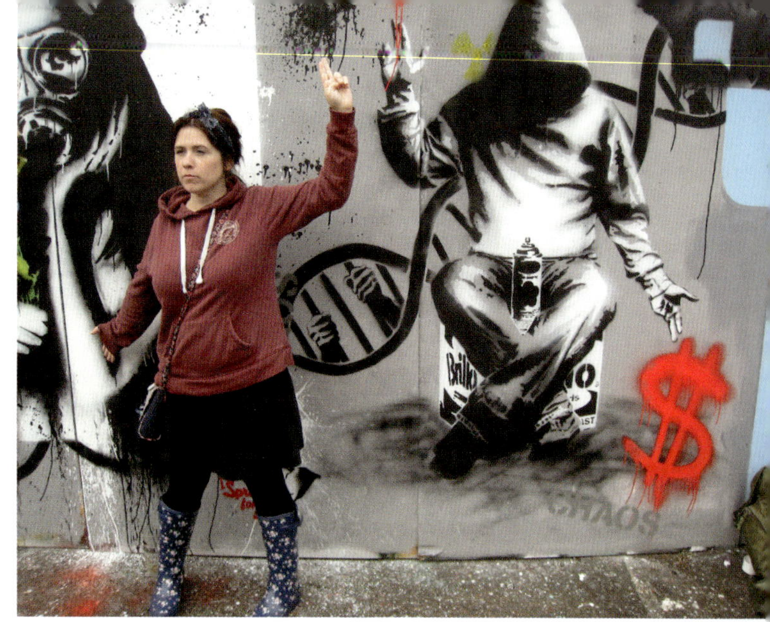

Visitor enjoying the UPFest
at Bedminster, 2011.
(photographs: Paul Gough)

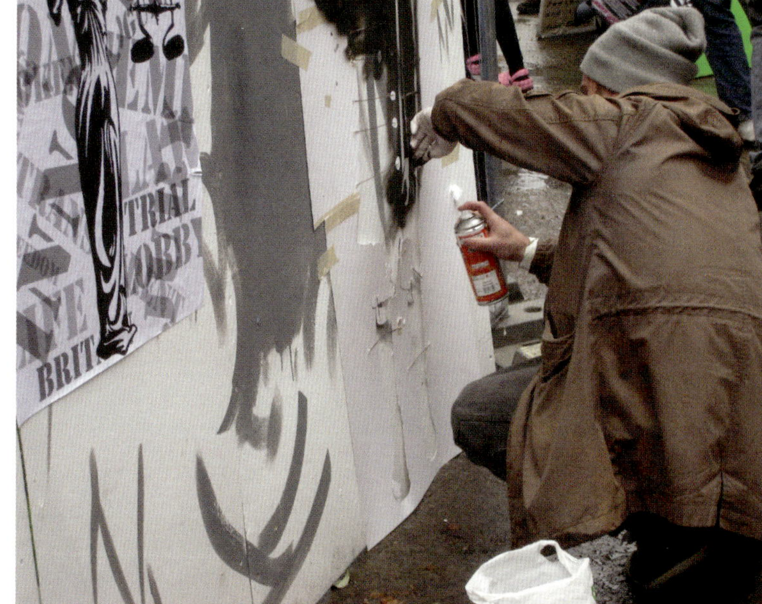

Street artist at work during
the UPFest.

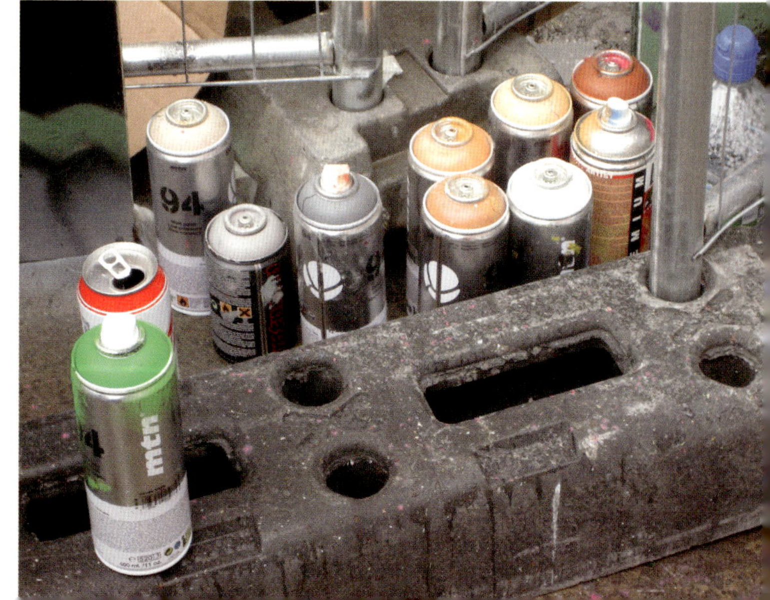

Spray cans ready for action.

Each of the contributors to this book has addressed the question of legacy and impact. The first section of the book sets the scene, starting with a potted biography of the world's most elusive artist by veteran correspondent John Hudson. This is followed by several essays that locate Bristol as a city with a rich history of radical dissent and division. Historian Dr Steve Poole discusses the hastily-scribbled or scratched calligraphic mark as the signature of urban protest, and in an essay on 'the versus habit' I trace the tensions that linger, and occasionally erupt, under the carapace of the city. The Banksy show, argues curator Kath Cockshaw, was preceded by an equally seismic event in an equally hallowed gallery. Her essay on 'Crimes of Passion' concludes this initial series of essays that set the context for the show and identify its wider origins.

The middle section of the book looks at the show itself. As principal architects of the exhibition Kate Brindley and colleagues throw some light – though not the full beam – on their front-line role in staging the exhibition. One person who spent possibly more time 'working the queues' than anyone else that summer was the curator Katy Bauer whose innovative book *The Banksy Q* captured the raw enthusiasm and sticking power of the tens of thousands who travelled from far and wide to see the work. Her reflective essay locates the Banksy phenomenon in the widest political context and examines its roots in the Stokes Croft social scene. Eugene Byrne, a writer who few can match for his granular reading of the city, examines the immediate impact of the show and the artist's ambivalent relationship with 'official' Bristol. Cultural impresario and historian Andrew Kelly offers a panoramic view of not only how the show immediately reverberated, but how it was also played out through a network of educational projects and associated events, which were deeply attuned to the many communities touched by Banksy's work. Aware that many consider the artist to be little more than a witty one-line 'quality vandal', Kelly celebrates his more generous attributes and, as someone who also stages exhibitions, events and arts festivals concludes, 'I long for the day when I can see those queues again.'

Which brings us to the third section of the book, where we attempt a judgment of the show from a number of vantage points. As someone deeply committed to bringing museum collections to life for the widest array of people, Dr Anna Farthing asks the knock-out question: who won? Her thoughtful and rhetorical answer is followed by a cool economic assessment by two business historians Anthony Plumridge and Andrew Mearman, who bring to bear evaluation and costing tool-kits to ask a number of questions about official statistics, hyperbole and civic sentiment. John Sansom explores one of the most visible manifestations of the Banksy legacy: the urban paint festival held in August 2011 under the rubric 'See No Evil' which took place in an inner-city front-line urban trench sandwiched between new shopping arcades and rather threadbare office blocks. He discerns an official anxiety to appear inclusive and cutting edge, and also reminds us that in these excitable times the question should be not 'is it art?' but 'is it good art?' Another sceptical voice concludes this evaluative section of the book: with characteristic wit and an inimitable approach, art critic David Lee offers a sobering assessment of Banksy's iconography. Drawing provocative comparisons with other 'amateur' art exhibitions held in the city more recently Lee draws some interesting broad conclusions suggesting that the 2009 Banksy exhibition may yet be seen to have marked a watershed in the State's reaction to popular art.

Drawing up the rear is an essay by lawyer John Webster who suggests that, given their cultural and financial value to a city, Banksy street paintings could benefit from the protection of listing through the British planning system. This is followed by a short essay on the art of stencilling, the urban calligraphy which has become Banksy's trademark. A bibliography of further reading and viewing drawn up by Dr Alice Barnaby concludes the book.

In truth, I could have included many other essays. Once word was out that I was embarking on this project I was inundated with stories, anecdotes, photographs and illustrations. The wave of generosity and interest was impressive and touching, although there were also those who wanted to express a personal note and room has been found for these voices too. The Banksy story shows no sign of abating – it is lively, current and dynamic. The 2009 exhibition was just a staging post in a longer narrative about the city, its streets and its mutating identity, or as Banksy puts it:

> *Graffiti ultimately wins out over proper art because it becomes part of your city, it's a tool; 'I'll meet you in that pub, you know, the one opposite that wall with a picture of a monkey holding a chainsaw'. I mean, how much more useful can a painting be than that?*

Dr Paul Gough is the Professor of Fine Arts and Deputy Vice-Chancellor at the University of the West of England, Bristol. A painter, broadcaster and writer, he has exhibited widely in the UK and abroad, and is represented in the permanent collection of the Imperial War Museum, London, the Canadian War Museum, Ottawa, and the National War Memorial, New Zealand. In addition to numerous roles in national and international higher education, his research into the imagery of war and peace has been presented to audiences throughout the world, and in numerous journals and books. He has published three books with Sansom & Company: a monograph on *Stanley Spencer: Journey to Burghclere*, in 2006; *A Terrible Beauty: British Artists in the First World War* was published in 2010, and *Your Loving Friend, the Great War correspondence between Stanley Spencer and Desmond Chute*, in 2011.

Notes

1. I am making the popular (but unjustified) assumption that Banksy is male. Sam Downie, a digital noisemaker based in Bristol, has told me that 'Banksy' is not so much a single individual, rather it is a network of Bristol characters, a 'family tree' that would include Massive Attack, Tricky, many artists, writers and performers. However, every encounter I have had with those who have worked with the artist describe him as male.

2. Emily Truman (2010) 'The (In)Visible Artist: Stencil Graffiti, Activist Art, and the Value of Visual Public Space'. *SHIFT: Queen's Journal of Visual & Material Culture*. Issue 3, 2010, pp.1-15.

3. Banksy, *Banging your Head against a Brick Wall*, Weapons of Mass Distraction: London, 2001.

4. Banksy, *Wall and Piece*, Century: London, 2005, p.85.

5. Janet Wilkinson, correspondence with the author, June 2011. I am also grateful to Nicola Donovan for her observations about the exhibition which have been incorporated into this section of the Introduction.

6. www.youtube.com/watch?v=lRai9x8aD3A&feature=player_embedded/ accessed 7 October 2011, by which dates there were 949,122 hits, of which 2,061 were 'likes', 44 'dislikes'.

7. Agenda item 2 at the Bristol City Council Museums and Archives Select Committee held on 23 March 2009 (a few months before the Banksy show opened) contained a letter signed by over seventy museum staff which posed six penetrating questions regarding the future staffing of the service. The first stated:

> *Was the Select Committee aware that in December 2008, the three unions which represent the staff of the service lodged an official letter of 'dispute' with the senior management, on behalf of their collective membership, over the proposed new staffing structure?*

In addition to letters of protest from eminent organisations and individuals, the last page of the official record carried an angry letter from Professor Bernard E Leake, FRSE, which read:

'I am appalled at proposals to reduce the dedicated Geology curatorial staff in the City Museum. I lived in Cotham for 17 years & I know, as former Keeper of the Geological Collections in the Hunterian Museum, Glasgow, that you cannot look after the very valuable collections that have been donated to you over nearly 200 years without expert Geologically-trained staff. At a time when there is unprecedented interest among the public & young people in environmental matters, to reduce the City support for geological material, which is the main source of information about past Earth environments, & leave the displays to 'fossilise' in neglect, due to diverting the resources into 'visual arts' or other matters, will not receive the support of most Bristolians or scientists in general. It will result in an outcry nationally as well.' (p.14)

8. Not many months earlier the telephone number of the City Council's Chief Executive had been daubed on a wall which once sported some impressive graffiti but which had been cleaned, despite local protest, by the municipal authorities. Even during the course of the Banksy show the Council had to apologise after a piece of street art in Bristol was painted over for a second time. (see BBC Bristol, 22 July 2009)

9. Banksy, quoted in numerous websites. Most of the material attributed to Banksy is pithy and rather memorable: 'The artist Paul Klee said "drawing is like taking a line for a walk", but for me it's always been more like drowning a photocopier in a canal' and in *Time Out*, 'I plead not guilty to selling out. But I plead it from a bigger house than I used to live in.'

10. Kate Brindley, heavily redacted email headed 'Fwd: Freedom of Information Request' to Banksy (?) sent 22 June 2009, available as four PDF attachments on-line from www.culture24.org.uk/art/art71021/ accessed 8 October 2011.
Page seven of the May 2009 version of the Contractual Agreement includes the detail of the costs (£1) paid by the Museum to the artist to stage the show, although paragraphs 5.2, 5.3, and 5.4 are all excised in what is the most heavily redacted portion of the paperwork that was released.

11. In the email exchanges certain names and highly-sensitive information such as the value and insurance costs of individual works were obscured with black ink. There are no direct references to the artist, but passages carry the initials of the Pest Control Office (PCO) responsible for verifying Banksy works. There is also a letter from Bristol City Council's legal team which describes the artist's anonymity as 'crucial to his commercial interests'. The papers released under the Freedom of Information Act were made available from 14 August 2009. The handling of the Banksy team, the press and the public was made the basis of a case study by the MLA (Museums, Library and Archives), and is available on: www.research.mla.gov.uk/case-studies/display-case-study.php?prnt=1&prjid=558/ accessed 10 October 2011.

12. This phrase is taken from the *Yellow Railroad* report created for 'Destination Bristol' in 2010. The sentiment is endorsed in a number of other sources amongst them the 2010 McKinsey/World Economic Forum Innovation Map, which states: 'Bristol is a hotspring of innovation in the global innovation 'heat map'.'

13. Bristol, *The Rough Guide to the UK* 2010. Opening the Bristol and Bath Science Park (SPark) in April 2008, Lord Sainsbury said: 'Bristol is unique in combining excellence in new technologies and creative content. It is this cross over which marks it out.'

14. 'Design Against Crime' is a socially responsive, practice-led research centre located at Central Saint Martins College of Art and Design, University of the Arts, London. 'Buffing' is the street-art term for a piece of graffiti removed by the authorities; a 'green wall' is a public space grown with plants or trees to prevent it being painted or tagged. See 'A Graffiti Glossary', www.graffiti.org/faq/graffiti.glossary.html/ accessed 12 October 2011.

15. Jennifer Harris (2011) 'Guerilla art, social value and absent heritage fabric', *International Journal of Heritage Studies*, Vol.17, No.3, May 2011, 214-229, p.219.

16. Christine Dew (2007) *Uncommissioned Art: an A-Z of Australian Graffiti*, Melbourne: The Miegunyah Press, p.13.

17. Banksy, *Banging your Head against a Brick Wall*, Weapons of Mass Distraction: London, 2001.

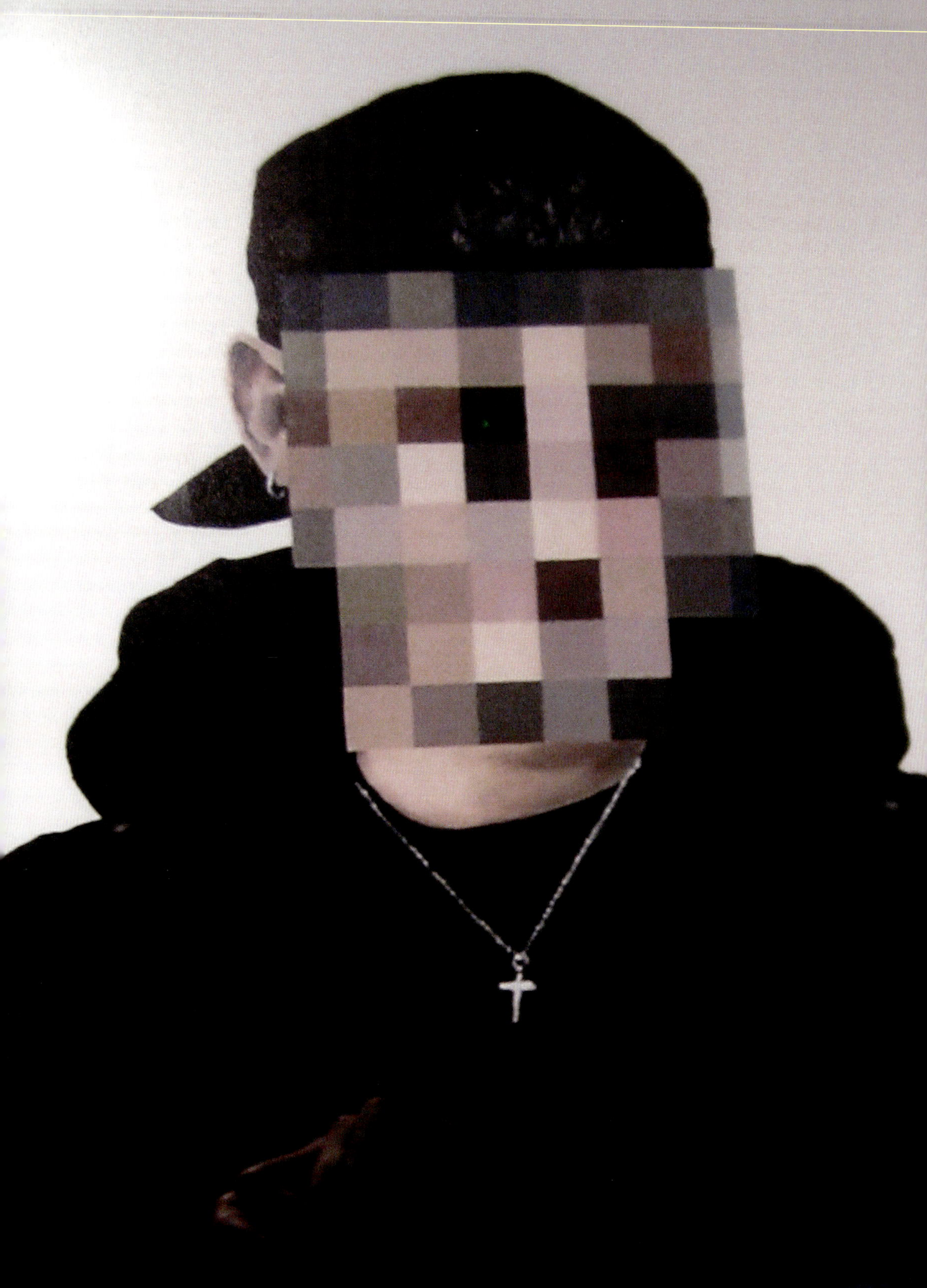

Is this the mystery man? This image is to be seen at the dockside MShed Museum, Bristol. [photograph: Paul Gough]

Banksy: the story so far ...

John Hudson

To the press and public, the question of Banksy's identity is at least as intriguing as the legitimacy of his work and the price that celebrities and other wealthy patrons are prepared to pay for it. His and his circle's great triumph has been in their ongoing ability to keep that identity swathed in mystery, even though the artist's name is now in the public domain beyond all reasonable doubt, freely available on *Wikipedia* and subject to myriad press revelations in the past five years.

Speculation about Robin Gunningham, born at Bristol Maternity Hospital on 28 July 1973, had been kicking around the media for some years before a British Sunday newspaper felt it had gathered all the proof it needed to 'out' him as Banksy a few days before his 35th birthday in 2008.

What it failed to do was track him down in person, and that has remained the case. Certainly, in the early years, his reticence was all too understandable for pragmatic and practical reasons, but today it smacks far more of an extremely finely-tuned publicity stunt. After all, any local authority that pursued him on criminal damage charges would risk attracting widespread ridicule and opprobium; and even if by chance it did so and won, Banksy would not have to dig very deep into his coffers to pay the fine.

No. At this stage of his career, the artist is far more likely to shun the spotlight for the very sound commercial reason that being the Man of Mystery is greatly more intriguing than allegedly being Robin Gunningham, ex-Bristol Cathedral schoolboy now allegedly married to a parliamentary lobbyist.

Maybe it is something of a gamble. After all, if he had come clean immediately after he had been named he could instantly have made a million pounds out of his autobiography, scooped a further six-figure sum from newspaper serialisation rights, been the subject of multiple television documentaries and sat on endless chat show couches to be quizzed by everyone from the highbrow heights of Mark Lawson and Kirsty Wark to the buffoonery of Graham Norton and Alan Carr.

He clearly believes that a rejection of such a lifestyle is a gamble well worth taking. Or maybe his life really does reflect the anti-materialist, anti-capitalist, anti-establishment stance of so many of his images and slogans. Maybe, but what casts doubt on the latter proposition has been his ready

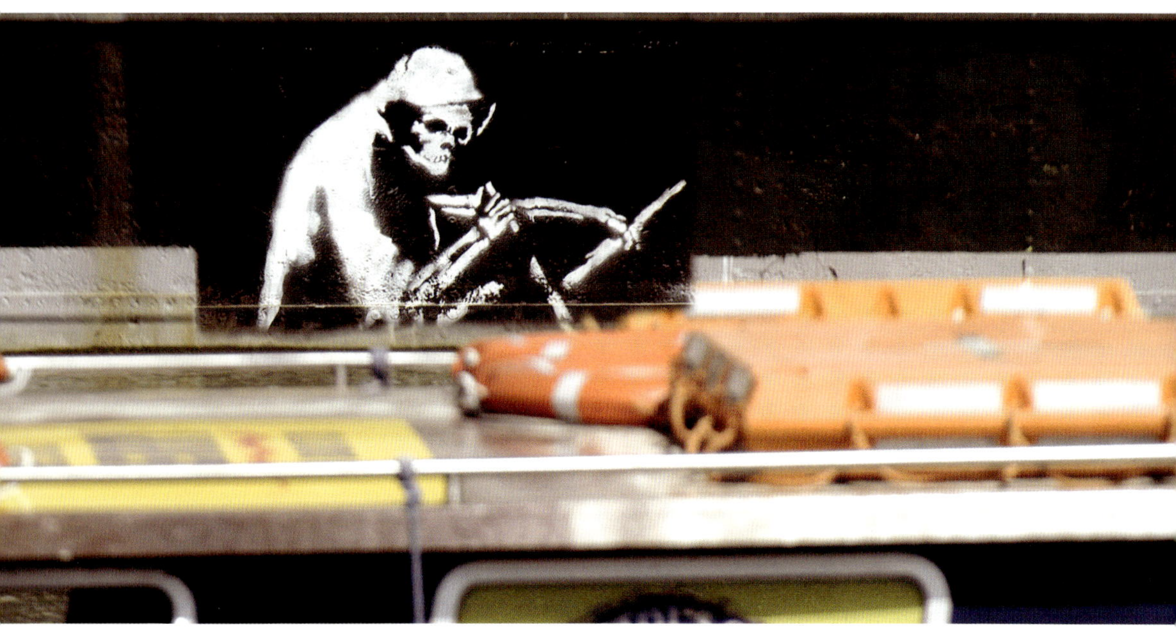

Banksy in the city's Floating Harbour: The Grim Reaper on the *Thekla* moored alongside The Grove. [photograph: Stephen Morris, from *Further off the Wall*]

transition from stencilling English provincial backstreet walls to producing canvases of the kind – and displayed in the kind of galleries – that prompt the likes of Tom Cruise, Christina Aguilera and Angelina Jolie to part with hundreds of thousands of dollars for them. Much of his focus is now on America, and it was a fan from across the Atlantic who paid a record £288,000 for his *Space Girl & Bird* at auction in 2007.

What is noteworthy, though often overlooked, is how swiftly he has scaled these heights of commercial success. Those whose neighbourhood's walls he first adorned in Bristol, London and Brighton two decades ago or more might feel he has been on the scene for ever, but the fact remains that he allegedly does not reach 40 until 2013. That other *enfant terrible* of the British art world with strong West Country ties, Damien Hirst, is eight years his senior, Tracey Emin a full ten.

Humour, bitter and dark or otherwise, has always been central to Banksy's armoury, and indeed one of his saving graces as far as some less enthusiastic observers are concerned. His tag itself is no more than a schoolboy joke: *Get Rich Quick* by Robin Banks, a time-honoured and some would say tired old spoof title that takes its place on the bookshelf alongside *Into The Jungle* by Hugo Furst and *Dangerous Cliffs* by Eileen Dover.

He has displayed an equally light touch in some of his public pronouncements. 'We can't do anything to change the world until capitalism crumbles. In the meantime we should all go shopping to console ourselves' is characteristically

 Banksy, The Bristol Legacy

double-edged, as is his list of people who should be shot: 'Fascist thugs, religious fundamentalists, people who write lists telling you who should be shot.'

'Sometimes I feel so sick at the state of the world, I can't even finish my second apple pie' is another quip with tough undertones. But he was back to the schoolboy gag book when, at the end of his extraordinary mixed-media exhibition at the Bristol City Museum and Art Gallery in 2009, he told the local evening newspaper: 'In some ways I'm sorry it has to end, but I promised my mum she could have her leopard-skin coat back.'

Before Banksy there was not a long history of graffiti being accepted as art, and local authorities around the world still view it in a variety of ways, most of them with severe reservations. London boroughs do not tend to be sympathetic, a great deal of his street art in Australia has sunk without trace, and survival rates in the United States and Canada are also patchy.

The council in his home city of Bristol, whatever the private thoughts of some individual members and officers, has learned to put on a happy face, even though there have been times since the late 1980s when it has seemed that some streets have been in danger of sinking in a sea of spray paint, by no means all of it applied by Banksy.

For some years the city fathers' most high-profile signal of acceptance was the survival of Banksy's image of June 2006 which showed a naked man hanging one-handed off a high bedroom windowsill while a scantily clad woman inside seems to be having a tricky conversation with her husband. It was on a wall clearly visible from busy Park Street and directly opposite the council's headquarters, but was so wittily presented that the local authority knew that its removal would strike many as po-faced and heavy-handed.

The council's solution was to leave it to the public to decide whether the mural should stay or go, and in a web-based poll 97 per cent of respondents voted to keep it. The fact that this fêted and treasured piece of work has now been attacked, the victim of fellow graffiti artists, is a reminder of the extreme transience of much of Banksy's street output, and puts into perspective his move to canvases in galleries – and not only from a financial standpoint. Not all revere his art, or even know about it. In the summer of 2011, the new owners of a house in Eastville, Bristol, having never heard of the artist, blithely painted over an early Banksy of a gorilla in a pink mask. 'I thought it was worthless,' said Saeed Ahmed, 'I didn't know it was valuable and that's why I painted over it. I really am sorry if people are upset.'

> **... the local press estimated that the 'Banksy Effect' put millions into the city's economy**

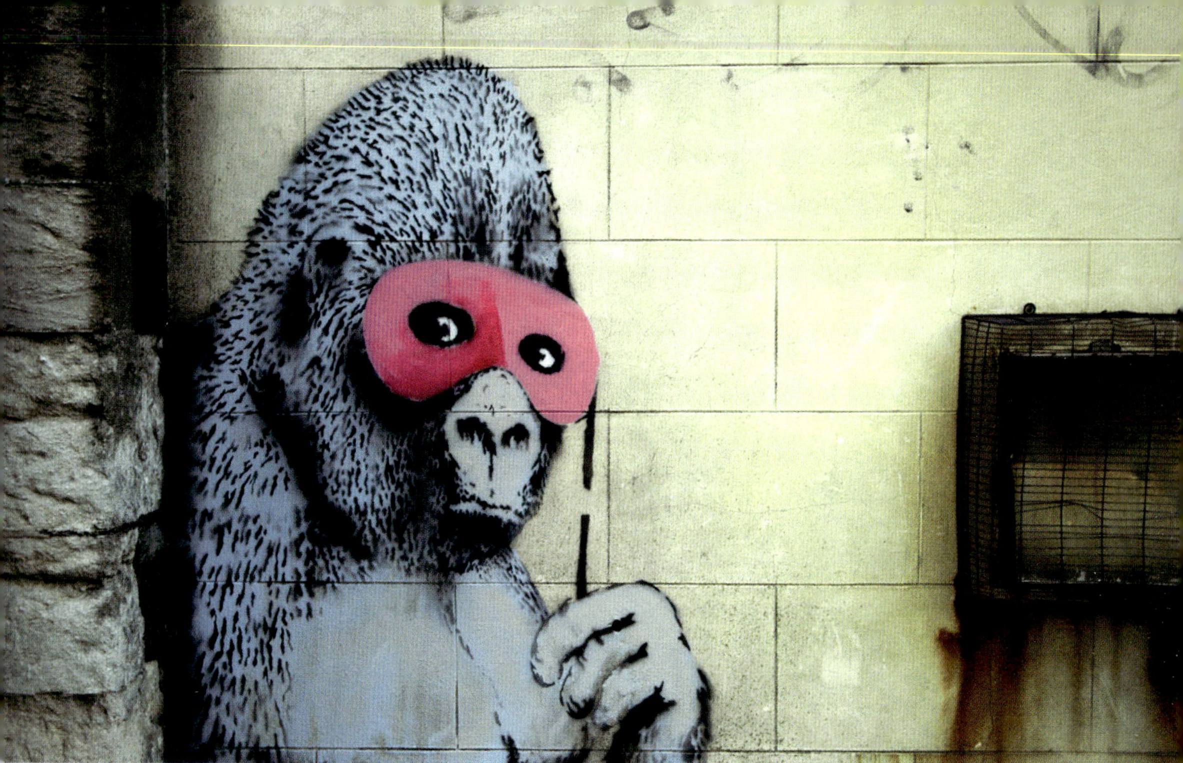

The ill-fated *Gorilla in Pink Mask* on Fishponds Road, Bristol erroneously painted out by a new owner. [photograph: Stephen Morris]

Since 2006, however, his home city has shown its affection in a considerably more substantial way, with the 'Banksy vs Bristol Museum' exhibition in the summer of 2009 attracting more than 300,000 visitors in twelve weeks, when enthusiasts queued for up to six hours to view the 100-plus works. As others have examined in detail in this book, the local press estimated that the 'Banksy Effect' put millions into the city's economy and doubled the turnover of a number of neighbouring businesses during recessionary times. Donations to the museum topped £45,000 – nearly four times the customary annual amount, though that good news was tempered by the fact that it had been forced to take on an extra thirty temporary staff over the three months. As Banksy 'told' a reporter:

> It's nice to see it's been so popular, but it makes me a bit suspicious. Throughout history all the great artists have been overlooked in their own lifetime and only appreciated once they've gone. I'm starting to worry I'm not one of the good guys.

Whatever Banksy's status as a 'guy', there is no shortage of dissenting voices around to assure him that he need never confuse himself with a great artist. The campaign Keep Britain Tidy is 'concerned that Banksy's street art glorifies what is essentially vandalism'; in this book David Lee dismisses Banksy for his shallow, trite anti-capitalism, and the outspoken critic Brian Sewell is so harsh in his assessment of him that in 2009 he pointed to the popularity of 'Banksy vs Bristol Museum' as a sign that 'the art world has gone absolutely crazy'. 'Any fool who can put paint on canvas or turn a cardboard box into a sculpture is lauded,' he complained. 'Banksy should have been put down at birth. It's no good as art, drawing or painting. His work has no virtue. It's merely the sheer scale of his impudence that has given him so much publicity.'

So far, so predictable – but the super-right-on satirist Charlie Brooker was of much the same mind about Banksy. 'His work looks dazzlingly clever to idiots,' he said in *The Guardian*. However, there were many dozens of readers who rejected this position, using his on-line column to bark back at Brooker for being so sour-faced.

An artist, then, to divide opinion across the spectrum, and there is no harm in that. It is what creative spirits should do, but the question now is how he will continue to achieve that objective in the years ahead. There seem to be any number of avenues open to him. Public art with a message in controversial venues – he has already adorned the Israeli West Bank barrier and flood-devastated buildings in New Orleans – might be one way of keeping his views in the news.

Then again, his closeness these days to the United States seems to be taking on a life of its own, with a cameo part in 'The Simpsons' and a string of accolades – including an Academy Award nomination – for his 2010 documentary *Exit Through the Gift Shop*, billed as 'the world's first street art disaster movie'. If part of the motivation for this recognition has been the prospect of luring the man into the spotlight it has failed miserably.

An inventive young mind that has progressed from painting freehand on walls to stencils to canvases to film surely has a trick or two still in store; and if by chance Banksy should ever find his career apparently stalling, he can always out himself and set the merrry-go-round spinning more crazily than ever. More positives than negatives would undoubtedly ensue from such a move, whatever the likes of Messrs Sewell and Brooker might think and say.

A long-standing journalist in the West Country, **John Hudson** has followed the Banksy story from its earliest days.

Drawn in chalk, but graffiti all the same: street protest in eighteenth- and nineteenth-century Bristol

Steve Poole

Graffiti and street art are not new in English cities and neither is the moral outrage they have frequently provoked. A century or two ago, there were few things quite so irritating to 'respectable' opinion and local authority as the unsanctioned decoration of public walls with crudely carved initials, challenging proclamations and rude rhymes. In eighteenth- and early nineteenth-century Bristol however, where, unsurprisingly, access to print media was effectively restricted, a simple piece of chalk was all it took to confound and frustrate the censors. In many ways, chalked messages on walls were the social media of the age, whether summoning the crowd, defying authority or mocking the privileged. But what messages did Bristol's chalk authors leave on the city's walls and what measures, if any, did local elites take to combat them? This chapter explores some of the surviving evidence.

TV has made going to the theatre seem pointless, photography has pretty much killed painting, but graffiti remains pretty much unspoiled by progress. (Banksy, 2006)

In March 1839, Lant Carpenter, the liberally minded minister of the Unitarian chapel at Lewins Mead, in Bristol, launched a spirited tirade against Bristol graffiti artists. A proposal to increase public subsidies to the Maynooth Catholic College had reignited anti-Irish and anti-Catholic feeling in many urban centres, but Carpenter was alarmed to find it on the genteel streets of Clifton. Chalked on its walls in 'very large and well-executed letters', was the slogan, DOWN WITH MAYNOOTH AND POPERY!

'I am calling on the chief magistrate, as conservator of the peace of the city,' wrote Carpenter, 'to direct the police to obliterate these offensive words wherever they are perceived.' Carpenter recognised that however unrepresentative the secretive authors of declarations like this may have been, the sentiments they expressed posed a genuine challenge to public order in the age of Chartism. It was, after all, just ten years since Bristol had last seen fierce anti-Catholic rioting, and only eight since the reform riots had left two sides of Queen Square and many public buildings in ruins. 'With such language commenced the riots in London in 1780 and those in Birmingham in 1791,' Carpenter insisted. 'Do the mischievous instigators of these inscriptions desire to renew *here* the horrors of 1831?'[1]

We may think of graffiti art as a modern phenomenon, and as 'art' perhaps it is. But public declarations of the kind that bothered Carpenter had been present on the streets of Bristol for centuries. They were not exclusively the work of lower-class democrats and rebels, as the daubing of the city's streets with the Tory slogan, 'True Blue and Trade' had demonstrated during the general election of 1832; indeed they were not always concerned with political matters at all.[2]

Chalk, rather than paint, was the usual medium; accessible, instant and impermanent; an archive often erased within weeks of its birth. Some examples nevertheless found their way into the historical record. *The Merry Thought or the Glass Window and Bog House Miscellany*, published in four volumes in 1731, was perhaps the earliest attempt to preserve and circulate the nation's graffiti in print, although we learn little of popular politics from its pages. Its sole intention was to entertain with amusing doggerel collected from the walls of the country's pubs and privies. From an interior wall of Bristol's premier coaching inn, the White Lion, for example, comes the following:

> *I'm witty, I'll Write,*
> *I'm valiant, I'll Fight,*
> *And take all that's said in my own Sense:*
> *In Liquor I'm sunk,*
> *And confoundedly drunk,*
> *So there is the Source of this Nonsense.*[3]

It was not unusual to find wordy proclamations of this kind in eighteenth-century buildings and the streets were a widely-used scribblers' canvas. 'My first relish for letters I got by conning over those elegant monosyllables which are chalked out upon walls and gates,' asserted a Londoner in 1755, and 'the knowledge which I have thus picked out of the streets has been very extensive.'[4] Wall writing in past centuries was not only common but, as Juliet Fleming observes of Elizabethan and Jacobean England, 'sanctioned in ways that are foreign to ourselves', even on the interior walls of private houses, where mottoes of various kinds offered friendly commentary on domestic *mores*.[5] Although it was generally accepted in early modern towns however, the Victorian middle classes baulked at street writing, conflating it with 'primitive' foreign cultures and the decadence of Pompeii where, as one scholar put it, 'We discover without surprise that a large proportion of the graffiti are of an indecent character.'[6]

The desire of many Victorian municipal authorities to erase crude popular decorations like these was mirrored by a parallel discomfort over the posting of unlicensed bills. The crowding of vacant walls and fences with legions of gaudy and shabbily executed paper advertisements clashed untidily with every attempt to clean up and gentrify the Victorian urban environment and seemed, to social elites at least, to encourage lower class vulgarity and vice. A number of painters in the 1830s and '40s were sufficiently struck by it to produce 'street scene' commentaries in which iconic bastions of rational architecture in London became dwarfed and obscured by handbills and the motley, unrespectable crowds they attracted, beginning with John Parry's *Street Scene with Posters* (1835) and Charles Hunt's self-explanatory *Cross Readings at Charing Cross* (1838). The first pits popular culture against the dome of St Pauls; the second against the new National Gallery. The regulation of fly-posting presented problems for authorities anxious not to impede the free marketing of goods and later legislation against print media would accordingly focus its attention on the less controversial target of 'obscene' publication and display.[7] Scrawled messages in chalk and paint however, could be tackled more easily, and appropriate restrictive bye laws were framed in various English towns throughout the nineteenth century. At Bristol, chalking was effectively criminalised by the passing of a local Encroachment Act in 1837, a typically complex piece of nineteenth-century legislation which created 286 new categories of street offender, and made liable to a £2 fine anyone 'who shall write or describe any obscene or indecent language or figure on any wall, door, post, pavement or public place… or write upon or otherwise deface or mark by means of chalk, paint, or any other material whatsoever', any building in the city.[8] Strengthening laws were passed in a number of places to obstruct the militant women's suffrage movement in the early years of the twentieth century. Four years after Emma Sproson was fined five shillings for chalking suffragist slogans in the capital in 1907, a 'London Various Powers Act' increased the penalty to £2.00. The intention, it was explained in *The Times*, was specifically to tackle, 'the pavement artist for the display of whose talent the City was not an appropriate place, and the chalking of "Votes for Women" on the pavements'.[9]

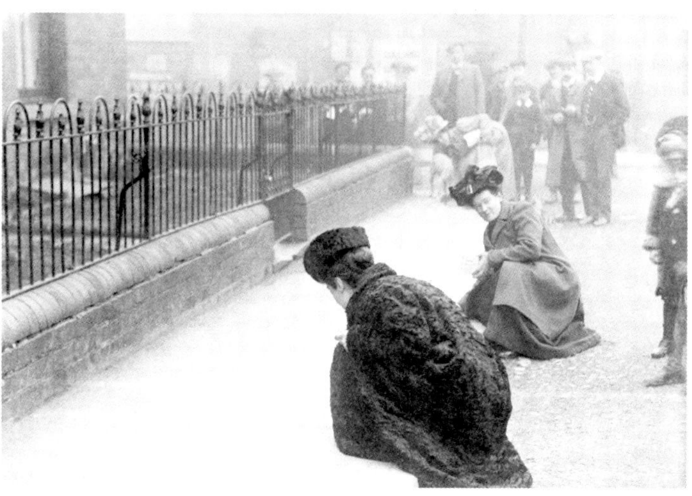

Suffragette Emma Sproson
chalking a pavement.
[courtesy Museum of London]

 Banksy, The Bristol Legacy

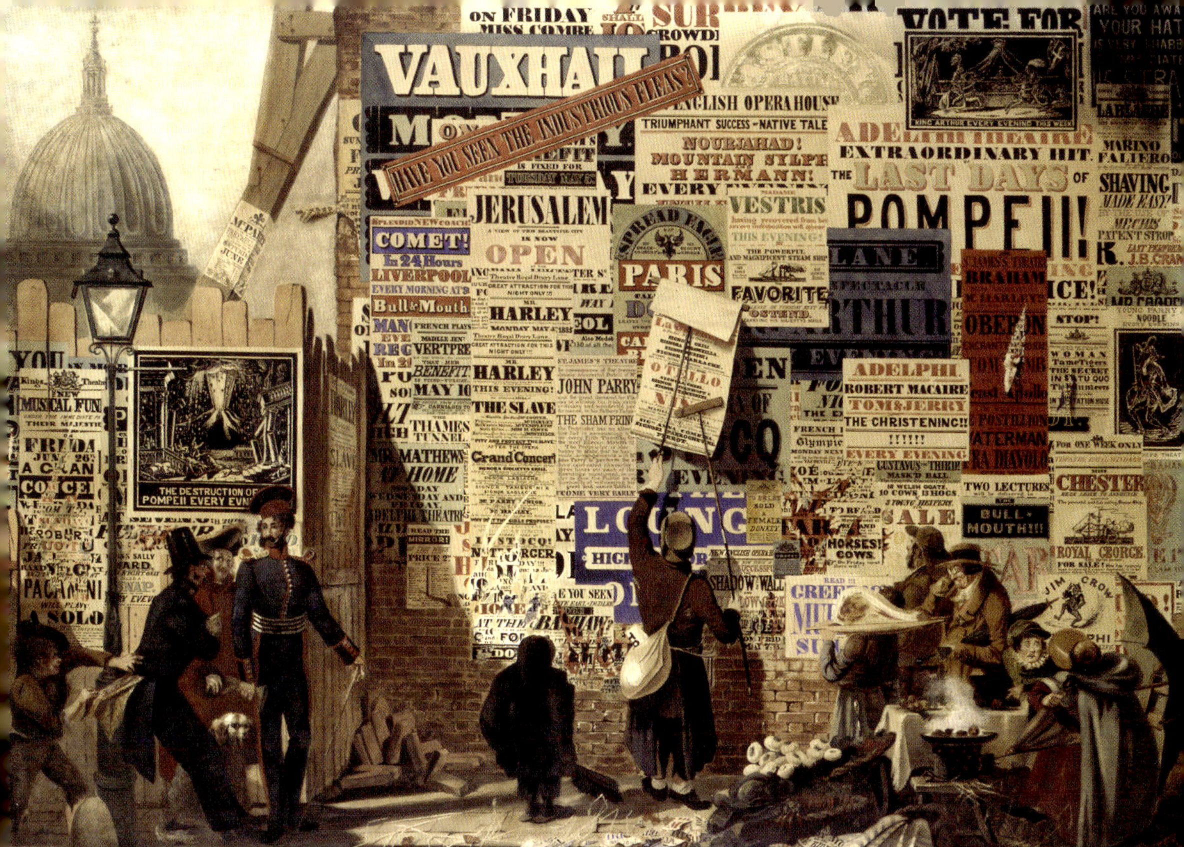

John Orlando Parry, *Street Scene with Posters*, 1835. [courtesy Alfred Dunhill Museum and Archive]

Not surprisingly, in-situ examples of graffiti from this and earlier periods
are elusive, but some eighteenth-century survivals may be seen in Bristol's
Redcliffe Caves, left behind when the caverns were being back-filled with
builders' waste from residential developments above ground. Protected
from the daylight outside, the chalk script is as fresh and bright as the day it
was written. 'Joseph Coles Where are we now 1774', runs one, while nearby
a second date has been added above an archway in large numerals: '1789'.
These are prosaic gestures perhaps, recording nothing but the subterranean
presence of two long-dead Bristol labourers. Yet, however little these writers
may have known of events elsewhere in the world, in the fifteen years
separating their interventions, other men and women much like themselves
were forging modern participatory politics in Washington and Paris, and the
framework of their working and social lives would be profoundly changed
by the knowledge of it. Other survivals may be seen scratched onto the
lantern window of the Wesleyan New Room in Broadmead where, in flowing
characters, eighteenth-century visiting preachers or their assistants left
testimonies to their faith on the glass. Hardly a subversive act perhaps, but
then in some respects Methodism itself was rebellion enough and, in the face
of frequent prejudice, in some need of public re-iteration. 'On brittle glass
I grave my name,' runs one, 'A follower of the blessed lamb; But thou canst
show a nobler art, and grave thy name upon my heart'.
Signatory, political, comedic or bawdy, graffiti was woven into the fabric
of urban life, and though rarely as inflammatory in its effects as Lant

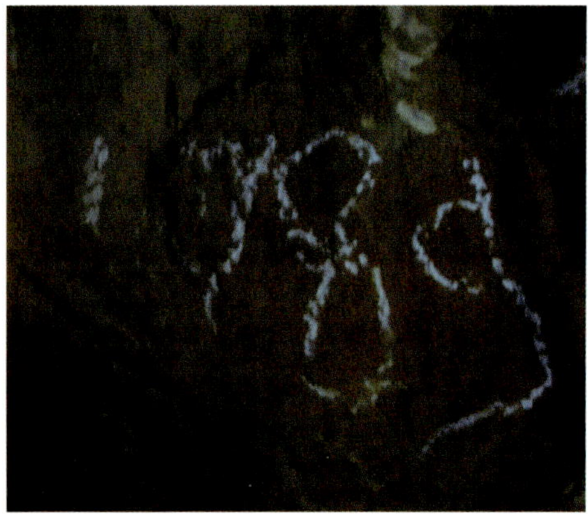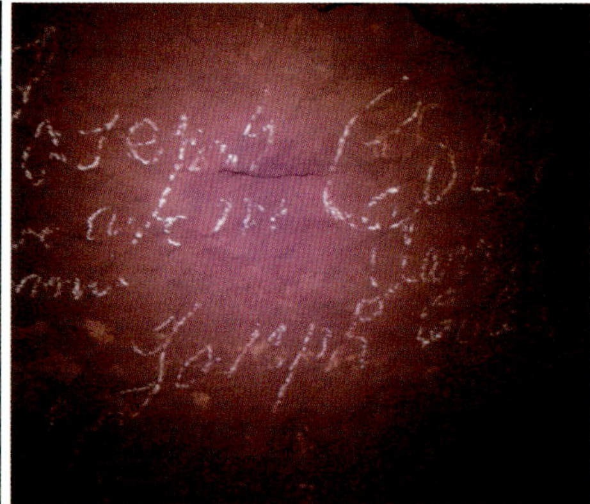

Eighteenth-century wall scribblings, Redcliffe Caves, Bristol.

Carpenter feared in 1839, it remained nevertheless an irritant to power and a barometer to 'unofficial' popular opinion. Its exercise offered the marginal and the poor every opportunity to freely publish, to exercise wit, fortitude, or intolerance, and to set aside, however temporarily and surreptitiously, the deference of normal social relations. Chalk could be unobtrusively hidden in the pocket and its use defied surveillance. And we may read both assertive bravado and humour in the chalked memo left behind by two burglars in a Bristol counting house in 1829. Finding nothing but a few spoons, some ceiling wax and five shillings in cash, they scrawled their disappointment on the lid of a desk. 'The next time, leave the key of the Peter behind', they suggested, 'It is a shame to disappoint us'.[10]

Message inscribed on the lantern window of the Wesleyan New Room, Broadmead, Bristol. [with kind permission of the Trustees of the New Room]

It was undeniably an indiscriminate social leveller. 'The ceiling and walls are covered with graffiti,' it was noted of Shakespeare's birthplace at Stratford in 1895, 'where plebeian and peer, mediocrity and genius shoulder one another.'[11] Such shouldering seldom brought advantage to the peer, however. In Bristol's Gloucestershire hinterland, Earl Bathurst had magnanimously opened his extensive Cirencester pleasure gardens to visitors in 1800, only to be confronted by 'the wanton, licentious and outrageous behaviour of some who have been admitted to this favour in scrawling upon the walls and breaking the windows of the buildings and resting places'.[12] Libellous and mocking attacks upon the reputation of authority figures were quickly made in chalk and the outrage they caused predictable. 'We have recently observed the names of respectable inhabitants associated with epithets which proclaim or insinuate the foulest imputations', growled a newspaper editorial following an epidemic

 Banksy, The Bristol Legacy

of 'incendiary and obscene inscriptions' on the streets of Bath in 1815[13] yet disapproval might sometimes be ameliorated by pity. The appropriation of other people's walls by at least one voiceless victim of poverty had caused a minor sensation at Bristol some years earlier when the body of a drowned man was pulled from the Avon at Sea Mills. He was later identified as James Doe, a journeyman ceramic painter who had drifted to Bristol in search of work in 1797 and taken up temporary residence in a ruined building beside the river. There he spent several days contemplating suicide and scrawling his troubled thoughts across the walls, first in pencil, then when it ran down, with an old nail. 'Never oppress the poor. Do as you would be done by,' ran one entry, and another, 'Oh God give peace to all nations and stop the amities of war.' Doe's helpless wall writings touched the city's reading public deeply and they were posthumously, and somewhat ironically, published in pamphlet form.[14]

The Reverend Carpenter's anxiety was directed less at signature writing, bawdry or vandalism then, than at the more overtly subversive use of unregulated street art, and this too had plenty of precedents in Bristol. In 1810, the City Recorder, Vicary Gibbs was expected in Bristol to open the spring assize, but his arrival was heralded by a campaign of hostile chalking. Once a popular figure at Bristol for his role in the defence and acquittal of London democrats arraigned for treason in 1794, Gibbs had since taken silk, become Attorney General and changed his colours. In April his ruling on the seizure and detention of the radical baronet, Sir Francis Burdett, provoked a storm of protest, and the streets of Bristol were emblazoned with the slogans 'Burdett for Ever' and 'No Gibbs!' in anticipation of his arrival. He was escorted into the city under heavy guard, but the windows of the Mayor's Mansion House in Queen Square were shattered that night and several anonymous threats posted about the streets detailing Gibbs's most recent crimes against civil liberties and urging Bristolians to show him 'proper respect' if they saw him.[15] There was similar activity, though of a more welcoming kind, when the prominent radical orator Henry Hunt came to address a mass public meeting of parliamentary reformers at Brandon Hill on Boxing Day, 1816. The Bristol watch were put on full alert but were unable to catch any of the city's plebeian 'chalk authors' who were at large for a fortnight, scrawling 'incendiary inscriptions' about the streets.[16]

There was more hostile 'chalking on walls' in April 1831 when Sir Charles Wetherell, a later Recorder, came to open the spring assize. Like Gibbs, Wetherell had forsaken an earlier reputation as a political liberal and spoken in parliament against reform. 'The words, "Hoot Sir Charles Wetherell today" were liberally bestowed on the walls', noted a Tory newspaper, 'and mostly in the same handwriting'.[17] Wetherell escaped without incident, but when he returned for the autumn assize the Reform Bill had fallen and his reception was worse. 'The shutters and walls are very generally chalked "resist taxes", "down with the peers", "down with the Church", "fight for reform" etc', it was reported a fortnight before he arrived. Wetherell was hooted and pelted as he made his way to the Mansion House; windows were broken, and the building ransacked. The Recorder opened the assize, then fled the city as the most severe three days of rioting in Bristol's history got underway. When it was all over and a Special Commission was ordered to try more than one hundred Bristolians for riot offences, the authorities let it be known that capital charges would be pursued. This brought a fresh spate of indignant and challenging graffiti. 'Many places were chalked "a House for a Neck",' it was reported; a variation on a vengeful inscription that had appeared under the gallows at Winchester after death sentences were announced for several agricultural 'Swing' rioters a year earlier: 'Murder for Murder! Blood for Blood!'[18]

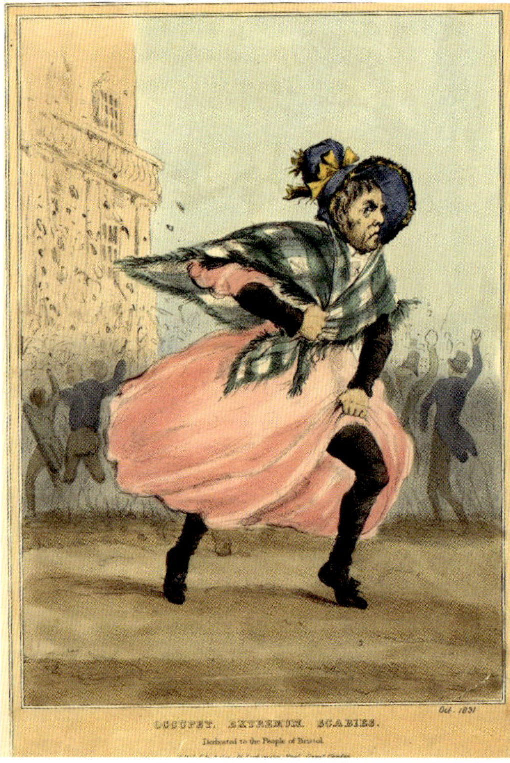

An unpopular Recorder Sir Charles Wetherell, much graffitted against, fleeing the wrath of the Bristol mob in drag.

The elaborate, colourful and ambitiously staged street art of the twenty-first century owes much to audacious proclamations such as these. Despite the relative ease with which alternative web-based news forums like Indymedia have provided a platform for the circulation of dissent, it is the very public and declamatory nature of low-tech street intervention that ensures its survival. As Banksy would have it, 'A wall has always been the best place to publish your work', which is why advertisers spend so much money on enormous street hoardings. 'Well,' he says, 'they started the fight and the wall is the weapon of choice to hit them back.'[19] Today's graffiti artists began stencilling because it was quicker than free painting, making discovery less likely. But the chalk authors of nineteenth-century Bristol, who had neither stencils nor the internet at their disposal, took to the streets partly because publication in print was considerably more hazardous. Tax-evading radical newspapers like Cobbett's *Register*, Carlyle's *Republican*, and *The Black Dwarf* did offer a platform, but provincial authorities vigorously prosecuted anyone who tried to sell them and Bristol's magistrates were no exception. Two men caught selling the *Register* outside

A wall has always been the best place to publish your work.

the Exchange were (unlawfully) jailed for two months under the Hawkers and Pedlars Act in 1817 for example, and Mayor John Haythorne believed the radical press 'much impeded' by it. That same month, Haythorne also arrested and summarily convicted a Bristol printer, Joseph Arnold, for using an unlicensed press to publish pamphlets critical of the Prince Regent. Terrified that his business would be ruined if he persisted, Arnold resolved never to publish radical titles again and was rewarded with a £5 fine for his good sense.[20] Selling or publishing critical political opinion required nineteenth-century radicals to adopt a public profile and risk prosecution. Clandestine chalking, on the other hand, was quickly effected, difficult to prevent and impossible to control, however robust the by-laws framed to tackle it. In this respect at least, little has changed.

But radical visual interventions in public space should not, perhaps, be seen only as two-dimensional scripts. Queen Square, for example, built at the beginning of the eighteenth century around an equestrian statue of William III, was designed to embody those constitutional rights and liberties of citizenship wrested from the autocratic Stuarts during the Glorious Revolution of 1688. In the later eighteenth and nineteenth centuries, the ownership and interpretation of these 'rights' was regularly contested between the city's oligarchic Corporation and its more democratically inclined citizens and the Square became an arena for radical performance. When the government of Pitt the Younger suspended *habeas corpus* and passed two draconian Acts to obstruct free speech and public assembly in 1795, the physician Thomas Beddoes called for William's statue to be draped in mourning cloth, 'till our liberties be secure'. Then, during the acute food shortage of 1800, a blood-soaked loaf was impaled upon the statue railings by nocturnal visitors and a note pinned to it. 'My dear, dear friends,' it read, 'your country bleeding at every pore, your Familys starving, your husbands and sons sent to foreign countrys to be murdered, and for what, why to keep pitt and his gang in place what care they... will you spend your last shilling and last drop of blood, for gods sake withhold it.'[21]

Some of the most effective agitational street art adapts and plays with

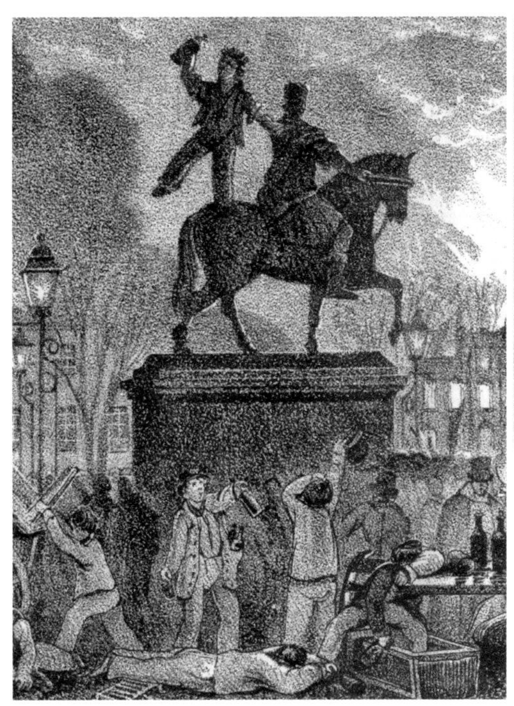

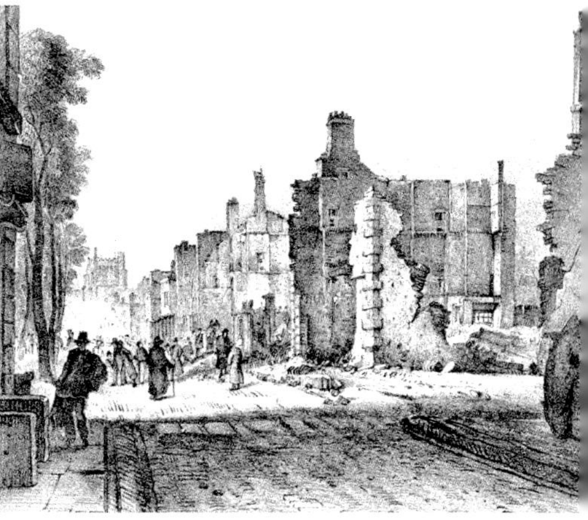

North side of Queen Square in ruins, 1831 as depicted by J B Pyne [Bristol Museum & Art Gallery].

Mayhem in Queen Square, as rioters go beserk. Detail from William Muller's *Queen Square on the Night of 30th October 1831* [Bristol Museum & Art Gallery].

the material culture of authority in ways like these. Just as demonstrators against cuts in public services in 2011 decorated the statue of Charles I in Trafalgar Square with a Unison waistcoat, a GMB flag and a banner proclaiming 'Hands off Libya!', and just as Banksy himself fixed a wheel clamp to the statue of Boudicca in her chariot outside Parliament in 2006, so an anonymous Bristolian during the reform riots of 1831 mounted William's statue in Queen Square and placed a French tricoloured cap of liberty over it. Another, who climbed up onto the back of William's horse, raised a bottle of stolen wine high into the air, and offered a toast to liberty as confusion reigned below, has since become iconic for he was later immortalised in the best-known and most poignant engraving of the entire event. 'It doesn't matter how great you were,' says Banksy of equestrian statues like this one, 'it'll always take an unfunny drunk with climbing skills to make people notice you.'[22]

Whether physically 'performed' like this, or posted in rough lettering across the public walls of urban England, graffiti has been making mutable mischief for hundreds of years. We might regard it as social activism of the most playful and creative kind, and if it is not often considered the stuff of history, it is perhaps because it has no permanence. 'The majority,' Banksy laments, 'is destroyed by zealous municipal officials who fail to recognise the artistic merit and historical value of daubing on walls.'[23]

Dr Steve Poole is Reader in social and cultural history at the University of the West of England, Bristol and Director of the university's Regional History Centre. His recent published work includes books and essays on Hanoverian popular protest, the Captain Swing agricultural rebellion, and the republican democrat John Thelwall and he is currently editing a book of essays for Redcliffe Press on the social history of the Bristol waterfront.

Notes

1. *Bristol Mercury* 23 March 1839.

2. *Bristol Mercury*, 22 December 1832.

3. *The Merry Thought or the Glass Window and Bog House Miscellany*, Part IV (London, 1731), p.6.

4. *The Connoisseur by Mr Town, Critic and Censor General*, 86, 18 September 1755, pp.518-9.

5. Juliet Fleming, *Graffiti and the Writing Arts of Early Modern England* (Cambridge: Cambridge University Press, 2007), p.29.

6. Samuel Manning, *Italian Pictures, Drawn with Pen and Pencil* (London, 1872), 165. For eighteenth-century graffiti see Lisa Forman Cody, '"Every lane teems with instruction, and every alley is big with erudition": Graffiti in Eighteenth Century London' in T. Hitchcock and H. Shore (eds.), *The Streets of London: from the great fire to the great stink* (London, Rivers Oram Press, 2003), pp.82-100.

7. For Hunt see Brandon Taylor, *Art for the Nation: Exhibitions and the London Public, 1747-2001* (Manchester, Manchester University Press, 1999), pp.41-3. On the 'cleansing' of London's streets see also Lynda Nead, *Victorian Babylon: People, Streets and Images in Nineteenth Century London* (New Haven, Yale University Press, 2000), part 3, 'Streets and Obscenity'.

8. *Bristol Mercury*, 1 April 1837.

9. *The Times*, 14 July 1911.

10. *Bristol Mercury*, 13 January 1829. For the Redcliffe Caves graffiti, I am indebted to Alan Gray for kindly taking me to see it.

11. Canniff Haight, *Here and There in the Homeland: England, Scotland and Ireland* as seen by a Canadian (Toronto, 1895), p.313.

12. Samuel Rudder, *The History of the Ancient Town of Cirencester* (Cirencester, 1800), p.127.

13. *Bath and Cheltenham* Gazette, 12 April 1815.

14. *Extraordinary Case of Suicide, Being a Narrative of the Life and Unfortunate End of James Doe, who was Found Drowned in Sea Mill Dock near Bristol with an Exact Copy of the Manuscript Found Written on the Walls of an Uninhabited House...* (Bristol, 1799).

15. *Morning Chronicle* 16 April 1810; *Felix Farley's Bristol Journal* 21 April 1810; *Examiner* 22 April 1810.

16. *Bristol Mercury* 23 December 1816.

17. *Felix Farley's Bristol Journal* 16 April 1831. To 'hoot' was to boo.

18. *The Courier*, 10 October 1831; National Archives, HO40/28, Abraham Bagnall to Sir Richard Jackson, 27 December 1831. For Winchester see *Morning Chronicle* 17 January 1831.

19. Banksy, *Wall and Piece* (London, Century, 2006), p.8.

20. *Bath Chronicle*, 22, 29 January 1817; National Archives, HO 42/159, Haythorne to Lord Sidmouth, 8, 9, 21 February 1817.

21. Thomas Beddoes, *A Word in Defence of the Bill of Rights Against Gagging Bills* (Bristol, 1795); Bristol Record Office, *Corporation Letter Book*, 26 February, 1800.

22. *The Bristol Riots, Their Causes, Progress and Consequences*, by A Citizen, (Bristol, 1832), p.96 and frontispiece; Banksy, *Wall and Piece*, pp.208-9.

23. Banksy, *Wall and Piece*, p.185.

The 'versus' habit:
Banksy and the Barons
Paul Gough

Banksy has described his interventions as a form of 'brandalism', a calculated act of subverting familiar images and icons so that they are twisted into novel and provocative forms. But is this a new phenomenon? Moreover is it new to Bristol – a city that has a quiet history of schism and strife. Paul Gough examines the origins of Banksy's contrariness, suggesting that the 'versus' in his title tells us a great deal about the artist, the city and its civic habits.

Unconventional. Unorthodox. Unaccustomed to appearing on the front page of a British newspaper, let alone the *Ethiopian Times*, Bristol has a reputation for being slightly cool, tinged with green, and cannily creative. It also has a reputation for being a little removed, even rather complacent, a myth underlined by a widely shared tale which suggests that whereas northern English cities – Leeds, Liverpool, and its arch rival as an 'ideopolis', Manchester – had to fundamentally re-invent themselves in the wake of crushing recession in the 1970s and 80s, Bristol was selling the very stuff that people relied upon when they were feeling fed up: alcohol, chocolate and cigarettes, commodities then stacked high in the bonded warehouses that encircle the extensive docks at the heart of the city. As a city some say it has lacked homogeneity; it's a federal arrangement of precincts which inspire great loyalty. There are people who think of themselves as from 'St Pauls' or 'Clifton', 'Montpelier' or 'Redland', as much as from 'Bristol', though this is changing as the city galvanizes itself and starts to project a coherent image and identity.[1] It is though still rather self-effacing. It lacks the braggart city-narrators of the other 'Ideopolis' up north, it has two pretty lowly soccer teams with a deep-rooted fanbase (not for this federal city a 'Bristol United'), its tourism has for long been overshadowed by the Georgian munificence of nearby Bath, and its principal cultural stars are a curiously modest bunch: Wallace and Gromit borrow their aesthetic from Lancashire; the lead singer of Portishead prefers to remain aloof at the back of the stage; its other headline ambient trip-hop band, Massive Attack, release an album every blue moon, and, of course, its most famous son (other than the French-born Isambard Kingdom Brunel) is the world's most famous anonymous painter, Banksy.

As others have observed much more eloquently in this book Banksy has amassed a significant reputation for his provocative, wittily politicized interventions, what one critic has termed his 'red nose rebellion': he has painted peace motifs on the West Bank barrier in Israel; secretly located an inflatable figure of a Guantanamo Bay prisoner in Disney Land's *Rocky Mountain Railroad Roller-coaster Ride*; and hung hoax artifacts in the greatest museums in the world. He is, as the *New Yorker* described, 'both a lefty and a tweaker of lefty pieties', he is a champion of just causes and in the same breath a caustic lampooner of those very same causes. His art appears to takes sides, but he rarely does. At a London anti-war demonstration in 2003, he distributed signs that read 'I Don't Believe In Anything. I'm Just Here for the Violence.' He has that disarming habit of 'satirising his own sanctimony', or to put it in his words: 'I have no interest in ever coming out, I figure there are enough self-opinionated assholes trying to get their ugly little faces in front of you as it is.'[2]

Contrary by nature and with a love-hate *rapport* with his home city, it was no surprise that he chose an adversarial title for his retrospective show: 'Banksy *versus* Bristol Museum'. 'This is the first show I've ever done', he is said to have commented, 'where taxpayers' money is being used to hang my pictures up rather than scrape them off.' Few of those hundreds of thousands of visitors were put off by the title. Indeed its anti-cultural message may have aroused and encouraged them to queue patiently to

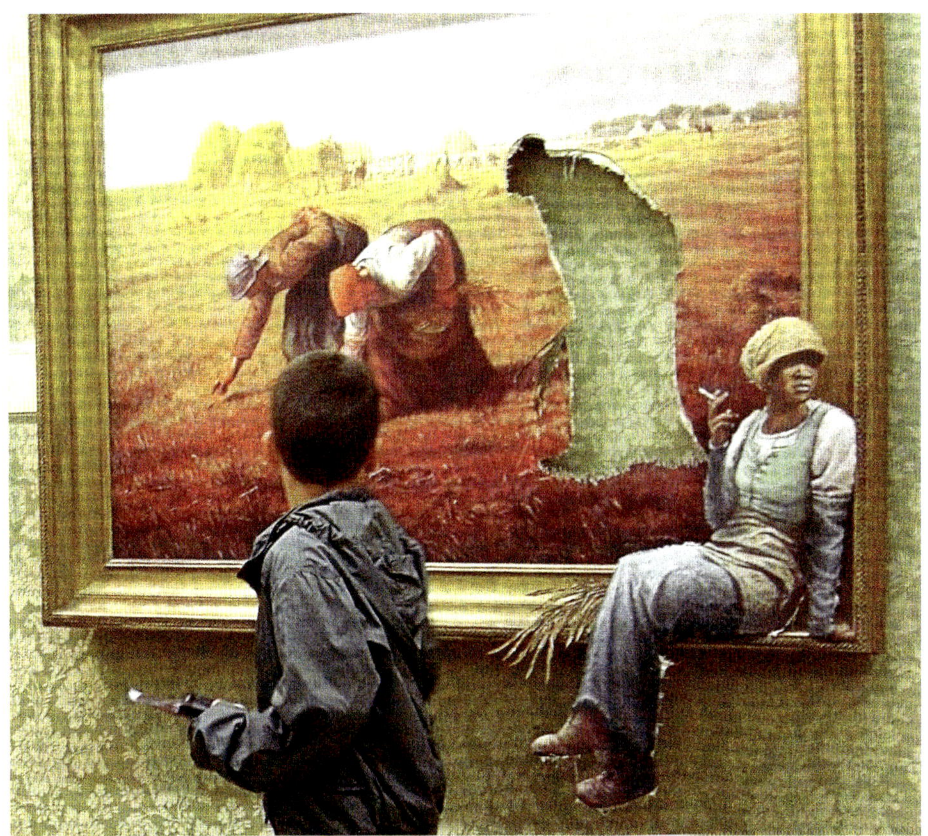

Banksy, J.F. Millet's *The Gleaners* modified, 'Banksy versus Bristol Museum', 2009. [photograph: Katy Bauer, *the Banksy Q*].

enter, possibly for the first time, the civic grandeur of the Bristol Museum and Art Gallery. Greeted by a burnt-out ice cream van, which doubled as an information booth and anchor-piece for the show, the artist's work was secreted throughout the labyrinth of rooms, corridors and galleries, hidden amongst the fossils, the stuffed animals and the museum's notable collection of Chinese pottery. Few visitors were disappointed; not only had Banksy radically re-mixed the permanent collection but he, and his team of fabricators and animatronic engineers, had mastered the art of surprising and irreverent juxtaposition. In addition to his trademark stencilled paintings there were walls of canvases and a menagerie of life-sized animated beasts: a muzzled lamb; a cheetah transformed into a fur coat; aquaria full of wriggling fish fingers; a full-size policeman clad in riot-gear gently bobbing on a child's rocking horse, and hotdog sausages that wriggled inside their buns.

Criticism of his civic-sponsored show might have been anticipated; after all, a significant segment of Bristolians have little time for cocky graffiti artists with their mindless scribble, their unreadable 'tags' and their wanton vandalism of 'innocent' property. And above all Banksy refuses to be cosy: his work is held to be offensive by some, criminal damage by many. However, all this quickly evaporated once the queues lengthened, the press became hooked, and the acclaim spread. Yet to a few discerning observers and sensitive city-elders, the 'versus' word rankled. It seemed to strike a jarring note in a city that had recently been short-listed for European City of Culture where the visual arts, music, news media, film, and animation had been courted, sponsored and presented as the new, authentic face of a city that had largely re-invented itself from an ageing port with some dubious trading links into an environmentally switched-on, culturally diverse, attractive city, hailed in 2009 as 'England's Best City to live In'.[3]

So why 'versus'? How had Banksy arrived at a phrase so guaranteed to irritate those who wanted to protect the city's image? What unhealed wounds if any, did it expose in Bristol's distant (or even recent) civic memory?

Cultural historian Paul Fussell has explored these questions. Writing of countries at war, he suggests that the confrontation between 'us' and 'them' is an example of gross dichotomizing, or polarization, that can best be understood as 'the modern *versus* habit'. One thing must always be opposed to another, he argues, not in the Hegelian hope of achieving some synthesis, or a negotiated peace, but with a determination that neither side should concede, that total submission of one side or the other is the only resolution.[4]

Perhaps in choosing the 'versus' word, Banksy was more cannily attuned to the historical fractures that have divided Bristol than many could have guessed. Bristol, as Steve Poole has examined in this book, has a history of being divided against itself. Certainly, there were many other examples that summer of art and artifacts being used to mark territory, to declare positions and oppose unnecessary change, to arouse polemic rather than create dialogue. As the queues were winding their way around the Georgian corners of conservative Clifton, a collective of neighbours in Windmill Hill (a grid of terraced houses in the south of the city, deep in a staunch Labour-held constituency) were galvanizing support to preserve a red pillar-box that was being threatened with removal by the Post Office. As the Banksy show started to gather the world's attention, residents in Windmill Hill transformed the much-vandalised postbox into a shrine, bedecking it with flowers, plastering it with farewell odes, decorating it with RIP messages, funerary images and a model of the Virgin Mary. A passage from one of W.H. Auden's poems was pasted to one side: 'And no one will hear the postman's knock/ Without a quickening of the heart. For who can bear to feel himself forgotten?'

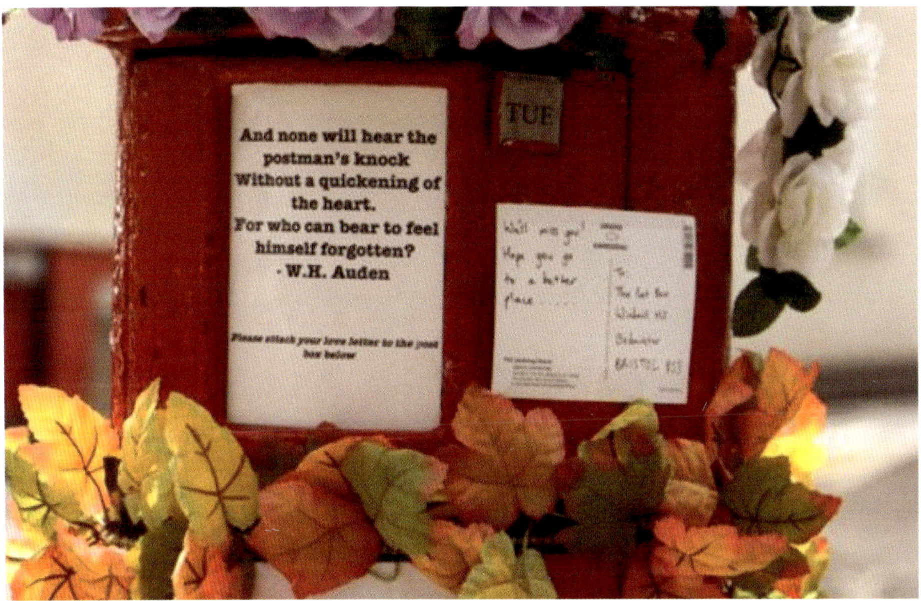

Decorated pillar box, Windmill Hill, Bristol, 2009. [photograph: Paul Gough]

Little is ever forgotten in Bristol. The historic enmity between the two halves of the city is well documented: during the eighteenth century, gathered to the north around Georgian Clifton, lived the high Anglican, high Tory, merchant class, their social standing epitomised by the Society of Merchant Venturers. Over centuries they became the most powerful mercantile cartel in Bristol and the region; their wealth and status partly founded on the trade in slaves and other 'goods' from the west coast of Africa. On the other side of the city lived and worked the Non-conformist, Whig/Liberal industrialists of Bedminster, the separate town that eventually became South Bristol, strongly associated with Dissention and the development of tobacco, sugar and chocolate industries owned by Non-conformist families such as the Frys and Wills, dynasties linked to the Quakers and rooted in manufacturing rather than maritime trading.

The merging of the 'Hundred of Bedminster' with the City of Bristol around 1900 brought the two ruling élites into direct competition for control of the central commemorative landscape of a new Bristol. The built environment is still bedecked with their claims to the high ground. Two edifices mark the skyline: Cabot's Tower, an 'ornate Victorian minaret' was built in 1897 to mark the 400th anniversary of the discovery of Nova Scotia by another of Bristol's adopted sons, the Genoese adventurer Giovanni Cabotto (renamed John Cabot for Bristol purposes). It proclaims and celebrates the spirit of the city's mercantile entrepreneurialism. Quarter of a mile away stands the 1925 Wills Memorial Building of Bristol University, which was substantially funded by the eponymous South Bristolian family, and further aided by the Frys. At 215 feet high its massive tower is over 100 feet taller than the Cabot Tower, it dominates the city horizon, not merely a monument to the spirit of education but to the munificence of the Wills dynasty and a remarkable way of imposing one family's identity onto the civic landscape.[5]

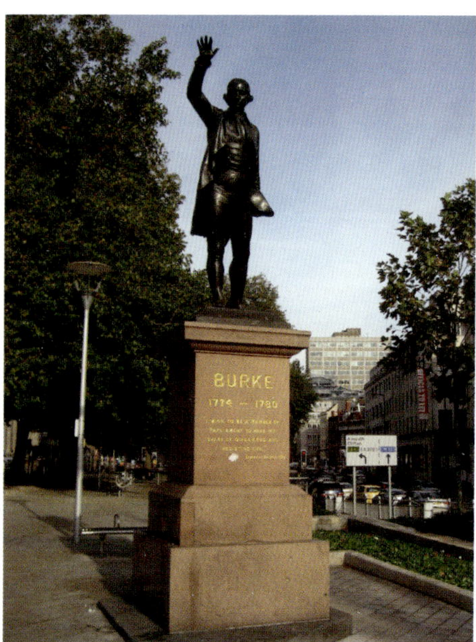
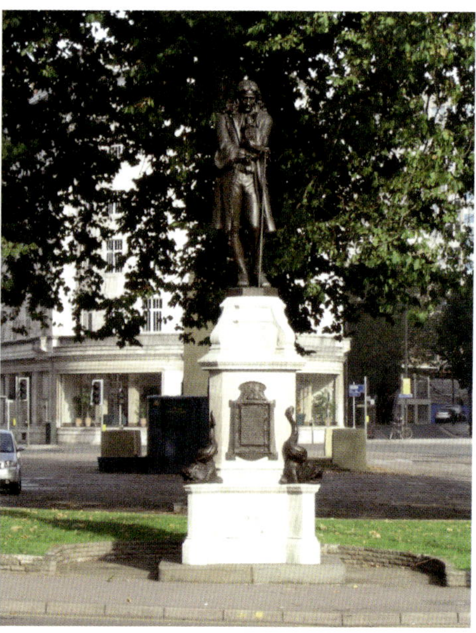

Statue of Edmund Burke MP, by James Havard Thomas, 1894, on St Augustine's Parade, central Bristol. [photograph: Paul Gough]

Statue of Edward Colston, by John Cassidy, 1895, St Augustine's Parade, central Bristol. [photograph: Paul Gough]

Elsewhere in the city, other monumental forms perpetuated the adversarial *frisson* between the rival factions. In 1894, the year that W.H. Wills was returned to Parliament as MP for East Bristol, he marked the occasion by commissioning a statue to the mid-eighteenth-century radical Whig MP for Bristol, Edmund Burke. One year later, by way of response, John Cassidy's statue of Edward Colston, paragon of the city's mercantile and Anglican values, was erected in the centre. Today, the two statues stand a hundred metres apart locked forever in a historical dispute which rumbles on. Although the hunched posture of Colston seems to suggest he is talking into a mobile cellphone, there is no dialogue with the bronze politician, no dialogue: instead they perform parallel monologues reciting the inequities of Bristol's past.

Such tensions erupt periodically but persistently. In 2006 the city held the great 'apology debate', a mass gathering of historians, politicians and other public figures, chaired by A.C. Grayling, intending to arrive at a conclusive declaration. 'It's time the city said sorry,' proclaimed *The Bristol Evening Post*, but in the event no clear consensus emerged. On the contrary, the debate stirred up further anger and upset. Seven years earlier, with rather less fuss, Liverpool City Council had passed a formal motion unanimously acknowledging and apologising for the city's part in the slave trade.[6]
It is not difficult to see, then, how the mnemonic landscape of Bristol offers a difficult setting for any monumental intervention. Take for example its war memorial. Given its speckled history of internecine rivalry it will not surprise us that Bristol was the very last major city in Great Britain to erect its own Cenotaph, a monument to the 6,000 men and women who died in the Great War. Designed to unite disparate factions in one inclusive act of mourning it was not unveiled until 1932, fourteen years after the Armistice. The delay was due not to its cost, to its design or inscription, but to its very location. It now stands on a traffic island on reclaimed land over the river Frome, a 'neutral' spot lodged between the mercantile north of the city and the Nonconformist south, a tomb to no one on no one's land.[7]

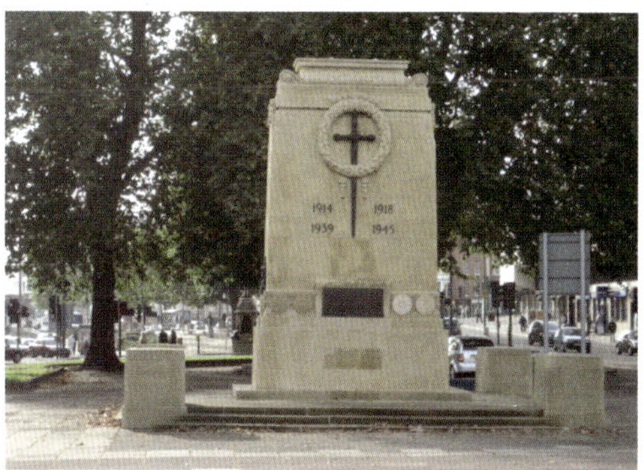

The Bristol Cenotaph, St Augustine's Parade, Bristol. [photograph: Harry Gough]

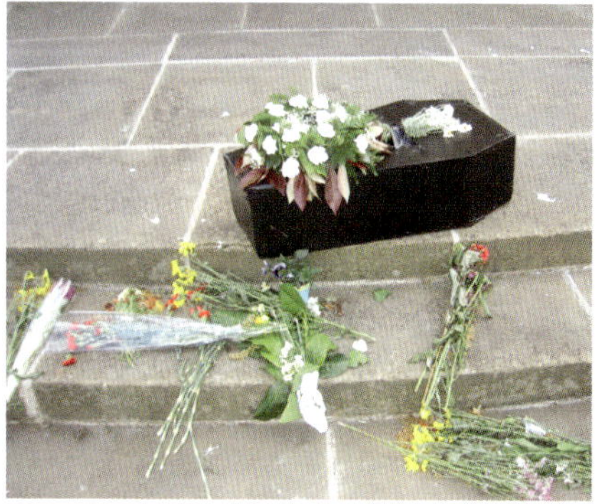

Cardboard child's 'coffin' on the steps of Bristol Cenotaph, April 2003. [photograph: Paul Gough]

As major markers in the urban landscape, memorials encapsulate and perpetuate memory. The very sites and spaces they command and control are important. Rarely are they arbitrary assignations, they are 'consciously situated to connect or compete with existing nodes of collective remembering.'[8] Containing and conveying memory, memorials exist not only as aesthetic devices but as an apparatus of social memory, as 'rhetorical topoi', civic compositions that set out our national heritage and our public responsibilities, positioned in the urban *schema* as the embodiment of power and memory.

However deeply submerged they may be in the collective sub-conscious of a city, such tensions explain why the rhetorical iconography embedded in monuments is capable of arousing such ire when they are first sited, defaced, removed or threatened with relocation. Statues, their chosen subjects and their positioning in British cities arouse passions that can seem disproportionate to the actual investment in bronze or stone. The livid protests that accompanied the erection of a statue to the RAF commander 'Bomber' Harris may seem rather extreme sixty years after the war, but that is to underestimate the role played by public artefacts in sustaining certain power bases, especially in moments of contemporary anxiety or dispute.[9] Power, as Foucault points out, creates its own points of resistance and the power over memory and identity held by any dominant social group is rarely left unchallenged.[10] That which is designed to provide a locus of 'inclusion', also proclaims exclusion, and can arouse disruption from a rival faction or from discontented individuals.

Banksy's exhibition was clearly attuned to the vexatious histories of his home city. His work is aligned to, indeed perhaps derived from and nurtured by, the spirit of dissent that drives the counter-cultures of Bristol. During this same period – the tail-end of a Blair government and a Bush administration – there was increasing evidence in the city of visual dissent that drew its energy and iconography from the stencilled street art of Banksy and other 'unknown' urban calligraphers.

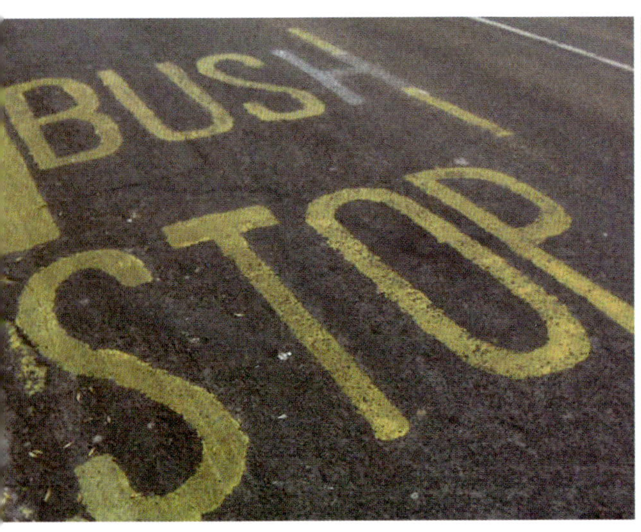

'BUSH STOP', street marking. Bedminster, Bristol, autumn 2008. [photograph: Paul Gough]

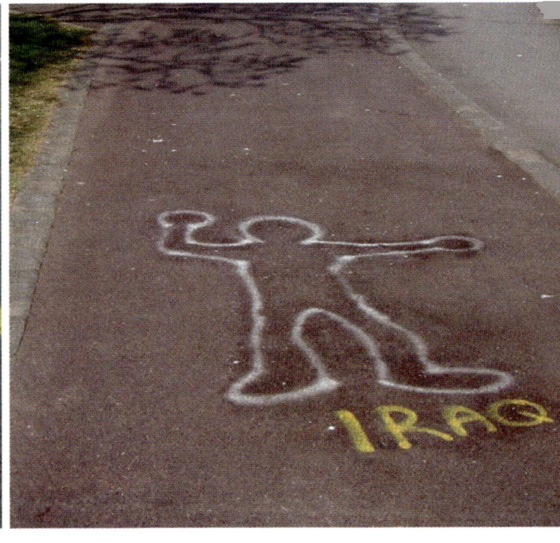

'IRAQ', street marking, St Peter's Park, Bristol, 2004. [photograph: Paul Gough]

A number of these interventions took the temporary form of signs, symbols or letters painted onto road surfaces – the letter 'H' appended to the words 'BUS STOP' for example, to create the phrase 'BUSH STOP', or the outline figure of a corpse marked with the words 'IRAQ', painted on the cycle path that runs through the peace park near St Peter's Church in central Bristol.

Other interventions appear to be more systematic, targeted at the billboards surrounding the controversial commercial development at Cabot Circus. A band of guerilla-artists operating under the banner 'Subvertise' regularly re-label and re-word billboard signs on many of the approach roads into the city. The forms used by these guerrilla interventionists are sophisticated and knowingly applied: the typography mimics the graphic conventions of corporate advertising, and engages in wordplay linking commemoration with commerce, protest with politics. The same group may have been responsible in 2003 for depositing a cardboard facsimile of a child's coffin on the steps of the Bristol Cenotaph, around which were strewn bouquets of flowers with a typed label: 'For Those Who Died for Oil'. A commemorative artwork shown in a foyer gallery at the Watershed was appropriated by guerilla interventionists protesting against US and UK military interventions in Afghanistan. South of the river a tagger who signed himself in two-metre-high capital letters as 'The True Baron of Bedminster' laid down a challenge to those other Barons who had marked the city with their own large scale, self-aggrandizing monuments.

Banksy's exhibition was clearly attuned to the vexatious histories of his home city.

Do such gestures constitute an organized counter-culture or are they spontaneous forms of politicized, anti-corporate tagging? Are they truly contemporary manifestations of a city that is not at peace with itself or its historic past? Or are they more generalized anti-capitalism gestures? The apology debate was inconclusive; Banksy has attained the status of canny anti-hero; Massive Attack still refuse to perform at a music venue named after Edward Colston.[11] Should much of this surprise us? Such historical disputes mark every cityscape. In Bristol, however, they are rehearsed repeatedly in proxy through its mnemonic landscape, through the network of sculptures, statues and plinths that already litter its precincts, and more markedly by temporary and irreverent markers that cast a necessary shadow across the official history of the city.

Notes

1. An assessment of 64 UK cities, conducted by the 'Centre for Cities' in 2010 indicated that Bristol appeared well placed for the economic recovery given its highly educated workforce, strong private sector and high level of graduate skills. It has a large number of knowledge-intensive businesses and is ranked eighth highest for employment in K-I Businesses (2008) – 91,100 employees (24.7% of the total); it is also ranked 8th for lowest youth unemployment (16-24); 8th fastest growing city by population growth (1998-2008).

2. Lauren Collins, *The New Yorker*, 14 May 2007, www.newyorker.com/reporting/2007/05/14/070514fa_fact_collins (accessed 8th August 2011).

3. www.news.bbc.co.uk/1/hi/england/bristol/8330514.stm (accessed 8 August 2011).

4. Fussell, P., *The Great War and Modern Memory* (Oxford, Oxford University Press, 1975) p.79.

5. Morgan, S.J., (1998). 'Memory and the Merchants: Commemoration and Civic Identity', *International Journal for Heritage Studies*, vol.4 (2), pp.103-113.

6. See for example: www.liverpoolmuseums.org.uk/ism/srd/liverpool.aspx (accessed 8 August 2011).

7. Gough, Paul and Morgan, Sally J. (2004) 'Manipulating the Metonymic: the politics of civic identity and the Bristol Cenotaph, 1919-1932', *Journal of Historical Geography*, no.30, pp.665-684.

8. Boyer, M. Christine, *The City of Collective Memory: Its Historical Imagery and Architectural Entertainments* (Cambridge Massachusetts and London, MIT Press, 1996) p.343.

9. Johnson. N. (1995) 'Monuments, Geography and Nationalism', *Environment and Planning D: Society and Space*, no.13, pp.51-65.

10. Foucault, M., *The History of Sexuality*, vol. 1 (London, Penguin, 1981) pp.95-96.

11. The accommodation of Banksy into Bristol's new sense of itself is evident in the officially sanctioned literature. *The Bristol 20:20 Plan, Bristol's Sustainable City Strategy* includes a section on 'creative genius' which lists Banksy as the most brilliant star in its cultural constellation:

> *This Bristol effect is the product of dissenting politics and racial and cultural mix. It even owes a lot to the St Pauls Riot. There is no better example of this than Banksy, once condemned as an inner city vandal, but now feted as an artist of international stature, whose exhibition at Bristol City Museum in 2009 produced huge queues each day. (p.30)*

A shorter version of this essay was published as: Gough, P.J. 'The 'versus' habit: Bristol, Banksy and the Barons', in '*Lest We Forget*', editors Maggie Andrews, Charlie Bagot-Jewitt and Nigel Hunt (London, Black Dog Press, 2011).

Challenging the institutions:

Street art and Bristol passion

Kath Cockshaw

The 2009 exhibition, 'Banksy vs Bristol Museum' was a runaway success in terms of visitor figures, providing a boost to Bristol tourism and the local economy. This chapter considers the challenges facing Bristol artists, and the conditions of production, funding and exhibiting opportunities for artists of all kinds who live and work in the city. Following the Banksy exhibition, the evaluation analysis carried out by Bristol City Council proved the extent of the financial and cultural benefits resulting from the project for the city, clearly illustrating that Bristol must invest more in its artists to gain future return. To further illustrate her argument, the author explores the importance of 'Banksy v Bristol Museum' and the RWA exhibition, 'Crimes of Passion: Street Art in Bristol', which immediately preceded it, in the context of the international street art movement.

When I lived and worked in Bristol as an arts fundraiser and curator, I realised that the stories which people told me of their associations with Banksy were a form of civic pride. Shortly after I moved to the city in 2006, a taxi driver said to me, 'I had that Banksy in my cab the other day'; I laughed. How did he know? A few days later, the window-cleaner told me he'd been Banksy's best mate at school. Similar claims were made by a variety of people I spoke to in all sorts of situations during my time in the city. If they were all to be believed, never was there such a popular kid in the playground, but his friends tell me a different story. There is immense local support for Banksy, and for street art, in Bristol.

Five years ago, the monetary value of Bristol street artists' work began to rocket, as international interest grew

An early graffiti exhibition: Arnolfini, 1985.

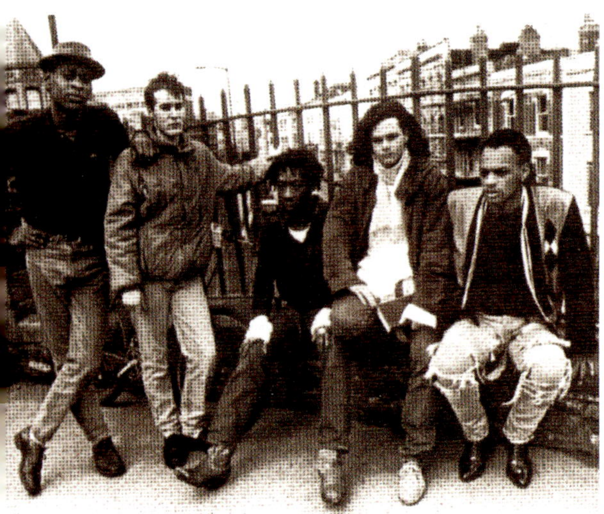

Music makers, The Wild Bunch, who metamorphosed into Massive Attack, part of the Bristol counter-culture which spawned the Arnolfini exhibition. [reproduced courtesy *Naked Guide to Bristol*]

in the city's urban art scene, largely driven by online forums, pop-up exhibitions, and a series of high profile auctions. However, until 2009, there had not been an urban art exhibition hosted by a *public* gallery in Bristol, since a show entitled 'Graffiti Art in Britain' at the Arnolfini in 1985[1].

Raising money and developing audiences for new creative projects of any kind in Bristol is hard, no matter the strength of support for the idea. It's a tough call to raise arts funding anywhere in the UK now, but in Bristol, despite a burgeoning arts scene with international respect across several art-forms – street art; animation; circus; classical, pop and jazz music, to name but a few – local funding sources are extremely limited and heavily over-subscribed, and existing public funding structures are restrictive, ill-conceived and out-dated.

Despite the lack of local public funding for arts projects, and continued lack of interest from Bristol's business community, pockets of enterprising individuals have been producing their own independently funded public street art projects and exhibitions in the city's disused buildings for several years, and continue to do so.

In December 2007, an urban art exhibition 'The 12 Days of Xmas', produced by Jono Boyle and Lucie Akerman of the artists collective Steal from Work, took place at the Old Police Station in Broadmead.[2] Following a strategic web-based PR campaign targeting the street art forums and fanbases, news of the show spread like wildfire. Over 1,000 people turned up on the opening night; the atmosphere down in the cells was electric. Queues stretched around the block. Steal From Work went on to produce 'Not a Penny off Pay' at a disused motorcycle showroom building in May 2008. Queues of people trailed up Stokes Croft for six hours before the exhibition opened. Tens of thousands of pounds worth of art was sold at both exhibitions.

Eventually, in autumn 2008, the Royal West of England Academy (RWA), a public art gallery and registered charity, which receives no core funding from the Arts Council, nor any regular funding from Bristol City Council, caught on. In September that year, the RWA commissioned me to produce a large exhibition of street art and an education programme, and to help raise funds for it all to happen.

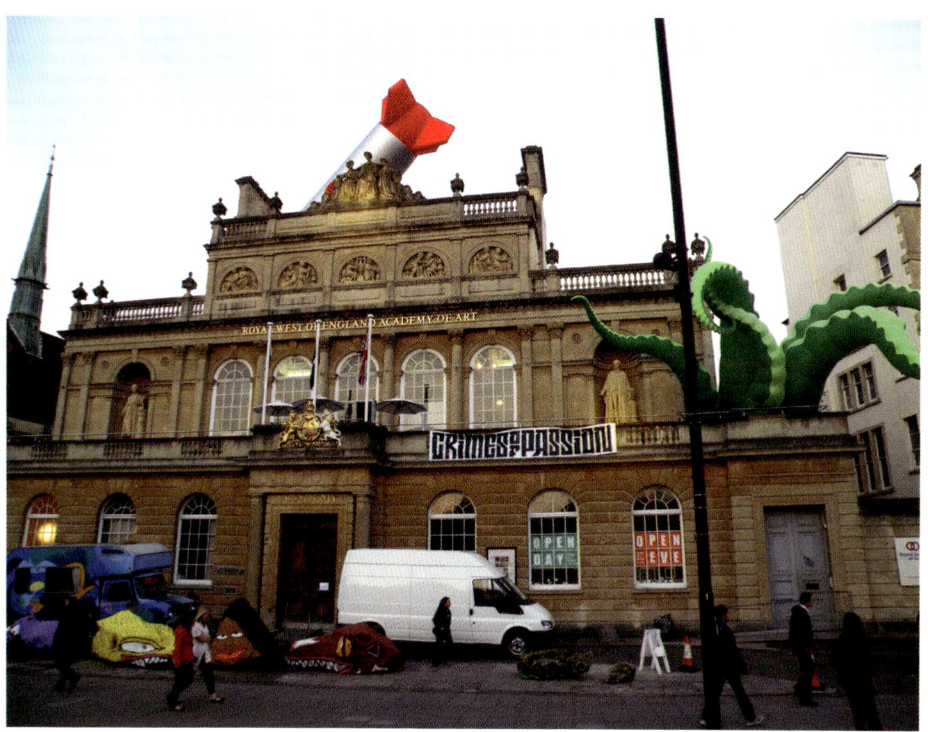

Royal West of England Academy: a great institution opens its doors to street art. (photograph: Kath Cockshaw)

The RWA sought to capitalise on the footfall and sales being achieved at other street art exhibitions in the city; in return, they offered Bristol graffiti artists an incredible platform on which to perform and exhibit, unrivalled in the city in terms of grandeur and square footage. I recruited graffiti artist Felix Braun and Jono Boyle of Steal from Work, also a street artist, as my co-organisers for the project. The title of the show, 'Crimes of Passion: Street Art in Bristol', was eventually approved by the RWA; it was felt that the wording illustrated what it meant to display street culture on the hallowed walls of an establishment institution.

The board of the RWA had two predominant aims in mind for their planned urban art exhibition – to make a profit from sales of work, and to bring in new, younger audiences. I was offered in-house resources in the form of premises and staffing, and a very small marketing budget, which was already in place for programmed exhibitions. There were no further financial resources available for the production of the show, or for anything 'out of the ordinary', shall we say. A proposal for an exhibition of street art at the RWA had previously been explored and turned down two years earlier, due to a lack of resources.

'Crimes of Passion' was essentially a labour of love for the organisers and forty-five artists who took part. Through piecemeal, cap-in-hand fundraising at the bottom of an economic downturn, we raised a total budget of

£85,000 all-in to cover costs for the production of the show, an exhibition catalogue, public events, and a successful education programme. There were no salaries as such for the organisers, but discretionary payments were made to us from profits raised by sales of work at the end of the project. Most of the funding for the development of the show came from the private sector, through local support for the exhibition idea. The Arts Council offered £5,000 and Bristol City Council offered nothing.[3]

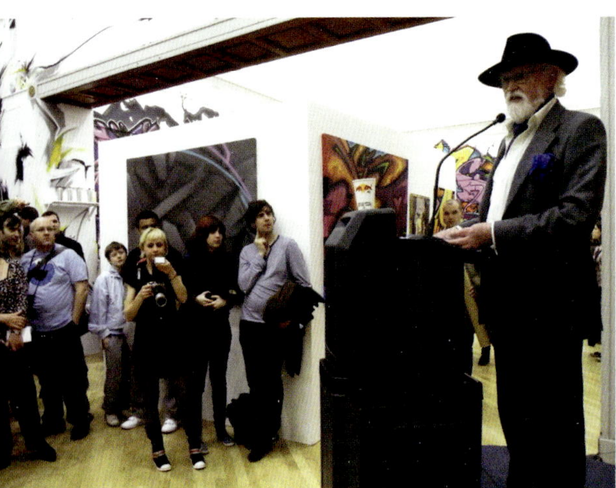

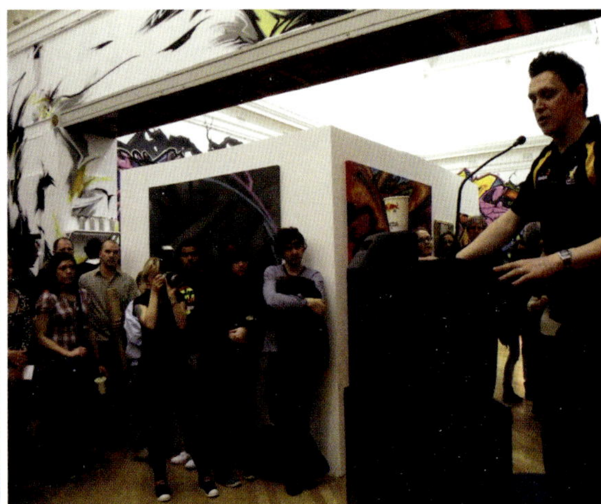

The then President of the RWA, Derek Balmer, opening the 'Crimes of Passion' exhibition.

Street artist, Jono Boyle (Motorboy).
(Both photographs: Kath Cockshaw)

'Crimes of Passion' opened on 21 March 2009. The exhibition was a tribute to street art in Bristol and the inventiveness and creativity of its leading local protagonists. Going by the cast-list, 'Crimes of Passion' was never going to be just a round-up of artists' tags and spray-can prowess. Outside the RWA building, the show was heralded by Rowdy's series of large, brightly coloured cartoon animal heads, painted on rocks mined from a local quarry (which proved to be incredibly popular with children and students, throughout the run of the exhibition), and Filthy Luker's traffic-stopping giant inflatable green tentacles, which waved nonchalantly in the wind. Inside, the artwork started on the marble walls of the grand staircase leading up through the building, and it didn't stop.

The main galleries featured work by internationally known artists, Inkie, Nick Walker, Sick Boy and Mr Jago, alongside work by forty other prominent and emerging Bristol artists. Huge spray-painted works, made directly on to the elaborately corniced, expansive white walls, loomed overhead. Vast, complex wrap-around group murals stretched high and wide, while wild-style graffiti, abstract art, stencil work, digital painting, MDF constructions, installations, taxidermy, junk art, polystyrene sculpture, detailed 3D models, crocodile mobiles, cast torsos, and surrealist art proliferated. Not to mention Mudwig's giant inflatable sausage.

Some 30,000 people came to see 'Crimes of Passion' at the RWA, more than the institution's entire annual footfall. Staff and board members were astounded by the steady flow of visitors and weekend queues, as word of the exhibition spread. There were two launch events for the exhibition; a buyers' preview, attended by 450 people, and the private view, attended by 1,300 people. Sales of prints and originals were good but not quite as high as we had projected; by the time the show opened, recession was in full swing. The exhibition was extended for as many days as was practically possible.[4]

A contribution by Banksy would have been the icing on the cake for the board of the Academy, and there was a certain amount of pressure on the organising team to procure this. A few of the artists in the exhibition were in contact with Banksy during the project's development. There was a whisper of an 'involvement', perhaps an external piece, perhaps an intervention of some kind. Then all went quiet.

Little did I know that around the same time that the RWA commissioned me in autumn 2008 to produce 'Crimes of Passion' Kate Brindley, then Director of Bristol City Museum & Art Gallery, had agreed to meet with a representative of Banksy's crew for a conversation which would lead to the development of the 'Banksy vs Bristol Museum' exhibition. Though we knew each other well, Kate herself did not tell me anything of the plan for the Museum until after the Banksy show opened, such were the levels of secrecy involved.

Six weeks prior to the opening of 'Crimes of Passion', however, I was passed information about the planned Banksy show, down the road at the City Museum. Following covert discussions, it was decided that the RWA and the Museum would work together to focus on the legacy of the shows; and that the new 'Museum of Bristol' would document the development and public interest in both projects, when it opened in 2011. At that point, Tim Corum, Deputy Head of Bristol's Museums and Galleries, offered the RWA a fixed amount of public funding for the documentation process.

On the morning of 13 June 2009, staff at the City Museum stared open-mouthed when they arrived at work to be confronted by a burned out ice-cream van, surrounded by a plethora of satirical installations, provocative visual stunts and practical jokes featuring costumed mannequins, customised toys, models and taxidermy. Without the knowledge of council officials, or most of the museum staff, a well-briefed, well-prepared 'crack team' had worked through the night to produce 'Banksy vs Bristol Museum', a large exhibition of the artist's 2D and 3D works, slick animatronics and 'interventions', which sprouted from the museum's collections over the entire building.

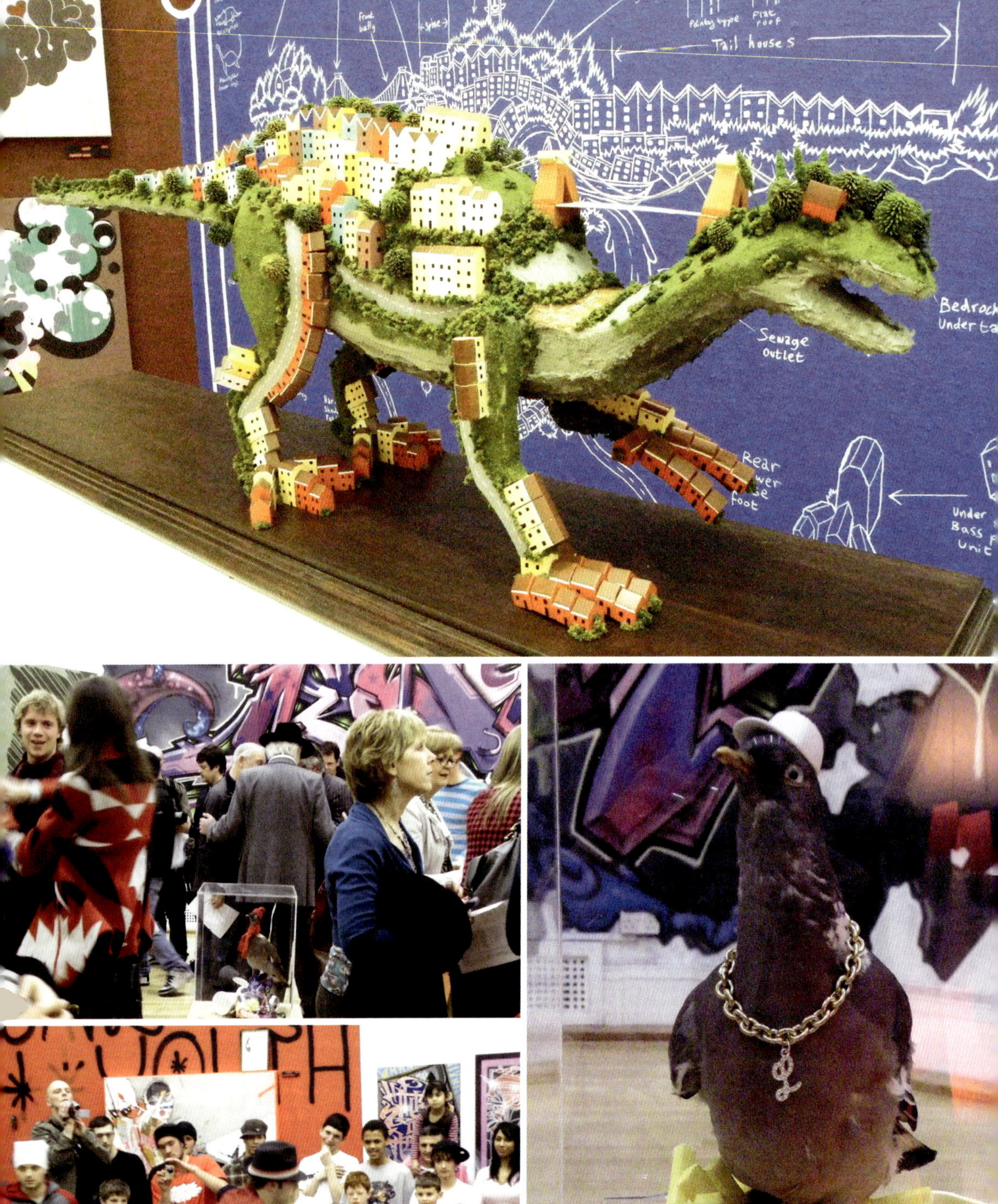

Scenes from the RWA exhibition. (photographs: Kath Cockshaw)

   Banksy, The Bristol Legacy

On the day of the press conference, prior to the public opening, the Museum's Director, Kate Brindley, told me that she stood, rooted to the spot from sunrise to sunset, fielding questions from the world's media. It was clear that the Banksy exhibition was going to be an unprecedented success, but no regional museum could possibly have been prepared for the forthcoming tidal wave of visitors, and the queue, which grew longer all day, every day, every week, for the entire run of the show, as news of the exhibition spread around the globe.

On the opening day of 'Crimes of Passion', three months before the opening of the Banksy exhibition, I sat on the forecourt of the RWA building, watching in amazement as hundreds of people streamed in through the doors. I knew then that what we had created had hit all the buttons for Bristol audiences, street art enthusiasts and tourists, attracting regional, national and international visitors across a broad demographic.

I remember wondering what other kind of exhibition would attract audiences in their droves like that. The majority of visitors to that exhibition had never visited the RWA before, and during the run of the show, many Bristolians told me that prior to hearing of 'Crimes of Passion', they had no idea that the prominent building was in fact a public art gallery.

Two and a half years on, I still get emails from people around the world asking me to comment or take part in interviews about my involvement in the 'Crimes of Passion' exhibition at the RWA. We received warm, positive feedback from local and regional audiences of all ages. Online comment forums show the extent of support for the show from the local community as well as the UK and international street art community.

I have been a curator, campaigner and fundraiser for public art galleries and the visual arts for over twelve years. Prior to these two exhibitions, I had never witnessed, or heard of, such demonstrable public interest in a visual art exhibition by local contemporary artists at a regional museum.

So how can we define Bristol's passion for street art and where does it come from? How can we place the city's street art shows of 2009 in a wider cultural context?

Many of Bristol's street artists, DJs, musicians, and underground performance groups, such as Artspace, Lifespace and The Invisible Circus (whose regular shows are attended by many hundreds of people), share common personality traits and an attitude of wilful independence. These characteristics are expressed in the ways they create, exhibit, perform and promote their work.

Talent, creativity, balls, originality, inventiveness, attitude, humour, determination, stubbornness, guile – call it what you like, but despite all the inherent insecurities which go with the territory of being an artist, Bristol's creatives seem to have it in spades, and their audiences love it.

Bristol breeds and attracts mavericks and people who want to do things their own way. As in most artistic enclaves, depression, a sense of rebellion, and a fighting spirit are rife in the city's arts communities. Local cynics often say, rather tragically, that Bristol is a 'graveyard of ambition'. This may be so for some, but success in any field of work is down to the talent and strength of the individual, and nowhere is this more true than the arts scene in Bristol.

Leading figures on Bristol's creative underground scene come and go. Big personalities, at their most magnetic on the crest of a wave, can attract followers easily in Bristol. There are some whose dogged determination knows no bounds, except their own repeated financial demise, and one or two who have learned to combine their talent with incisive business acumen – they don't tend to stay in the city for long. There are a steady few who get their heads down and get on with it, but in my experience, artists and creatives who make a living from their work in Bristol are only able to do so with single-minded, dogged determination, and bags of talent.

I think the terms 'Street art', 'Urban art', and 'Graffiti' do not really cover the diverse forms of contemporary art featured in 'Crimes of Passion' and 'Banksy vs the Museum'. The terms 'Underground art', or 'Outsider art' also apply to much of the work by Bristol's street artists and other kinds of artists working in the city. Undoubtedly, the laissez-faire attitude of Bristol's cultural establishment, and lack of public funding for the arts in the city, simultaneously permits and inspires a sense of rebellion in local artists, pushing them to work in and create an 'underground' culture.[5]

In terms of curatorial vision, we took inspiration for 'Crimes of Passion' in part from a show called 'Beautiful Losers', created by a group of self-proclaimed 'outsider artists' at the Contemporary Arts Center in Cincinnati, Ohio in 2004. That show, which featured work by the now internationally renowned street artist Shepard Fairey and film director Spike Jonze, continues to tour and inspire audiences and artists worldwide.[6] The 2011 street art extravaganza, 'Art in the Streets' at the Museum of Contemporary Art in L.A. (17 April-8 August 2011) was America's latest much-hyped public museum offering, born out of a world-renowned, longstanding, underground culture in the city.

As with the US shows, 'Crimes of Passion' at the RWA and 'Banksy vs Bristol Museum' were a natural progression of the street art exhibitions that had been happening in disused spaces and studios throughout Bristol for several years. The exhibitions were keystone events in a recognised international contemporary art movement which started in the eighties, with which there is an increasingly strong public affinity worldwide. The international significance of 'Crimes of Passion' and the Banksy exhibition is borne out by the level of international response which the exhibitions received in the form of online forums, media interest, numbers of visitors and continued public interest.

What can we learn from the public museum-based street art shows which took place in Bristol in 2009, and what is their legacy?

Following the launch of 'Banksy vs Bristol Museum', Bristol-based artists and curators were greatly encouraged when Tim Corum and Phil Walker of the City Museum consulted with them as part of a targeted public outreach programme, inspired by the exhibition. That period of consultation resulted in several new projects which brought the work of local regional, national and international contemporary artists in to the Museum, including a year-long series of six plinth installations, organised by Container duo, Paul Witt and Rob Manners; 'Wild Dayz', an exhibition about Bristol's music scene focusing on the legendary Dug Out club; and a large exhibition with a Californian commercial gallery, Corey Helford, entitled 'Art from the New World', which represented the work of emerging underground US artists inspired by street art and 'neo-Pop culture', many of whom were well known to Bristol street artists and illustrators. 'Art from the New World' (15 May-22 August 2010) attracted over 30,000 visitors in its first five weeks.

These developments in programming at the Museum in 2009 were highly significant for Bristol's visual arts scene and were a further morale boost for local audiences. Traditionally, the programming for Bristol's public museums and galleries has been agreed by a small handful of people who manage the city's cultural institutions and organisations and those who manage and decree the funding for new projects. In Bristol it is often the norm that new visual arts projects stay small because funds are small. In terms of programming and funding, it is not that the appointed individuals responsible for defining Bristol's visual arts programmes have always aimed too low, but their working processes and the shape of the networks in which they operate are outdated and restrictive. The lack of communication between the leading players and organisations on the city's cultural scene, has meant that new projects initiated by its visual arts institutions in particular are often ultimately self-serving and exclusive.

Art junkies in Bristol have a variety of options in terms of spaces they can go to to indulge their passion. Outside of the public structure, Bristol-based artists of all kinds show their work in pop-up shows, street shows, regular

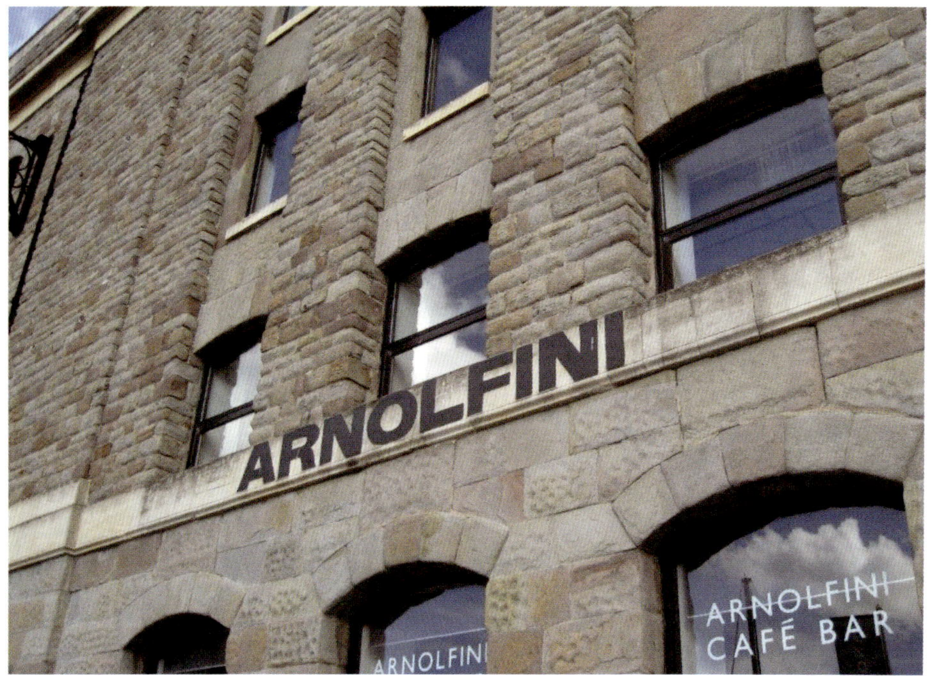

Arnolfini and Spike Island, Bristol: venues for cutting-edge work by international artists. (photographs: Paul Gough)

open studio events, commercial galleries and the city's year-round series of art trails and 'kitchen shows'. The trails are well attended, and the experience of interacting with and learning from artists, designers and makers who open up their houses in this way is generally deemed to be hugely enjoyable, even when the standard of art is questionable. The Arnolfini and Spike Island both programme cutting-edge work by international artists in exhibitions, installations and projects, and programme a range of public events.

The future and stability of Bristol's arts scene has been precarious for some time, because there has been too little public investment in culture for too long. Many local people feel that, like other European cities undergoing a process of regeneration, Bristol would benefit enormously in the long term from a landmark bridge, high quality public art, or a building by an international architect. Or citywide celebrations of the art forms for which Bristol is internationally known. Street Art? Dance music? Animation?

Following the success of 'Crimes of Passion' and the Banksy exhibition, and in direct response to a televised call by Councillor Simon Cook for further high profile 'joined up' arts projects in the city, there was considerable enthusiasm within Bristol's cultural establishment, and in the education and business sectors, for a citywide celebration of animation for 2012. The proposal that emerged included city-wide screenings and multi-site exhibitions, to include a touring show promoting Bristol as a world-renowned centre for animation. As with 'Crimes of Passion' at the RWA, various schemes had been proposed before and turned down due to a lack of funds. Now, the dearth of effective

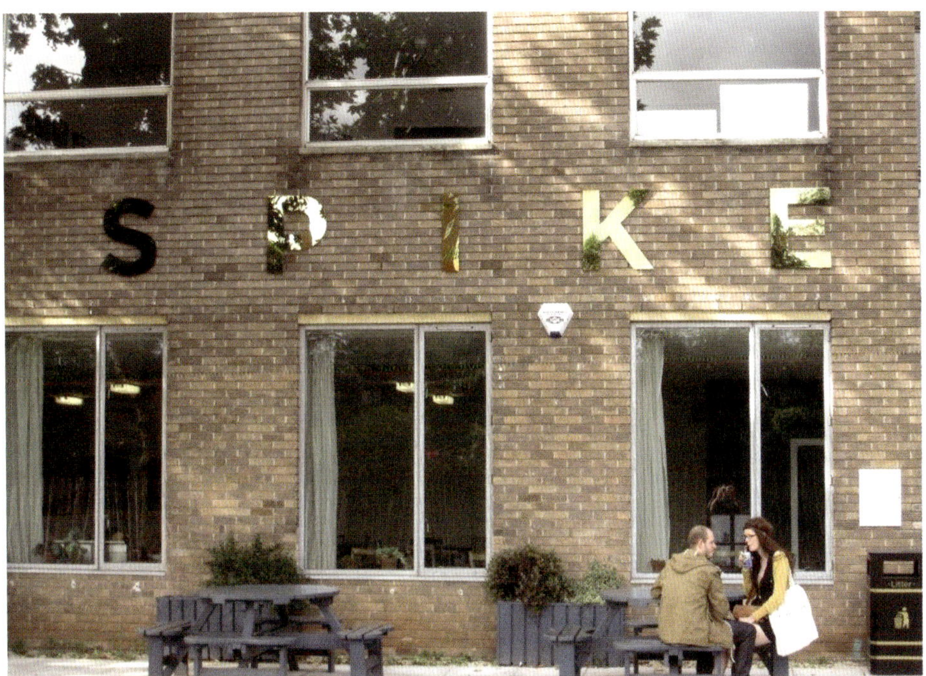

communication, a demonstrative lack of faith in a freelance team and an unwillingness to take risks on the part of cultural decision makers, ultimately stopped progress on the project.

Blockbuster exhibitions do not come to Bristol, and new touring exhibitions do not start in Bristol. Artists and musicians born, bred or based in the city have not been invested in, or properly celebrated by the city's cultural institutions. In order to change this, the current cultural establishment in Bristol needs to take more risks in its programming, especially in the areas of visual arts and music (the Banksy show was after all an unprecedented guerrilla exercise on the part of the artist *and* Museum Director), and the City Council and the city's arts institutions need to be more business-minded, and consult in useful, modern, pro-active ways with their audiences.

In terms of their cultural impact, the success of 'Crimes of Passion' and 'Banksy vs Bristol Museum', and subsequent exhibition projects inspired by them, proved that there is a tangible demand in Bristol for innovative programming, high quality substantial exhibitions, and public work by celebrated local, regional, national and international artists.

The seminal exhibition of work by Bristol's most notorious graffiti star, which took place in the summer of 2009 at Bristol City Museum and Art Gallery, was largely funded by the artist himself, and did not rely on public funding to make it happen. If it had, the exhibition could never have taken place in the form it did, when it did. According to a leaked copy of the contract between the museum and Banksy, the artist was paid a fee of £1 to exhibit his work. Councillor Simon Cook said, somewhat tellingly, that it was the '...best pound the Council ever spent.'[7]

Like one of its historic trading ships pitching on high seas, Bristol continues to weather its economic storms, but progress has been hard. If the City Council and its cultural establishment were to demonstrate a sense of civic pride and pay proper tribute to all the successful Bristol artists and musicians who continue to jump ship, the city would be able to help build and truly share in their legacy, reap the financial benefits and crucially retain local talent.

The recent appointment of creative businessman Mike Bennett as Bristol City Council's new Place-Making Director in September 2010 was a laudable, innovative, strategic move. He brings a modern approach to cultural investment and programming in Bristol, and to marketing the city and its image.

'See No Evil', an ambitious three-day street art project organised by 'Crimes of Passion' exhibitor Tom Bingle, aka the internationally celebrated street artist, Inkie, and backed by Bristol City Council under Mike Bennett's recommendation, was a major crowd puller in August 2011. As discussed elsewhere in this book, the project featured the work of top street artists from around the world, creating murals on buildings which currently form a concrete ghetto in and around Nelson Street in central Bristol, which the organisers hoped would receive international media attention and global interest. It is a further example of a highly successful Bristol-born artist 'giving back' to his city. This time though, there is a key cultural decision maker with his hands on the public purse strings, who has recognised the opportunity and its value.[8]

New, significant 'place-making' cultural projects can happen in Bristol, and we have seen how. The variety and creative potential of institutions in Bristol is there; effective communication between them, and with their audiences, is not. A brave, more creative approach to cultural funding, which forges new cross-sector partnerships, is key. Better communication between Bristol's cultural providers is key. Breaking down barriers is key. 'Crimes of Passion' and 'Banksy vs Bristol Museum' went some way in doing this, and this is their legacy.

Katharine Cockshaw is a visual arts curator, fundraiser and writer. She has worked across the public and commercial sectors, and extensively with museums and international charities. In 2008, Katharine was commissioned by Bristol's Royal West of England Academy to produce the landmark urban art exhibition, 'Crimes of Passion: Street Art in Bristol'. She is particularly motivated by organisational change and progression, and forging unexpected cross-sector partnerships to make big things happen quickly.

Notes

1. Felix FLX Braun, author of *Children of the Can* published in 2008, was one of the organisers of the 'Crimes of Passion' exhibition. On his 'Children of the Can' blog he discusses the 1985 graffiti exhibition at Bristol's Arnolfini:

'It was a warm July evening before they invented mobile phones, the Internet, or skunk, and Gallery 1 at the Arnolfini looked like the set of a New York cable TV hip hop show. The pieces on the walls were huge, train-scale, and painted in the mighty German 'art spray' Buntlack: all candy-pinks and oranges, and the deepest reds, electric blues and greens, the likes of which had rarely been seen in Bristol at the time. Enlargements of Henry Chalfant's New York subway graffiti photos hung in the foyer and the man himself was in town taking photos for his second book, *Spraycan Art*, and giving credence to the whole event. In the far corner by the stairs The Wild Bunch were holding court, dropping seminal classics such as T La Rock's 'It's Yours', and Run DMC's 'Sucker MCs'; whilst poppers, lockers and b-boys worked up a quick sweat in a large circle in the opposite corner, flanked by BSD's 'Wizard' piece and the Z-Boys' comeback comment on the whole issue of selling out, 'Traitor'. Documentary filmmaker Dick Fontaine was also in the house, working on his Channel 4 documentary 'Bombin'. Something was *definitely* happening, it was real, large and as fresh as a pair of red Puma States with matching fat laces.' October 2008

Bristol-based street artist AcerOne, who took part in 'Crimes of Passion', also commented on the 'Children of the Can' blog about the Arnolfini exhibition, 'This event has gone down in Bristolian history.'

A further comment on the subject of the Arnolfini show reads: 'That was the start of things for me. I was nine years [old] and was lucky enough to go there because my mum worked there at the time.' Mega Mega Mega, November 2008.

See: www.childrenofthecan.blogspot.com/2008/10/arnolfini-1985.html

The original 1985 promo for The Wild Bunch, who played at the Arnolfini event as described by FLX above, can be seen on YouTube, with a Bristol graffiti backdrop. The video, cut by Steve Haley, with several scenes shot by Julian Monaghan, 'shines a light on the vibrant early hip-hop scene in Bristol and features many of the city's unsung heroes, without whom there would never have been a "Bristol Sound".' Steve Haley, October 2008

www.youtube.com/watch?v=uQ2j2OV-6aM

2. Further information about Steal from Work's '12 Days of Xmas' and a substantial folio of images by Sarah Connolly can be accessed at: www.arrestedmotion.com/2011/03/openings-steal-from-work-flogging-a-dead-horse-the-showroom-bristol/www.stealfromwork.org/Archived-events/12-days-of-xmas-07/

3. Until recently, the Royal West of England Academy was regarded as a rather private arts institution, which relied heavily on the support of its 150 artist members, the 'Academicians'. In the past five years, much has changed. The 'Crimes of Passion' exhibition took place during a major re-appraisal of the institution. The RWA recently received an injection of public and private funds, including significant long-term support from the University of the West of England, and capital funding from the Heritage Lottery Fund. The RWA has never received regular or core public funding, so it usually charges admission fees to exhibitions.

4. A full-colour catalogue, featuring profiles and reproductions by all of the exhibiting artists was published. The fullest record of the exhibition is available on the website: www.crimesofpassion.info Sarah Connolly's comprehensive collection of photographs from the exhibition can be accessed on: www.flickr.com/photos/knautia/sets/72157615855041128

5. By the term 'cultural establishment', I am referring to the City Council and the city's arts institutions, museums and organisations, known in local government terms as Bristol's 'Key Cultural Providers', which all receive annual funding from Bristol City Council.

6. The story of the 2004 exhibition, 'Beautiful Losers', was made into a film featuring interviews with the artists: *Beautiful Losers* Dir. Aaron Rose, 90 Mins, 2008, produced by www.en.wikipedia.org/wiki/Sidetrack_Films Sidetrack Films in association with www.en.wikipedia.org/w/index.php?title=BlackLake_Productions&action=edit&redlink=1"BlackLake Productions.

'The greatest cultural accomplishments in history have never been the result of the brainstorms of marketing men, corporate focus groups, or any homogenized methods; they have always happened organically. More often than not, these manifestations have been the result of a few like-minded people coming together to create something new and original for no other purpose than a common love of doing it. In the 1990s, a loose-knit group of American artists and creators, many just out of their teens, began their careers in just such a way. Influenced by the popular underground youth subcultures of the day, such as skateboarding, graffiti, street fashion and independent music, artists like Shepard Fairey, Mark Gonzales, Spike Jonze, Margaret Kilgallen, Mike Mills, Barry McGee, Phil Frost, Chris Johanson, Harmony Korine, and Ed Templeton began to create art that reflected the lifestyles they led. Many had no formal training and almost no conception of the inner workings of the art world.' (Anonymous) www.imdb.com/title/tt0430916

7. This quote is taken from the Museums Libraries and Archives website, 'Case Study: Banksy vs Bristol Museum'. The site is a good source of information about the economic impact of the exhibition for Bristol. Also see 'Banksy: the economic impact' in this present book. www.research.mla.gov.uk/case-studies

8. For further information about the 'See No Evil' project, see: www.seenoevilbristol.co.uk.

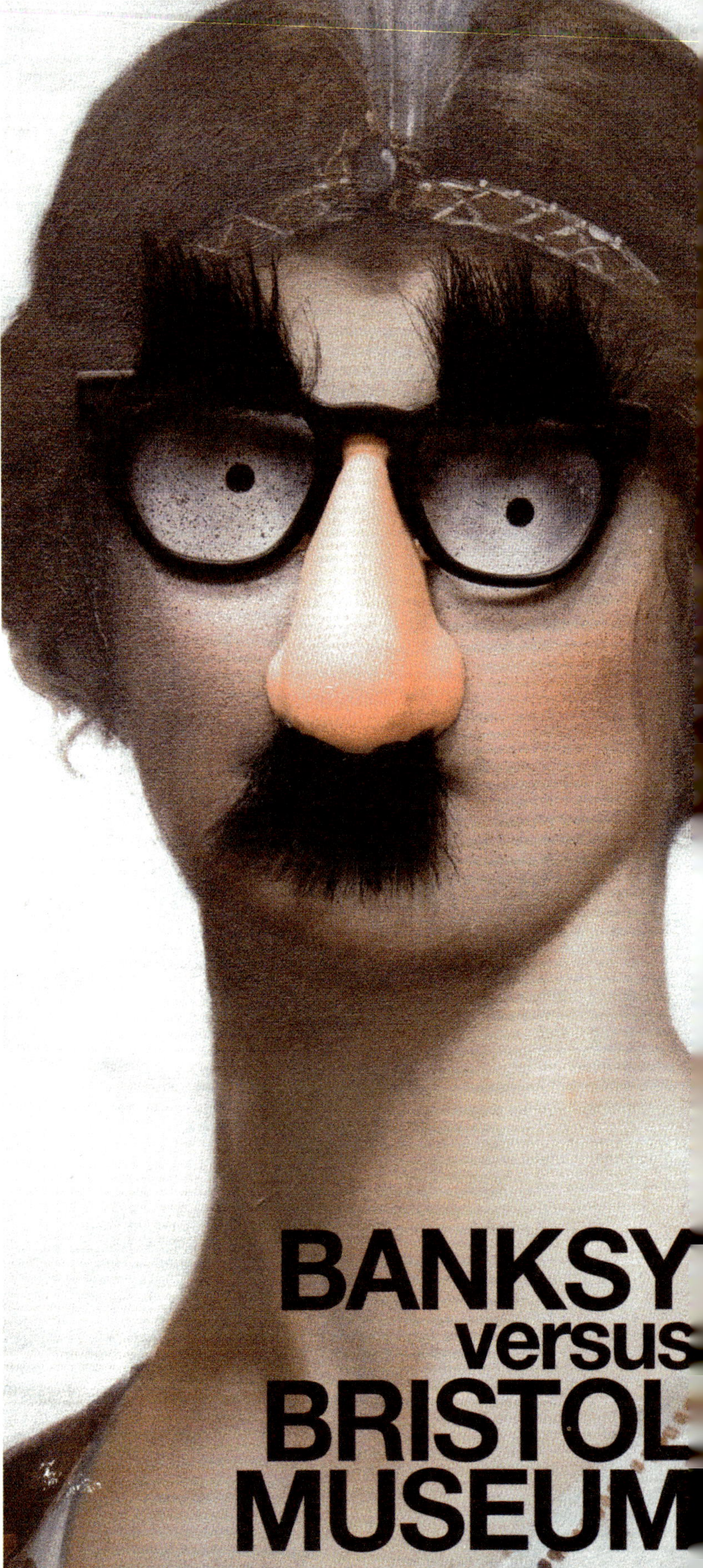

The official leaflet for the exhibition included a PG warning: 'contains scenes of a childish nature some adults may find disappointing.'

Bristol's great art heist
A view from inside the museum

This piece explores the major changes that the Banksy exhibition has caused in museum attitudes. It points to the shows by contemporary artists that have followed – which would not have happened without the trail blazed by the museum service – and how the experience revealed new ways of engaging people with collections and spaces. 'By our giving up control of the galleries we seemed to have enabled our visitors to engage more closely than ever before with both the collections and with gallery staff.'

Many people have asked how the whole thing was pulled off: everyone has a theory, many have made educated (others wild) guesses, few match the reality. Everybody wants to know and everybody has a view.

Unfortunately we can't tell the whole story of Bristol's greatest art heist, it is an extraordinary tale but like so much of Banksy's work must remain shrouded in mystery. Of course to be a part of the exhibition was exciting, it transformed the city museum overnight and made us the centre of world attention. More importantly for the museum as an organisation it has had a lasting impact on both the public's expectation of the museum and on our ambition to do more extraordinary things.

The impact of 'Banksy versus Bristol Museum' has been widely discussed, but most of the interest to date has been in the economic impact of the exhibition, occurring as it did in the midst of the 'credit crunch' and at a time when the cultural sector is increasingly seeking to demonstrate its financial value to the city's economy. The story we tell here is how the project enabled us to rethink the traditional model of the 'end of empire encyclopaedic any-town' museum. What we want to share in this essay is how the extraordinary experience of the Banksy show crystallised our rethinking of the city museum as a contested space, a space for ideas and creativity, for play and politics.

'Banksy versus Bristol Museum' was the first and quite probably the only collaboration between a museum and arguably the world's most famous artist.

During the weeks before the exhibition opened the web was full of rumour about Banksy's next great event. 'Something' was going to happen in June, 'somewhere' in Western Europe. In the fortnight leading up to opening there seemed to be a consensus that whatever Banksy was up to it looked like a 'homecoming' event, something for the city he reportedly comes

Banksy versus Bristol Museum

Bristol Museum and Art Gallery is proud to present a unique collaboration between the city's foremost cultural institution and one of the region's most overrated artists.

Banksy has gained notoriety in recent years by using stencils to paint images on a diverse array of outdoor locations. This is his first exhibition in a three storey Edwardian museum.

Tour highlights*

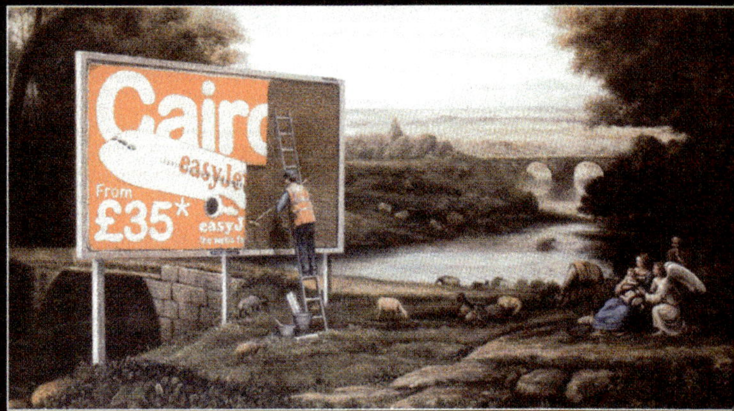

'The flight to Egypt' by Claude Lorrain. Unable to afford Lorrain original classic, Banksy has provided a no frills alternative.

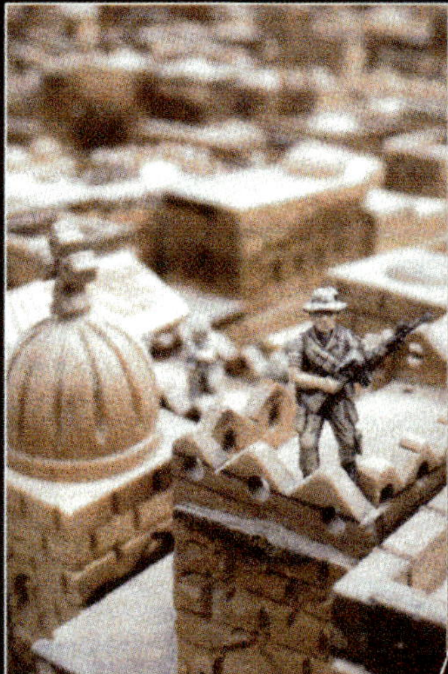

'Jerusalem' by Tawfiq Salsaa. Carved from native olive trees this intricate scale model was completed entirely from memory by a Bethlehem craftsman (Israel's security blockade has left him unable to visit the holy city for the past 12 years). A monumental achievement, it was purchased by Banksy and 'improved' by the addition of 284 toy soldiers. And one terrorist.

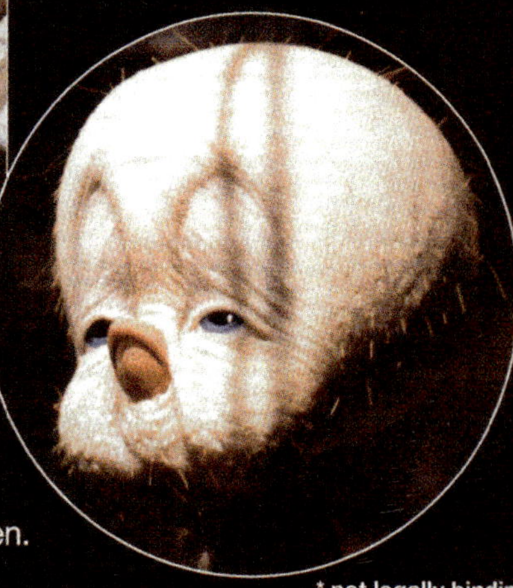

Tweety Pie
Visiting the west country for the very first time we present the star of such animated classics as 'I thought I saw a pussycat'. Please be aware this animal may bite, and dislikes children.

* not legally bindin

from, something for Bristol. With a week to go the web traffic indicated something extraordinary was going to happen somewhere in Bristol. But no one knew where.

On Thursday 11 June 2009 staff at Bristol Museum and Art Gallery turned up for work to find the museum transformed, the collection 'remixed' and that for the next 12 weeks Bristol City Museum had been handed over to Banksy. The work Banksy produced was extraordinary and demonstrated his breadth and ambition as well as his deft and witty manipulation of context. An entire gallery was hung with new stencil works and paintings; a recreation of his studio space gave a tantalising glimpse of how he operates; the museum's front hall was transformed into a crumbling urban square complete with wrecked ice cream van (which doubled as a reception desk). The rear hall had become a darkened and twisted menagerie of caged automata. Banksy also scattered his work throughout the permanent galleries, modified oils nestled amongst renaissance masters, a gypsy wagon seemed to have been clamped by an overzealous traffic warden, a hash pipe was nestled amongst the tea drinking paraphernalia in the ceramics gallery and our Assyrian reliefs now looked down on a scale model of Jerusalem populated by plastic soldiers and security watchtowers.

The whole stunt was pulled off with a subtlety, a sense of humour and professionalism that meant neither staff nor our regular visitors objected. By Friday evening the museum was filled with thousands of laughing, smiling visitors. And the queues didn't let up until we closed the exhibition almost three months later at the end of August. As others relate in detail in this book, over 300,000 people visited the show coming from all over the world and Bristol's economy boomed – an economic impact study estimated that over £10m was brought into the city as a direct result of Banksy's intervention. The exhibition was quite simply the single biggest event in the history of the museum service.

Naturally, we would like to take credit for this astonishing success but in truth the success was almost entirely down to Banksy. The stunt, his unique celebrity status, the accessibility, wit and humour of his work, his ambition and ability to deliver, all made the exhibition a success. The weight of tradition and public expectation often inhibits the development of civic organisations. There are few forces or people that have the appeal and dynamism to change the way people think about a place. Banksy is one of these. His impact is genuinely global and as attendance at the exhibition showed it reaches across generations. He is a translator and a mediator, an activist and comic. He demonstrated a deep understanding and respect of the museum's collections and its history as well as an uncanny awareness of its position in city life and its potential. In 'Banksy versus Bristol Museum' the public witnessed at first hand the clash of two utterly opposing archetypes, the bastion of culture, the authoritative institution versus the other, the outsider, the individual, the anonymous prankster.

The role of the curators

So what was our role? Put simply we helped create the environment which made this possible. When the opportunity arose we took the risk and managed it; we prepared the ground by developing the brand values that stressed new approaches, edginess and doing things differently. We created a narrative around Bristol Museum and Art Gallery (BMAG) which emphasised inspiration and creativity above all. We fostered a commitment to co-curation and a working culture that meant we were able to give up control of our spaces and to justify this to ourselves, to senior managers and to the city council as part of our long-term vision for the service. The truth is that we had always wanted to do something like this at BMAG. We had always wanted to break down the barriers between museum and visitor. We wanted to reinvigorate the museum's connection with artists and with Bristol; we wanted to create a buzz about the place. Banksy provided exactly that buzz.

Giving up control is anathema for a bureaucratic and hierarchical organisation like ours. Museums and local authorities have built their reputations on their reliability, authority and security. Professional ethics, procedure and academic rigour have provided a comforting cushion between users and the staff, and often ensures that even with the most inclusive and involving projects we are still asking our collaborators to work within our own boundaries rather than genuinely offering up control. Our world is full of constraints that many find baffling and obstructive. The result is that we tend to work with the same people, create the same projects and attract the same visitors.

The rewards for giving up control became apparent during the Banksy exhibition. We had lots of new visitors, but even our regular visitors seemed to appreciate a new-found freedom, seeing the museum and its collections in a new light, finding their way to displays they hadn't seen before and questioning those they were familiar with. By our giving up control of the galleries we seemed to have enabled our visitors to engage more closely than ever before with both the collections and with gallery staff.

Following on: the immediate impact

'The End of the Line', a show of contemporary drawings, was the name of the exhibition that followed Banksy. The irony of the title was not lost on the local press, who, having reported almost daily on the ever-growing line of people queuing to enter the museum, had hoped that the Banksy exhibition

A practical legacy. *Angel Bust* remained in situ in the front hall following the end of the exhibition. (photograph: Bristol Museum & Art Gallery)

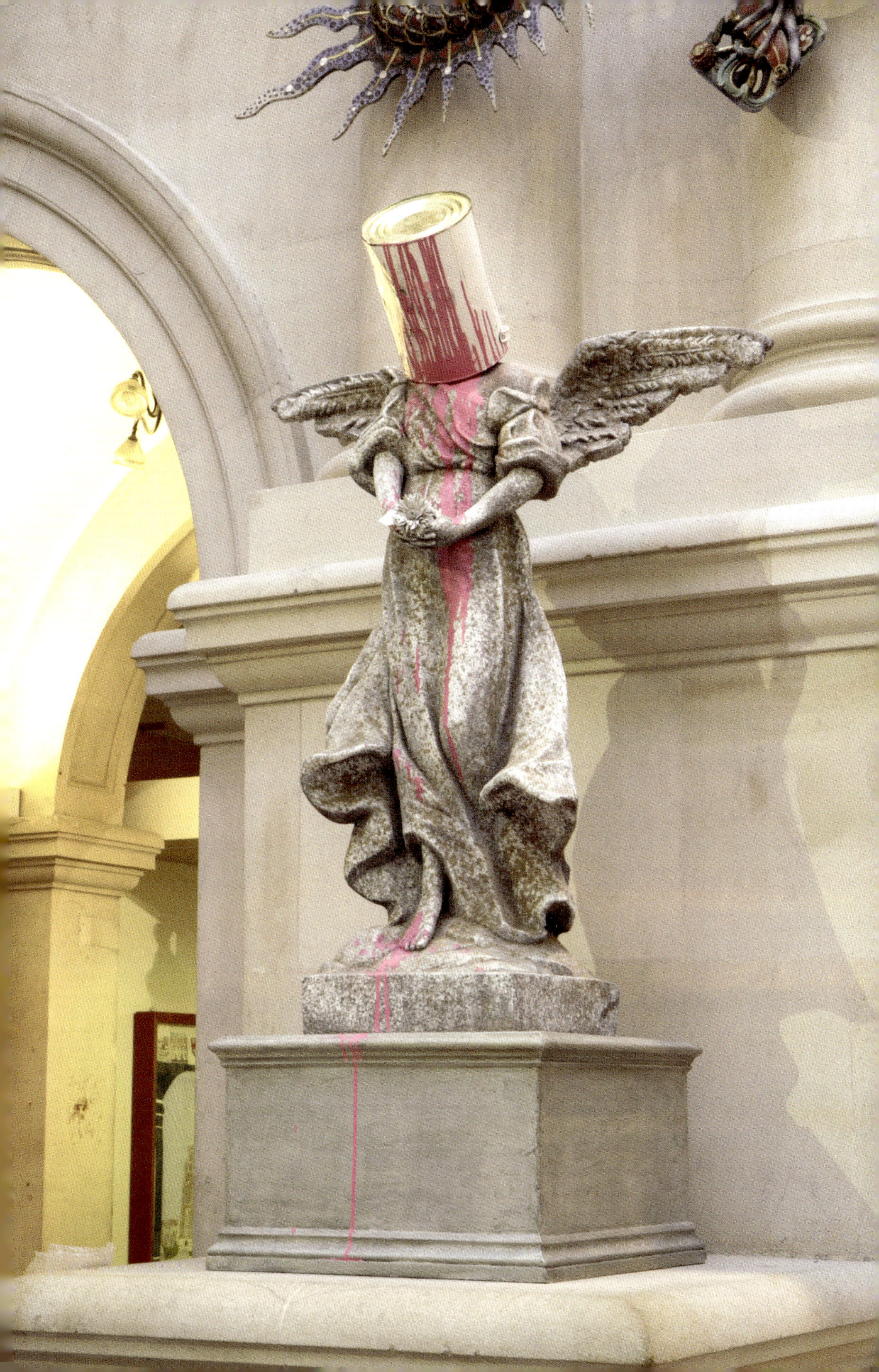

would never end. When it finally did come to an end, Banksy 'forgot' to take two of the works away. *Angel Bust* remains where he left it - on the plinth, the other - *Jerusalem* - is awaiting treatment before being redisplayed. But the lull that followed the closure of the show and the inevitable deflated feeling (a bit like the quiet morning after a glittering party) masked a fundamental change in the way the museum was perceived and the confidence and ambition of its staff.

In fact the legacy of the Banksy exhibition has manifested itself in a number of ways. The museum staff, visitors, artists, city, the cultural and commercial sectors have all been affected. Staff recruited for the summer have remained on to work across our venues, or migrated to other parts of the city council. Existing staff have emulated the Banksy infiltration of the museum, by creating hidden trails of museum collections in a more playful way - such as the numerous rabbits scattered liberally through the collections in celebration of the Chinese Year of the Rabbit. We encourage this playful approach to museum displays and aim to continue to re-mix our collections in future.

Visitors have begun to expect a fresh approach to the display of collections. They enjoy the game of discovery that Banksy introduced. By some there was a clamour for keeping the exhibition as a permanent feature, and for others a renewed enthusiasm for the historic collections that our regular visitors wanted to see afresh, once the Banksy exhibition moved on. The museum has now become part of the pilgrimage to discover authentic Banksy works in the city, so that there is a constant stream of visitors who pause to photograph *Angel Bust* in the museum's front hall, before musing upon the remainder of the collection and shaking their heads in disbelief over how it might have happened.

A whole range of artist projects have emerged; we were inundated by requests by artists and organisations wanting to work with us. We acted quickly to accommodate another local lad made good (and stable-mate of Banksy). Andy Beese (known as Beezer by all but his mum) was a young photographer from the early development of the club scene that helped bands such as Massive Attack to emerge onto the international stage. 'Bristol Wild Dayz' was another coup for the museum - it built on this entirely new audience that had been given a shot in the arm by the Banksy exhibition. Many post-clubbers of a certain age were delighted to take a stroll down memory lane. We were keen to capture some of the reminiscences and make a connection to this significant moment in recent Bristol social history as these would provide material for the new city museum M Shed that was in development at the time. The display was timed to coincide with the UK release of the *Bristol Wild Dayz* book - a cult publication of photographs from the 1980s Bristol club scene that had gone out of print and previously only available as an import from Japan. Other artists were included in the show. Two prominent graffiti writers and designers, Inkie and Cheo, had large pieces in the show as well as sculptor Ben Durnley and local artists Jef Row and Andy Stott together known as D*Frost – who'd collaborated on a series of Fridge door works, as well as the iconic pink record decks used by Massive Attack's sound system.

A succession of other exhibitions followed: the Bristol-studio collective known as Jamaica Street whose show culminated in an auction to raise money to purchase their studio building. This was followed by a major show – 'Art From the New World' – which gave a unique European platform for the Corey Helford Gallery from California to show an extraordinary ensemble of pop-surrealism and 'low-brow' street art. Their exhibition, which filled the galleries during the summer of 2010, attracted controversy on several fronts, not least a live performance from one of the world's leading burlesque acts Dita von Teese. Just as Corey and Halford had been attracted to BMAG because of its growing reputation for staging unusual, even slightly risky, exhibitions, so the curators were inundated with requests by artists and craft makers to create shows that addressed and responded to the collection. Rosa Nguyen's work, shown as part of a Crafts Council exhibition called 'The Shape of Things', placed her work amongst our glass and ceramics, and even the natural history collections, so that the line between the collections and the artwork became blurred, just as they had with Banksy. This was done in a perhaps quieter and more aesthetic way, but was as dramatic an intervention, albeit on a smaller scale.

... although the Banksy show was unique in many ways it was part of a trend in 2009 for British museums and galleries to rethink their role and challenge their practice.

There were other unexpected outcomes: we hosted a gathering of graffiti artists as part of a London-based research programme, called 'Design Against Crime'; we initiated a programme of site-specific projects, called CONTAINER, and of course, we prepared for the launch of M Shed where we further integrated artists' work within the fabric of the building and amongst interdisciplinary displays. We also made it possible to include works by such artists as Helga Gamboa, Graeme Mortimer Evelyn and Motorboy, and show them alongside more established artists like Richard Long and Kate Malone.

Final thoughts on the Banksy legacy

The Banksy show was unique but in many ways it was part of a trend in 2009 for British museums and galleries to rethink their role and challenge their practice. It was part of a growth of interest in what has been called the participatory museum. At the same time there has been a growing appreciation by museums of the value that creative people can bring to understanding the collections and promoting new ways of engaging with visitors. In particular the experience demonstrated the importance of the big event, the unique shared experience which reinforces how a community or in this case a city sees itself.

We have learned that we have to be prepared to share collections and spaces and be flexible in their use. Post-Banksy we are more committed

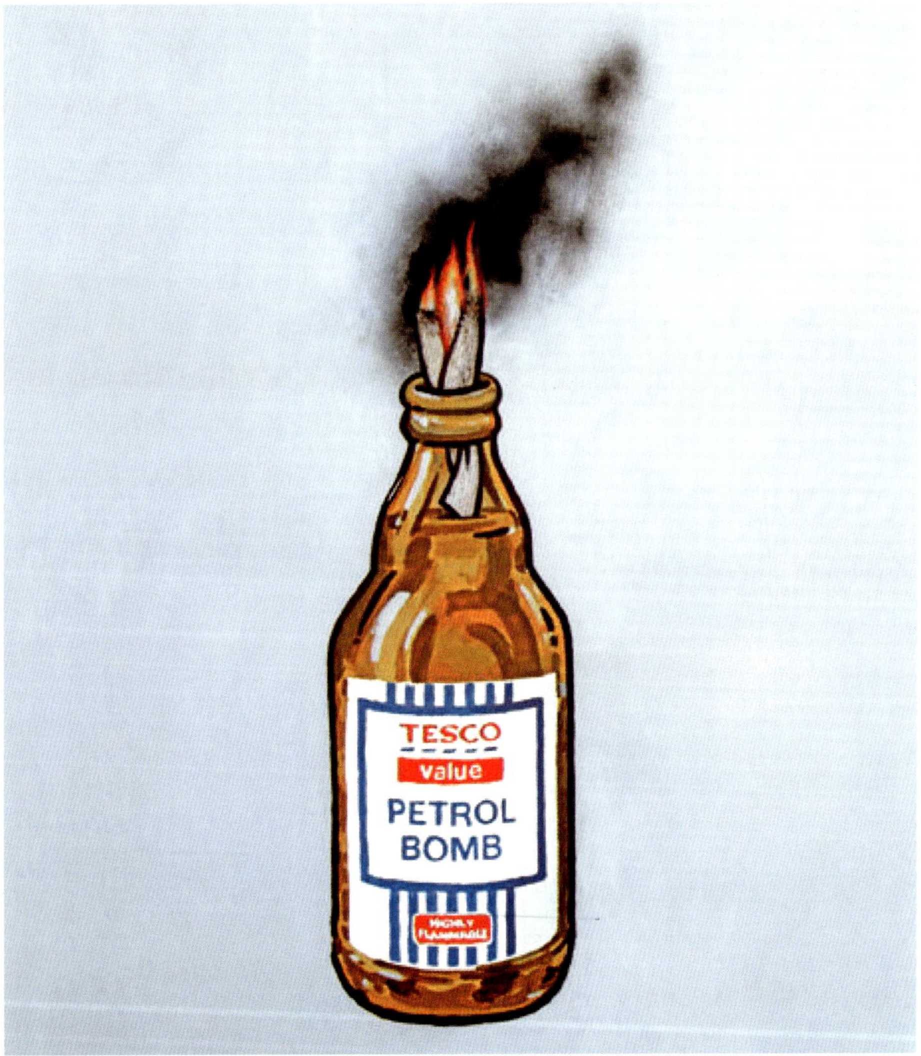

The controversial print displayed at MShed demonstrates that Bristol Museums Galleries and Archives continues to be responsive and does not shy away from controversy. (photograph: Bristol Museum & Art Gallery)

to finding new and imaginative uses for our objects and galleries and for involving people in the development of the service. In doing this we have to be open to both the creative and the extraordinary as well as the everyday. We want our collections and public programme to speak about people's lives, concerns and their sense of identity as well as offering something new and utterly fantastic.

How we do this is through partnership. We strive to create 'trusted' spaces, where people feel secure. We strive for all of these qualities, but one of the most important things we have learned from the Banksy exhibition is that the museum space isn't neutral. It's fought over and disputed, it's full of meaning, it's highly territorial, and there are complex procedural and professional boundaries that envelop it. It is this grain that was an essential component in 'Banksy versus Bristol Museum'. Visitors loved the tension and drama as well as the beauty and humour created in our contested spaces by their folk hero. It is these qualities and our openness and honesty in sharing the museum and its collections with them that will bring visitors back time and time again. All of these lessons have been used on the city's waterfront to create M Shed, a new kind of museum which holds both collections and engagement in equal measure. If we can use the complexity, the context and the grain of our collections, offer up our spaces, give them to community champions, artists, innovators, and entrepreneurs, the evidence is that you can genuinely transform any museum and give it a new place at the heart of the city.

This article was written by **Bristol Museums Galleries and Archives**.

Working with Banksy

Kate Brindley

I was the right person in the right place at the right time, who enabled something memorable and lasting to take place. In 2009 Banksy and his team could have worked anywhere and with anyone to produce his largest exhibition to date, and they chose to work in Bristol, with Bristol Museums, and I happened to be the Director of the museum he wanted to collaborate with.

I've worked in museums and galleries for twenty years, starting as a volunteer, cataloguing social history collections in Rotherham, working through the ranks to holding directorships of three regional museums and galleries over the last 10 years, I was born in Sheffield where as a teenager I had the good fortune to be introduced to the collections of the city's museums and galleries and became hooked on those places and their objects, so much so that I decided to study art history and take the path into a career working with museums and galleries and with artists.

I like to think Banksy, like thousands of kids growing up in regional cities, developed a relationship with his home-town museum and its collections. He has traded on infiltrating institutions, including museums, as part of his guerrilla activity. This approach changed when in late 2008 he approached us and started a dialogue, which while still overtly critical also demonstrated a playful respect and affection. I also like to think that he shares some of my belief that museums and galleries are key in our cultural experience and fundamental in societies that are creative, enquiring and inclusive in our towns and cities and which give birth to the Banksys and the host of other creatives and entrepreneurs of this country.

The project required me to draw on all my personal resources, I learnt a huge amount and it was fun. Keeping secrets from the majority of my team and superiors isn't the way I usually operate or feel comfortable with, but those were the rules of engagement. As Director I had to make that call when Banksy's people came knocking, but it was frankly a 'no-brainer'. Did I really want to become known as the Director who turned down what would become one of the most visited exhibitions in the world in 2009 and all the benefits that brought to Bristol?

Many moments from the project will stay with me vividly but those opening 48 hours were amazing, the moment I announced to the staff that Banksy had 'taken-over' much to their horror and delight, standing from 6am to 6pm in 4-inch Guccis to talk to the world's media, hosting a Banksy star-studded party until late. Then returning the next day to queues of fans waiting to come in, many of whom had never visited a museum before and had travelled miles – and this lasting all summer.

Even two years on, people track me down in my current role as Director of mima (Middlesbrough Institute of Modern Art) to ask me about Banksy. In the weeks and months following the launch in June 2009 I received emails and letters from all over the world, most from people I had never met, passing on their excitement and thanking me. I also received a few threats.

Banksy divides opinion in the art world and with the public at large; a smart artist or a one-trick pony, entrepreneur or entertainer, a maverick or a vandal, a flash-in-the-pan or a legacy. That discussion will continue. I guess I'm just part of that dialogue in history now however it turns out for him and me.

Kate Brindley, Director of Bristol Museums, Galleries and Archives from 2005 to 2009.

The view from Stokes Croft

Katy Bauer

[At Banksy's request, the publishers agreed to rewrite a reference on pages 72 and 73 to Banksy sending in a team to oversee the sale of the Tesco bomb poster. The Pest Control Office, on the artist's behalf, assured the publishers that this was not Banksy's team and that jocular comments attributed to Banksy staff were not made. Katy Bauer, the author of this chapter, adheres to her original version and wishes to dissociate herself from the changed text.]

'Banksy vs Bristol Museum' was an extraordinary show, but the part I liked best was the queue. About half a kilometre long, seven days a week for three months, it snaked up the road, and I joined a handful of buskers and advertisers in working it. But I didn't want money, I wanted drawings. I wanted the queue to leave a mark because I saw it as Banksy's most poignant statement yet. It was a vote for defiance and the voters could best be described as: The General Public.

The 3,500 drawings collected became 'The Banksy Q' and the exhibition was held in Stokes Croft in December 2010. All the drawings were put up and I am told Banksy visited the show more than once, though I wouldn't know whether that is true or not because neither I nor anyone else at the PRSC knows who he is. We still don't know him, but one day he instructed his office to call ours …

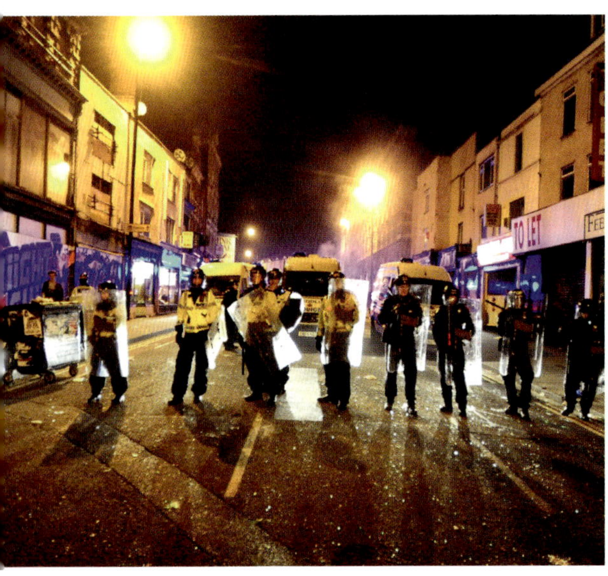

Mayhem in Stokes Croft: police response to the anti-Tesco riots in Cheltenham Road. [courtesy: *Bristol Evening Post*]

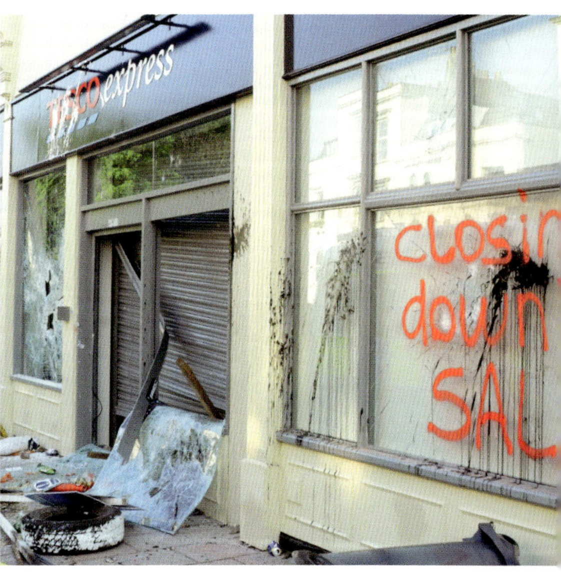

Wreckage at the Tesco store.
[courtesy: *Bristol Evening Post*]

No Tesco

The chain of events leading up to the unrest in Stokes Croft that started on
21 April 2011 and flared up two more times over the following fortnight, took
a year to build and would take more patience than either you or I have to
unravel here. Suffice to say the uprising became known as the Tesco Riots, and
brilliant, messy, revolutionary Stokes Croft was famous for fifteen minutes.

The saga held no surprises. The police action was at best a shambles, at
worst a sinister Tesco/Tory shambles. The squatters at Telepathic Heights
– the house opposite the much opposed Tesco Express on Cheltenham
Road and focus of the initial police raid – seemed bemused and fairly
uninterested in the broader political implications inherent in the events
taking place. Tesco played the brave, bewildered victim. And anyone who
never much liked the area's local flavour of painted walls and subdued
consumerism did the easiest thing imaginable and blamed the People's
Republic of Stokes Croft (PRSC) for 'getting people thinking'. It was like a
bad thriller, crammed with petty resentments and depressingly predictable.

Great. Thanks

...Then about half way through, the tale took an unexpected turn. Banksy's
people contacted PRSC chairman Chris Chalkley and told him that the
artist had created a poster to commemorate the riots and that he would
like to donate the money raised from the sale thereof to the non-profit
organisation. Chris's response to the riot until that point had been to sweep.
He took up his weapon of choice – the broom – and swept the glass-strewn
streets. He moved towards the litter chaos, and the human chaos moved
towards him. The police, the squatters, the furious, the Tesco spin-doctor

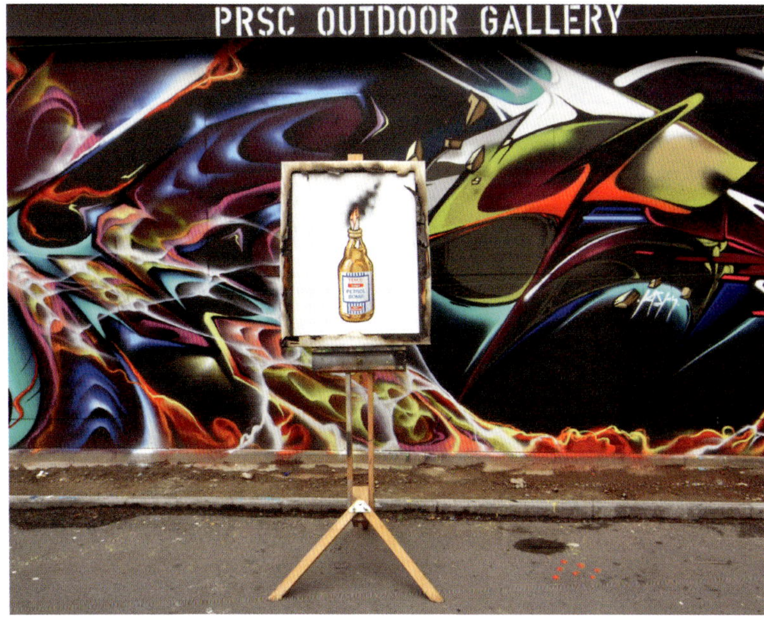

The controversial
Tesco image, outside
the PRSC Gallery.
(photograph: Chris
Chalkley)

all came knocking at 35 Jamaica Street. Nobody was exactly happy and mediation was a pretty much thankless task. Then suddenly, the Banksy call, and for a moment there was affirmation, real help, excitement. Great! Thanks! What was he supposed to say? It was Banksy. We love Banksy. Everyone with a heart and a brain loves Banksy. Besides, it was the first bit of cash anyone had ever offered the PRSC. It was a coup.

The Bomb

The following day the poster appeared in the press. There was no comment from the artist, only this release from his office:

> *After the recent Tesco riots in Bristol, Banksy has produced this fine commemorative souvenir poster. It's available exclusively from Bristol's Anarchist Bookfair this coming Saturday. All proceeds go to the People's Republic of Stokes Croft and associates ... Posters are five pounds each.*

As we gathered for our staff meeting at PRSC HQ we pulled the image up online. Responses ranged from laughter to cries of 'Blimey!', but a couple of people just stared – uneasy. They weren't enjoying it and they wanted to enjoy it. But this, a bottle with a Tesco label and a flaming rag stuck in the top, was not fun, it was too hard. They were right, it was hard. It said that Tesco was the danger, the threat to peace, ecology, diversity, stability and common decency. It said Tesco would sell anything. It said Tesco and its ilk were the bomb, not a couple of pissed off blokes with their jumpers tied across their noses.

We were just beginning to discuss things when a local graffiti artist came in ranting about the image, saying how he found it thoughtless and inflammatory and how he would have to distance himself from the PRSC if we accepted Banksy's offer. It was crazy. For a good twenty minutes we raged back and forth about the poster, then in a snap everything cooled down, everyone made friends and the image receded, but for a moment it had us and it was clear that more fury would be coming our way because of it. Bristol's only evening newspaper, the *Daily Mail*-owned *Evening Post*, had already decided to pin the unrest on the PRSC and had printed what we considered a libellous front page article to that effect. The release of the easily misunderstood Banksy image wasn't going to help. But there was no time to agonise. Two days later an entourage from the poster people arrived to oversee the sale of the posters, and the tale took another twist.

For twenty-four hours they chatted to everyone merrily, rolled up posters, admired pieces of Stokes Croft china, drank tea, and wrestled with a gazebo. Bearing gifts of books and posters, and asking lots of questions about our peculiar set-up, they were polite guests who seemed to be more interested in us than we were in them.

Banksy set particular terms for the sale of the posters, and suggestions about how the opportunity might be tweaked in order to further help the PRSC and possibly ebb the tide of misunderstanding about the image itself were barely noted, but beyond that there was an ease to proceedings, a friendly casualness. Banksy's name was hardly mentioned, and when it was, it was done with an affectionate irreverence. Banksy's the man. He's hip, he's magic. Brave, audacious, and kind. He's Snow White and the Seven Dwarfs. He saves us and tells us off and makes us laugh. He's also tough and single minded, and all the banter helped dissipate any suspicion that Banksy's gift might leave us wading through mud while he floated away to fresher pastures. Suspicion was replaced by certainty. Of course he'd ascend whether we drowned or not and if we'd loved him for it this long, to start getting irritated now that he was wafting around our own back yardwould have been churlish. In any case, wading through mud is what the PRSC does. It's the chicken that sticks its neck out. It speaks up, objects, encourages, and tirelessly woos its detractors, all of which brings it as much grief as it does joy. In 2008 Chris was arrested for stencilling a 'Welcome to Stokes Croft' sign on the monstrous 5102 building at the St. James Barton roundabout. The building is Bristol's Berlin Wall, creating a barrier between Stokes Croft and the city centre. The police went to the council and the council directed them to Chris, who took them straight to the stencil he'd used, happy to confess to having sprayed such a sign on the otherwise forbidding façade. But he pleaded innocent to the charge of Criminal Damage saying he considered it neither criminal nor damage.

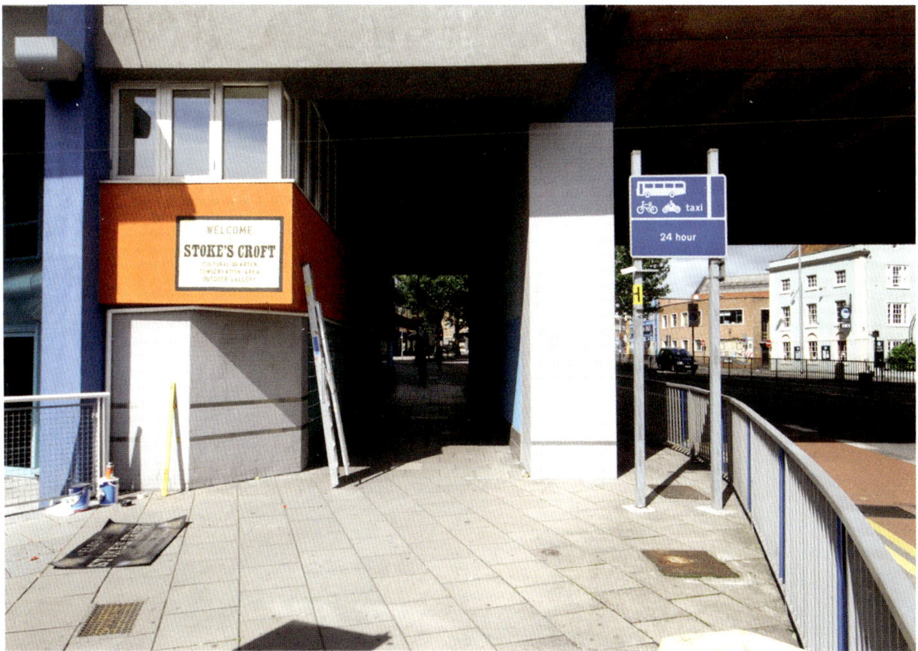

Chris Chalkley was prosecuted for placing this 'Welcome to Stokes Croft' notice at the St James Barton roundabout. (photograph: Chris Chalkley)

The owners of the building prosecuted, and the magistrate appeared uninterested, nay, irritated by the defence and found in their favour. The following day Chris wrote the owners of the building a letter asking for permission to reinstate the sign. He received no response.

Annoying?

It didn't take long for us to know two things for sure:

1. Banksy decides how things are going to go.

2. He's not too concerned about how that might affect how anybody else's things go. It's a method that gets people moaning into their pints. Who the hell does he think he is?

And worse still: who the hell is he? If only we could criticise his haircut or fancy his girlfriend it might offer some relief, but we can't, so we slag him off. But our frustration only grows when all we hear back is our own faint echo. However, there are those who do know what he looks like and still get twitchy. The furious graffiti artist who thought the commemorative riot image insensitive, is a good example. Why does Banksy annoy him? I'm

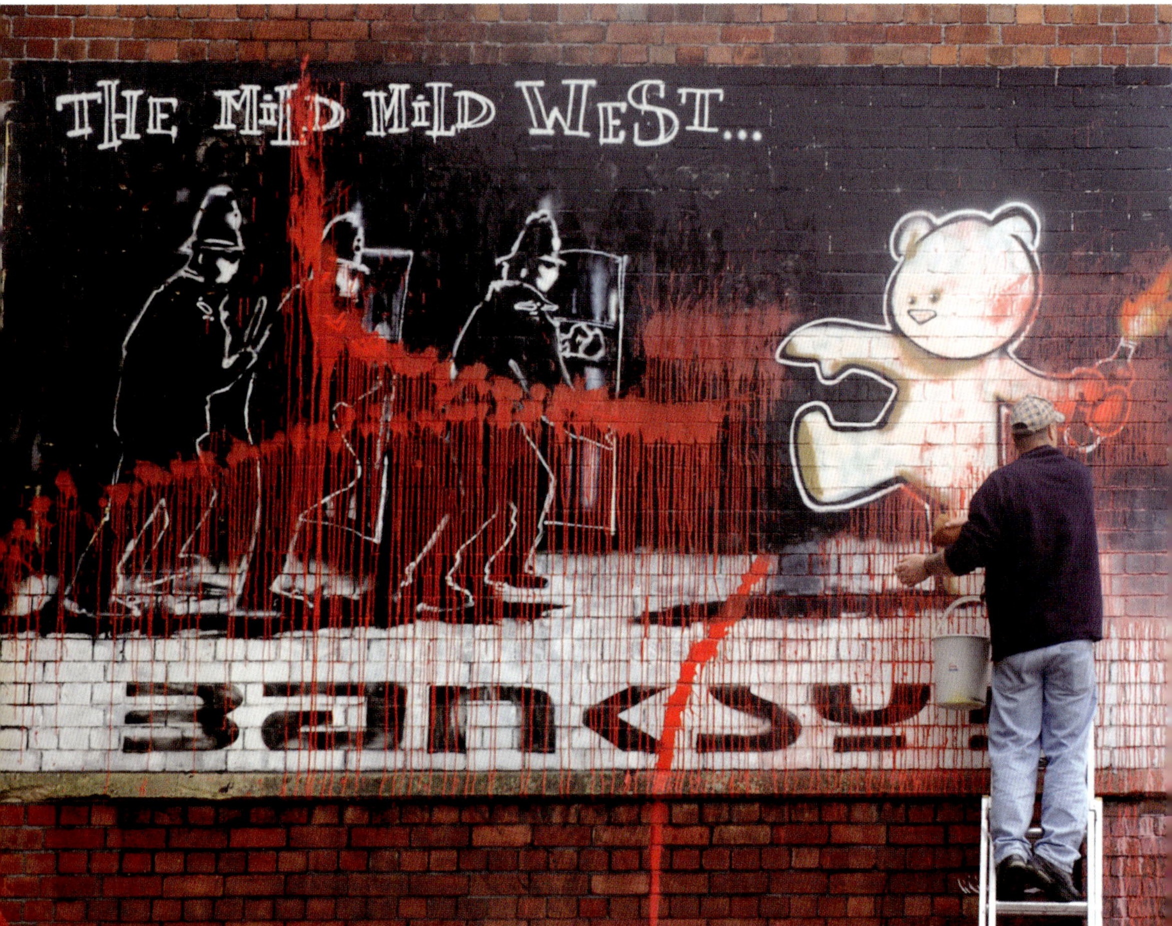

Chris Chalkley removing paint from the vandalised Banksy mural *The Mild Mild West.*

sure he has a perfectly valid list of reasons. We're all annoying to someone, but the more successful/rich/beautiful we become the more annoying we seem, if only by way of contrast. There's probably some law of physics that proves it.

In 2008 a group calling themselves Appropriate Media were so annoyed by Banksy they defaced his early freehand *Mild Mild West* on Stokes Croft. The morning after it happened Chris did a straw poll on the street below the piece, asking passers by whether they thought it should be repaired or not. As a result, the paint was cleaned off and parts of the image restored. Appropriate Media vanished after that. Despite having found Banksy's work/success/persona unbearable, they clearly had no good ideas of their own.

The New Banksy Queue

Our main concern about the commemorative posters going on sale in Stokes Croft so soon after the unrest was that it might spark another riot. To this end Chris persuaded Banksy to hire a locally based security team to keep an eye on things, and the police to stay away. The PRSC also organised free tea and cake all morning in order to placate anyone who might get stroppy if their sugar levels dropped.

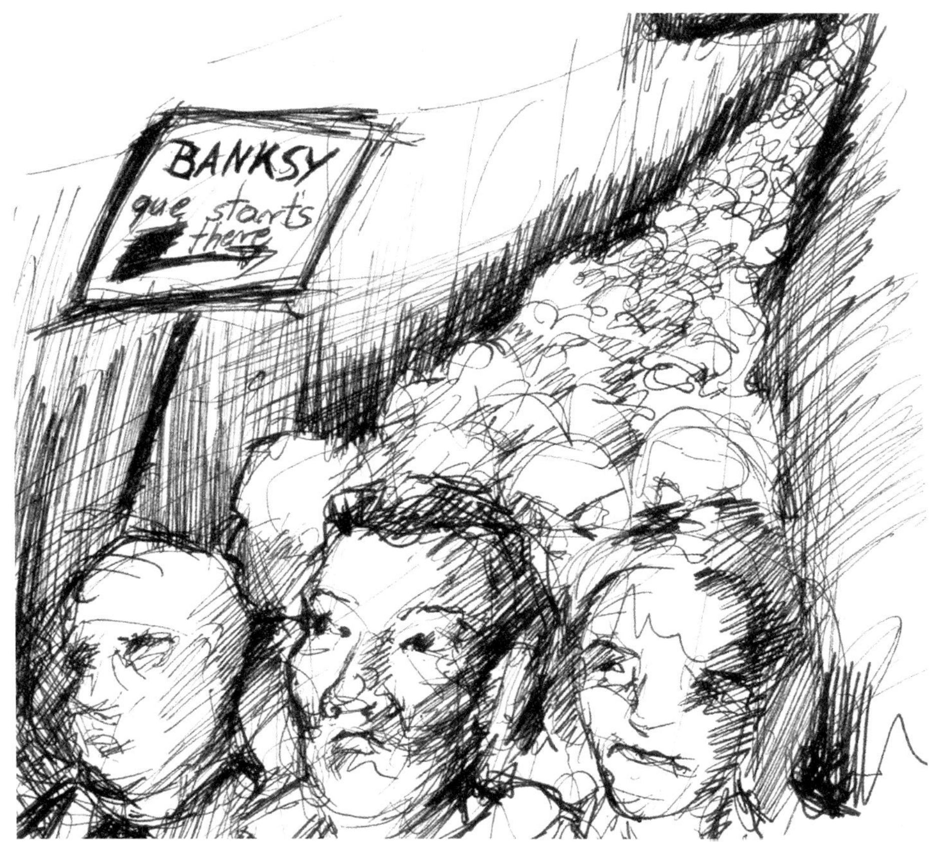

One of the 3,500 images Katy Dauel collected from the Queen's Road queue: Reata Lukasiewicz's *Just Banksy*.

A substantial queue formed, but the queuers were not in a rebellious mood, they were in a shopping mood, as we discovered when we tried with only mild success to get them to donate towards the Boycott Tesco Campaign. Plenty of blank faces told us they didn't have any money and a few even said they weren't sure they supported the campaign. I was outraged and told Chris I reckoned the queue was full of lousy Tesco shoppers, keen to make a quick profit by reselling their bargain posters on e-Bay as soon as they got home. I was subdued by large helpings of tea and cake, but before the sun went down those £5 souvenirs were all over the internet fetching £100 and upwards.

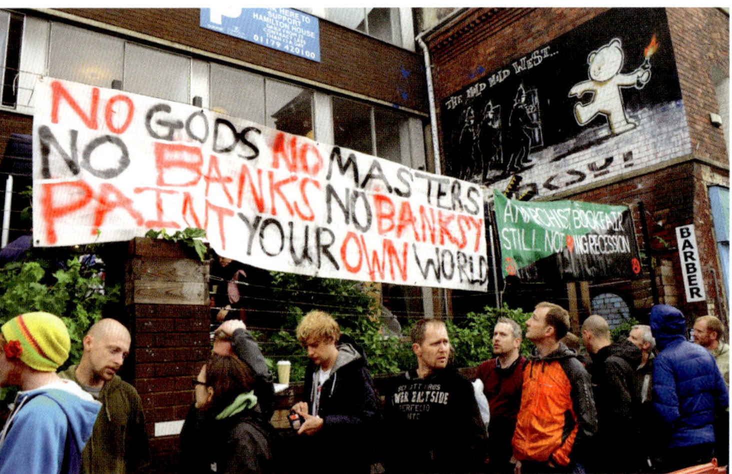
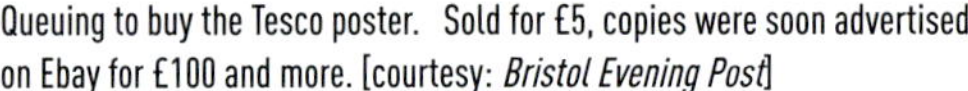

Queuing to buy the Tesco poster. Sold for £5, copies were soon advertised on Ebay for £100 and more. [courtesy: *Bristol Evening Post*]

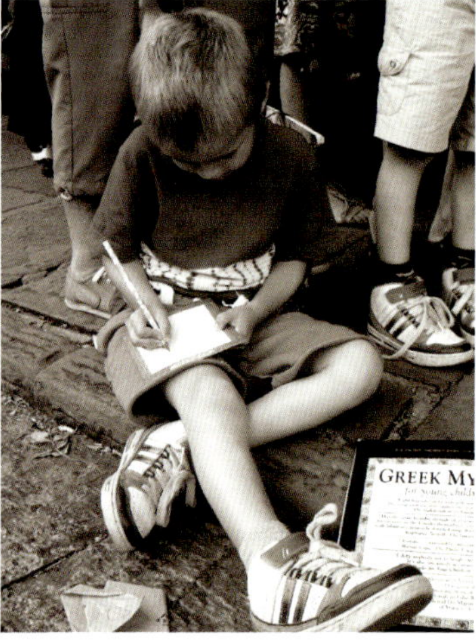

Helping create the *Banksy Q* book. [photograph: Katy Bauer]

The End

The posters sold out in about three hours raising £7,500. The PRSC got £3,000, the arrested squatters got £3,000 to help with legal bills, and local social enterprise company Coexist got £1,500. The whole thing was a bit stressful and it didn't solve our financial troubles, but that didn't matter. What mattered was that Banksy had thought of Stokes Croft and was hoisting his flag in our camp at a time when the people's republic was being accused and abandoned and that was grand. Anyway, what do we want? Our government is so corrupt we expect them to lie and cheat and steal and do as they please, so why demand perfection from an artist who actually gives a toss about us? Perhaps it's some residual Christian fantasy we cling to about virgins breeding the best humanity has to offer and a desire for someone truly good to pay for our sins because we can't be arsed to. Childish demands are best ignored, which is just what Banksy does. He keeps pumping, challenging and railing against human folly – the venality that lies at the heart of all controlling forces in particular – refusing to get bogged down in the detail, not interested in appearing perfect, and never asking permission.

Katy Bauer is a PRSC volunteer. Recent work within that context includes: Stokes Croft Museum, *The Banksy Q* (exhibition and book), *The Stokes Croft Toff (& Son)* (a newspaper), Crofts (a dog show), Think Local (portraits of local people) and various films.

The People's Republic of Stokes Croft (PRSC) is a Community Interest Company.

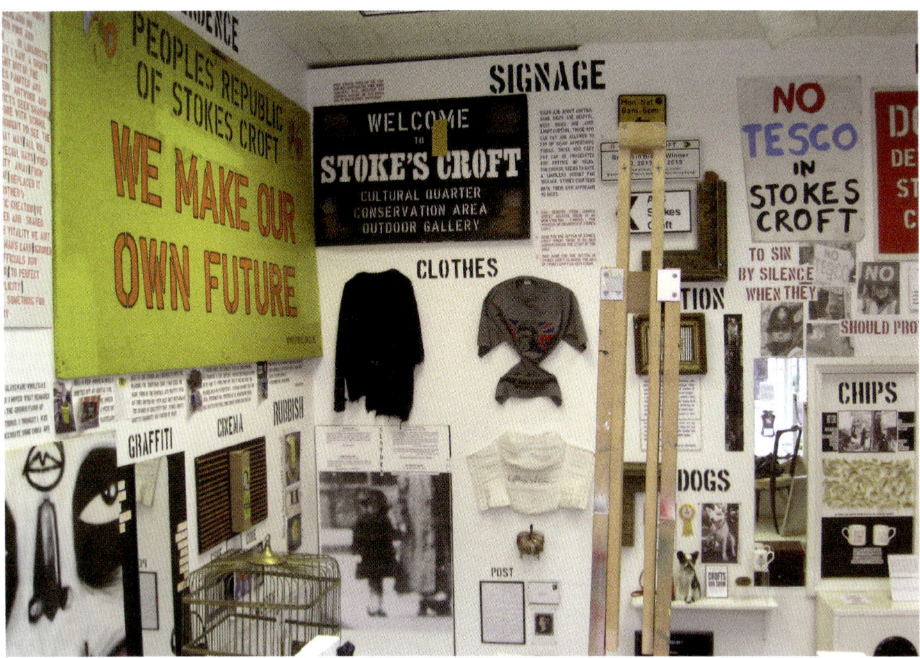

Katy Bauer's museum in *Stokes Croft*. [photograph: Katy Bauer]

Hanging out down the Council House: street art's outlaws and the Bristol establishment

Eugene Byrne

Thirty years ago, official Bristol persecuted graffiti artists with the full vigour of the law and the juvenile courts. Nowadays Bristol uses street art to market a cool and edgy image to everyone from tourists to businesses and potential undergraduates. The key moment in this transformation was not the Banksy exhibition at the Museum. It was rather, argues Eugene Byrne, a minor act of vandalism at the bottom of Park Street just before the show opened.

In August 2011, several leading graffiti artists from Bristol and around the world took over Nelson Street, Quay Street and Christmas Street for an event called 'See No Evil', during which several buildings would be transformed, a couple with some of the largest paintings in the world.

The event was instigated by Mike Bennett, Bristol's 'Director of Placemaking', who said the idea came about largely as a result of a brainstorm held just before Christmas 2010. This brought together councillors, council officers, members of the local arts community and people from education, business and the media. The agenda was to look at different ways of 'animating' Bristol.

'Everyone said how good it would be to continue the buzz that came out of the Banksy exhibition at the Museum,' Bennett told *Venue* magazine. 'Urban and street art are widely felt to be an important part of the city's creative DNA and the Banksy show attracted shedloads of people to come to Bristol to stand in a queue for three hours.'

'See No Evil' took place in a shabby, tired-looking area dominated by grey 1960s and 1970s concrete buildings. In the summer of 2011 many of the office units were empty and Bennett and his team had relatively little difficulty in persuading owners and landlords to allow their buildings to be painted. Said Bennett:

This is an unloved street, a run-down area right in the middle of town. It needs something big development-wise. If you talk to the business experts they will all tell you that with the economy as it is, the prospect of any serious development here in the next five years is almost non-existent. If we bring that attention to the street, then you get increased footfall and

John Sansom assesses the impact of the Nelson Street project elsewhere in this book.

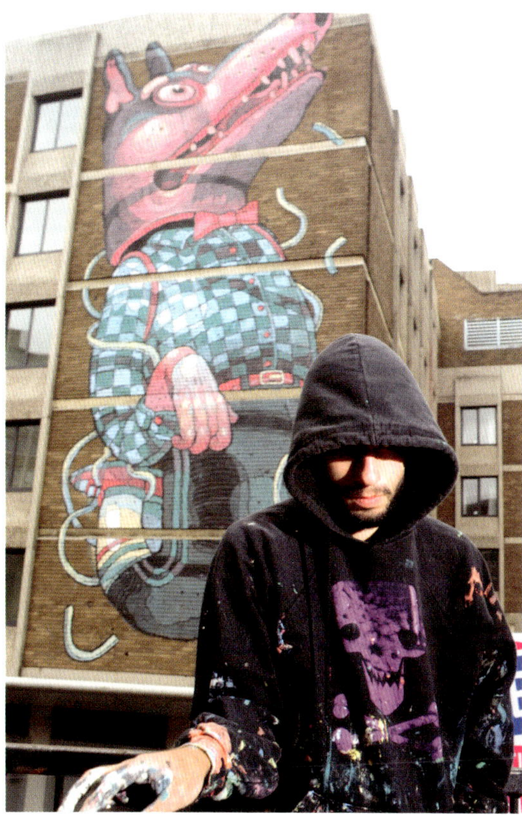

Monumental art in Nelson Street, Bristol: Spanish artist Aryz with his five-storey high *Wolf Boy*. (photograph: *Bristol Evening Post*)

By 2011 we had long passed the point at which street art was tolerated by official Bristol; it was now positively encouraged. Provided of course it stayed within certain well-defined boundaries. Street art is now part of the package the city offers to everyone from relocating businesses to tourists and even potential students. It's one of the things that makes Bristol interesting. It's even part of the official civic narrative of the moment. Bristol is creative, edgy and rebellious. Bristol, we tell ourselves, has always been like that. Thinking outside the box, not conforming, enterprising in business and the arts alike. We're different, a bit alternative.

So for instance in the introduction to *Bristol's 20:20 Plan*, the Chair of the Bristol Partnership, Dick Penny writes: 'Bristol has always had a radical edge, we have a unique opportunity to meld our diversity and creativity with the instinct for innovation to come up with new ways to deliver outcomes for everyone.'[2]

Bristol does have a distinguished history of innovation in science, technology and engineering which you can trace back to the Middle Ages. Its history of political, philosophical and religious nonconformity is astonishingly rich. Bristol's credentials as a cradle of socialism and trade unionism are respectable, its record in the women's movement is impeccable. And of course there's a goodly record of riots in recent and distant history.

In the arts, the city was always considered philistine, but that all changed in recent decades. The street art and music that came out of Bristol's inner city in the 1980s and 90s included some world-class names. More recently, as others comment in this book, a lot of attention has focused on Stokes Croft; here art, politics, business are blending in a melting pot that's coming up with some very exciting new ways of doing things. It's entirely appropriate that looking benignly down upon this scene is Banksy's *Mild Mild West* mural, with its message of cuddly insurrection. One might mischievously suggest that the Stokes Croft disturbances in the spring of 2011 have simply underlined Bristol's claim to be edgy, creative, rebellious (etc.)

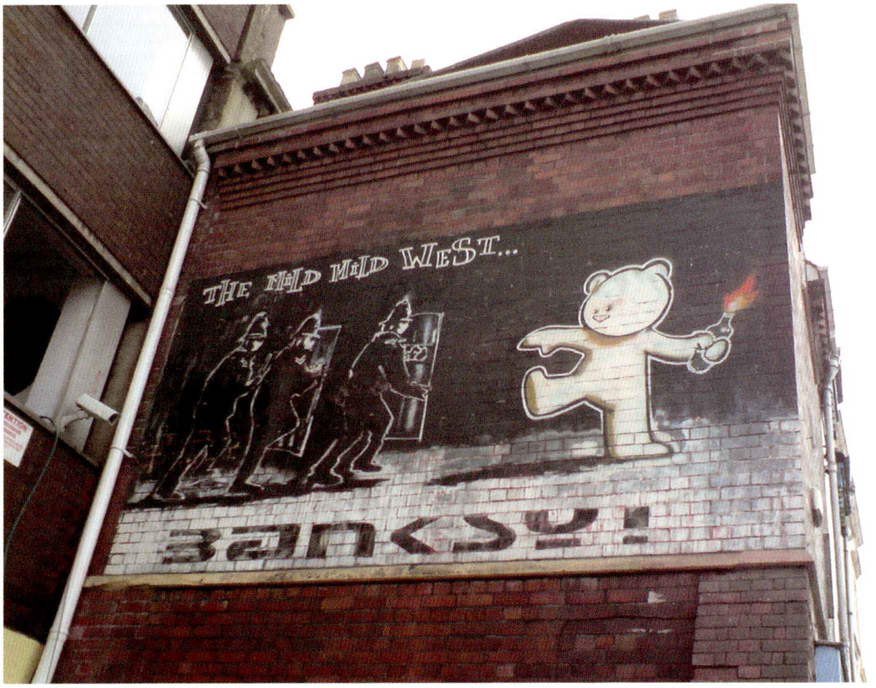

Banksy, *The Mild Mild West*, Stokes Croft, painted c.1999, before it was defaced by a Banksy rival and later restored by a well-wisher.

So how did it come to this? How did we progress from a quiet, pleasant, slightly philistine city in the 1980s which marketed itself on its 'colourful maritime heritage' and printed tourist brochures plastered with pictures of hot air balloons to the altogether more edgy, rebellious (etc.) and interesting place it is now?

Lots of reasons. Certainly many will suggest the meeting of youngsters from widely disparate race and class backgrounds from the 1970s onwards produced almost all of the city's most famous names in music and street art. The cliché is that white kids from the suburbs and black and mixed-race kids from the inner city found common creative ground, but there's some substance to it.

Street art is a key factor in Bristol's changing image. And this Banksy character (a white boy who – allegedly – went to the posh Cathedral School but who made his name with an inner-city art form) became the most famous exponent.

During the 1980s when Bristol's street art scene was in its infancy, the standard line was that it's all vandalism. News articles in the *Bristol Evening Post* would report the prosecution of artists and its leader columns would approve. *Venue* magazine, meanwhile, ran an article every two years or so between 1984 and 2004 which basically said, 'vandalism or art?'[3]

What a dumb question, you say. But hey – it took two or three decades before most people accepted it as art.

So how did this change of attitude happen? Lots of reasons, including, in no particular order:

- The obvious talent and artistic or entertainment value of a lot of pieces.

- Several efforts down the years by various well-meaning public bodies and community organisations to engage *da youf* with graffiti workshops and classes. If grown-ups are teaching you to do something, it must be respectable.

- Shops. By the 1990s a lot of business premises in Bristol started hiring graffiti artists to paint their walls. Not only did this draw public attention to them, but it was also usually successful in preventing the idiot element from tagging their walls. Street art thus became something 'normal'. There's a minor local urban legend that butchers' shops led the way to stop their premises being vandalised by animal rights activists.

- People who grew up thinking graffiti was cool just got older. Of course they still think it's cool, and some of them are now running this town.

- The *Evening Post* changed its mind. In 2005, Bristol-born Mike Norton returned to his native city to take over as editor; he'd left to go to university in 1982 and had then worked as a newspaperman elsewhere. 'I arrived at an *Evening Post* which essentially proclaimed Banksy to be a vandal, and I think perhaps being away from Bristol had benefitted my perspective on him ... I was quite proud of the fact that I came from the same place as Banksy, and when I got here the *Post* had this, if you like, traditional Bristol view, that he was overrated and a vandal. I'm not sure how the *Post* got to that conclusion. I think perhaps it listened to some of its more vociferous letter-writers on the subject.'[4]

So when 'Banksy vs. Bristol Museum' opened, street art was welcomed, or at least accepted, by the great majority of Bristol's population.

There is, though, a danger that in future the accepted view will be that it was the Museum show that turned official Bristol into enthusiastic converts to Banksy merely on account of all the media attention and money it brought in.

This is simply not true. Hugely popular though the show was, official Bristol officially took Banksy to its official bosom precisely three years before the Museum show opened.

Here's what happened …

In June 2006, Banksy came to Bristol and painted a picture on the side of a building in Frogmore Street. This was the now world-famous image of a naked man hanging from the ledge while the jealous husband and underwear-clad wife stand at the window.

The picture was directly facing the side of the Council House, at the bottom of one of the busiest, and most visited streets in town. This was a bold challenge, inviting Bristol City Council to come and have a go if it considered itself hard enough.

Liberal Democrat Gary Hopkins was at that time the councillor responsible for this sort of thing ('Executive Member For Sustainable Environment And Neighbourhoods'). Before he had seen the picture, the local TV asked to interview him. 'So the BBC were down there, opposite the Council House and live on air they asked what I was going to do about it. So I said, well, personally I think it's amusing and entertaining, I think people will like it, but let's hear what your viewers have to say.'[5]

Not long afterwards, he says, he realised that the Council could use its own *askbristol* website to sound out public opinion. In the end, more than nine in ten people who voted were in favour of keeping it.

Meanwhile, though, the Conservative councillor for Avonmouth, Albert 'Spud' Murphy, led the charge for its removal. He said: 'It is on a listed building and the council have condoned it by leaving it there. It's one rule for them and one for us … I think it should be painted over. Banksy should not be allowed to do it. Is the Council going to let the next person off who does it? It is not art.'[6]

Banksy's notorious naked man at the foot of Park Street, Bristol, painted 2006 and later defaced. [main photograph: Paul Gough, inset: Stephen Morris]

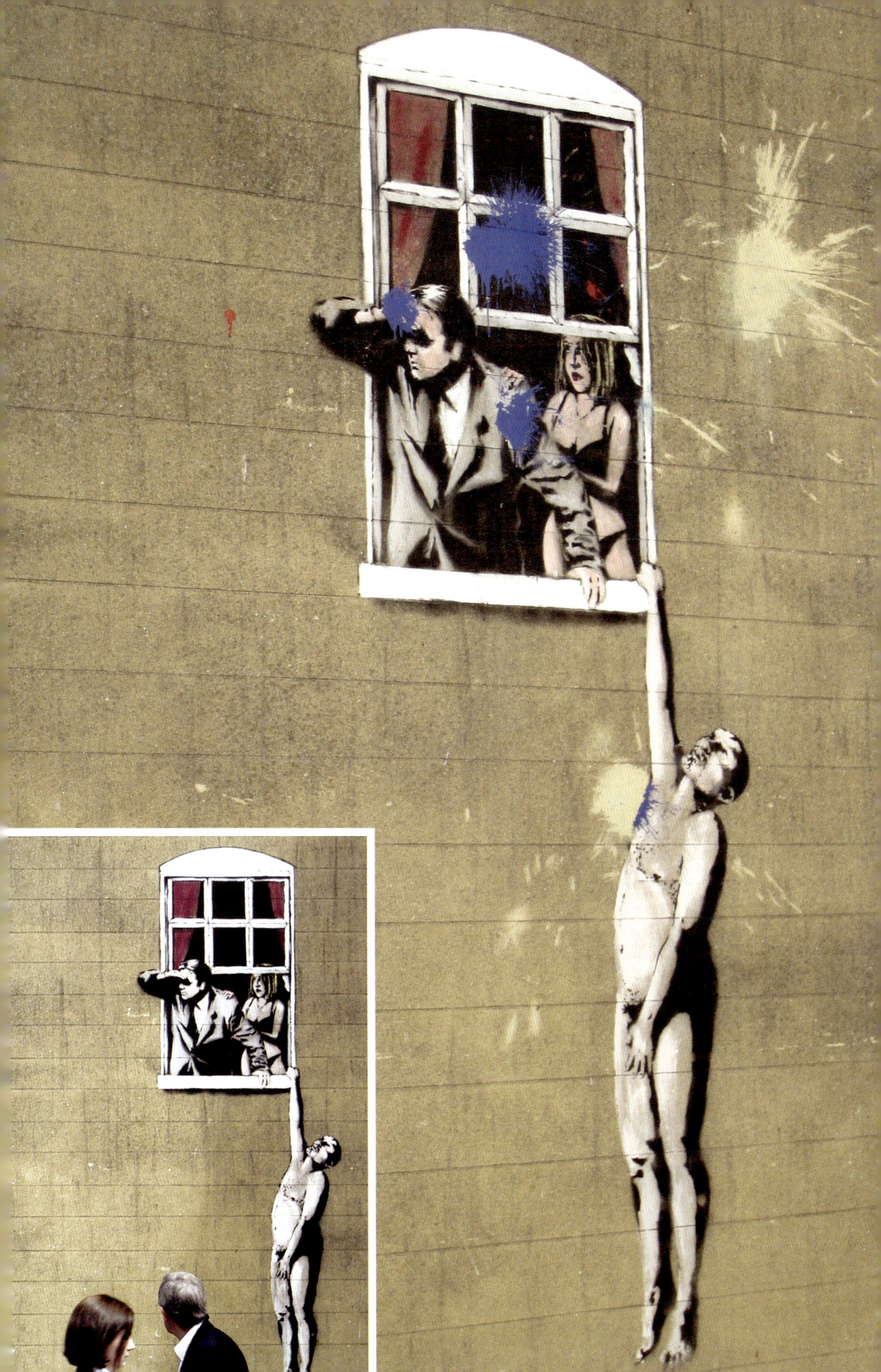

Fast forward three years. On 20 or 21 June of 2009, the mural was spattered with blue paint. The *Mild Mild West* on Stokes Croft was similarly attacked two days later. Who did it? Who knows? Various versions have it that it was done by Rovers fans (Banksy is apparently a City supporter), or that it was a statement by some other artists (maybe on account of the eternal charge that Banksy has 'sold out', man), or of course it could quite plausibly have been the work of Banksy himself.

Whatever. It really doesn't matter. What does matter is that this act of vandalism, carried out before the Museum show had opened, prompted a fair amount of outrage among Banksy lovers in Bristol. None more so that Councillor Murphy, who brought a cherry-picker from his own company in order to try and repair some of the damage. He told the BBC:

> *The council won't do it because they haven't got the facilities to do it and we have. We're going to remove the biodegradable paint first and then it can be cleaned off with soapy water and then we'll start on the picture. I'll do it myself, there's no cost to the council whatsoever.*[7]

In one of the greatest acts of political honesty in all of Bristol's history, the Council's sternest critic of Banksy had now performed a 180-degree turn. Banksy had now, before the Museum exhibition's true impact had been realised, been accepted into the official pantheon of A-List local heroes, alongside Isambard Kingdom Brunel (half-French and not from Bristol) and Wallace & Gromit (made of Plasticine, northern accent). However elusive the boy may be, at least he's actually genuinely from Bristol.

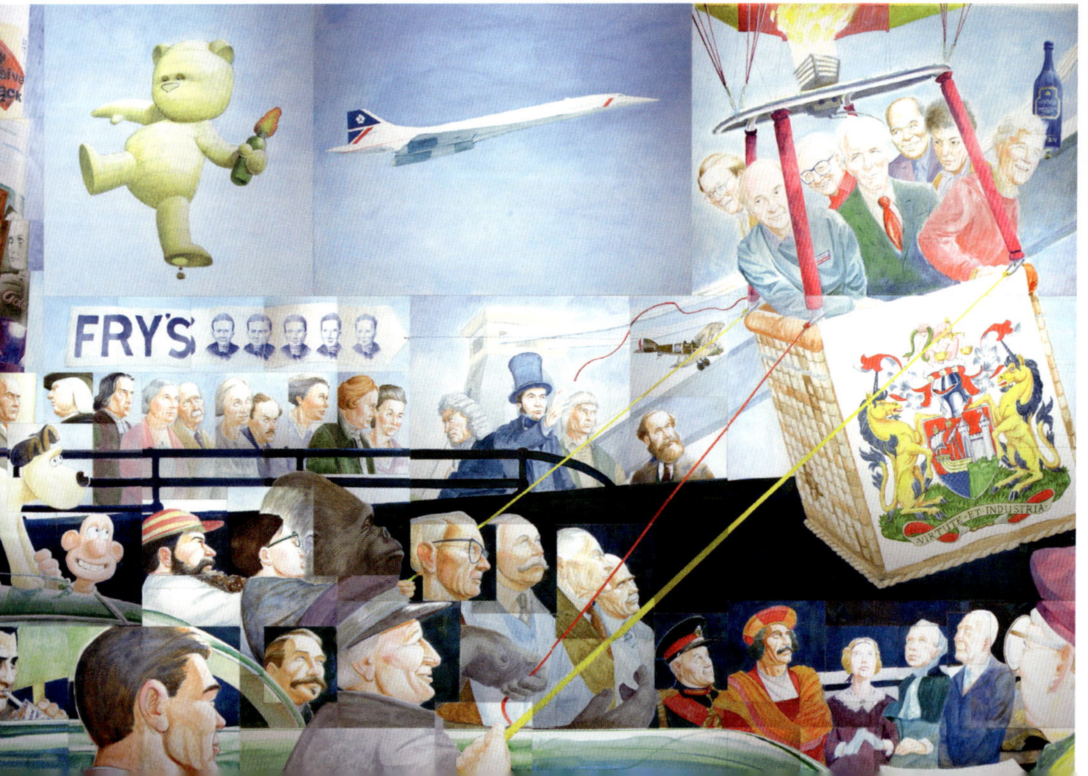

The effect of 'Banksy vs Bristol Museum', then, wasn't to make him acceptable to official Bristol because that had already happened. What the show did do was make everyone realise that street art in general and Banksy in particular were more potent global marketing tools for the Bristol brand than anyone had previously dared imagine.

Meanwhile, in 2011, the creative side of the 'See No Evil' event was led by Tom Bingle, aka Inkie, a leading Bristol artist who had cut his teeth back in the 1980s, working with the likes of Banksy and 3D. Inkie noted with pleasure that an old police building and the former juvenile courts were among the buildings the 'See No Evil' artists were to work on. As he told *Venue:*

> *Half the early graffiti artists in Bristol must have been through that court at one time or another. Now there's a really nice irony that we're going to be painting it!* [8]

So then ... Let's see if we've got this right. These artists have gone from delinquents up before the beaks to the vanguard of Bristol's global marketing and urban regeneration efforts in well under 30 years. That's what a successful show at the City Museum will do, but Bristol already loved Banksy and Co. long before that.

Eugene Byrne is an author and freelance journalist. He has written several science fiction stories and, with artist Simon Gurr, has produced a graphic biography of Brunel and a graphic history of Bristol. He is Consulting Editor of *Venue* magazine, for whom he has been writing about news and culture in Bristol since 1983. He does all his own ironing.

Notes

1. *Venue* magazine, August 2011

2. *The Bristol 20:20 Plan; Bristol's Sustainable City Strategy*, PDF file, www.tinyurl.com/3eorv2k/ accessed 6 August 2011.

3. *Venue* magazine is a monthly 'What's On' magazine for Bristol and Bath. Founded in 1982 by journalists who had once worked for *Out West* magazine, it gained a reputation for the quality of its coverage of regional arts, music and entertainment, as well as a name for investigative reporting of local issues.

4. Interview with Mike Norton by author, 21 June 2011.

5. Interview with Councillor Hopkins by author, 17 May 2011.

6. *Bristol Evening Post*, 16 October 2006.

7. 'Second Banksy city mural attacked', BBC News, 24 June 2009. See: www.news.bbc.co.uk/1/hi/england/bristol/8116060.stm, and www.tinyurl.com/nwvfyw/ accessed 6 August 2011. There is an interesting reflection on this issue on the *Bristol Graffiti* blog for July 2009: www.bristolgraffiti.wordpress.com/page/18/

8. *Venue* magazine, August 2011.

A Banksy image makes its appearance in Simon Gurr's *Some More Who Have Made Bristol Famous*, a new painting for the city of Bristol, 2011, Spielman Centre, Arnos Vale, Bristol.

Banksy and Bristol's cultural development

Andrew Kelly

It has taken a long time for official – government and business – Bristol to recognise the importance of Banksy. This is not surprising as it is only relatively recently that the city has begun to take arts and culture seriously. Bristol is a city of paradoxes and this is where Banksy best sits, but it sometimes leads to an uneasy relationship with the city wanting to celebrate heritage as well as the new, and where promoting radical, underground, street art can sometimes come back to bite – especially when caught up in the Bristol 2011 riots.

As I walked up Park Street early one morning a colleague rushed by me to join the queue for the Banksy exhibition. It was near the end of its run and, even though the crowds grew during the day, I thought that this was a bit early. She was right to rush: at 7.30am there was already a long queue. On the penultimate day before the exhibition closed, I saw the queue snaked back around the side roads to near the Senate House of the University. The person at the end was told it would be six hours before he would get in. He unpacked his folding chair, took out a book and drank his coffee. I don't think I saw a happier person that day.

Bristol had not seen anything like this – and certainly not for a museum exhibition. The two exhibitions I was involved with, on *Brunel and the Art of Engineering* and *Flight: 100 Years of the Bristol Aeroplane Company*, had over 65,000 visitors each. These figures were respectable, even good, but we could only look with envy at over 300,000 people wanting to see the work of a street artist who not so long ago was being criticised by local media, dubbed a criminal by some people and whose art Bristol City Council had made every effort to remove, often within hours of its having been created.

Now he is lauded: he has made Bristol the graffiti capital of the UK and is known worldwide; his work appears on official tourist trails; and the local media can't get enough of him – *Bristol Evening Post* got the crowd on the last day to hold up seven large signs spelling out the word 'Thanksy'. The adulation can also be feverish and sometimes stupid: there's been mention of a statue;[1] people enquired about tickets for an event we posted as an April Fool joke with Banksy being interviewed by Piers Morgan on stage; there's regular Twitter chatter about whether the latest piece of stencilled graffiti just encountered is another 'Banksy';[2] Persimmon Homes advertised a new flat in Ashley Down, Bristol as The Banksy apartment.[3] Even his

 Banksy, The Bristol Legacy

EVENING POST

★★★

thisis bristol.co.uk

7p · At the heart of all things local · Tuesday, September 1, 2009

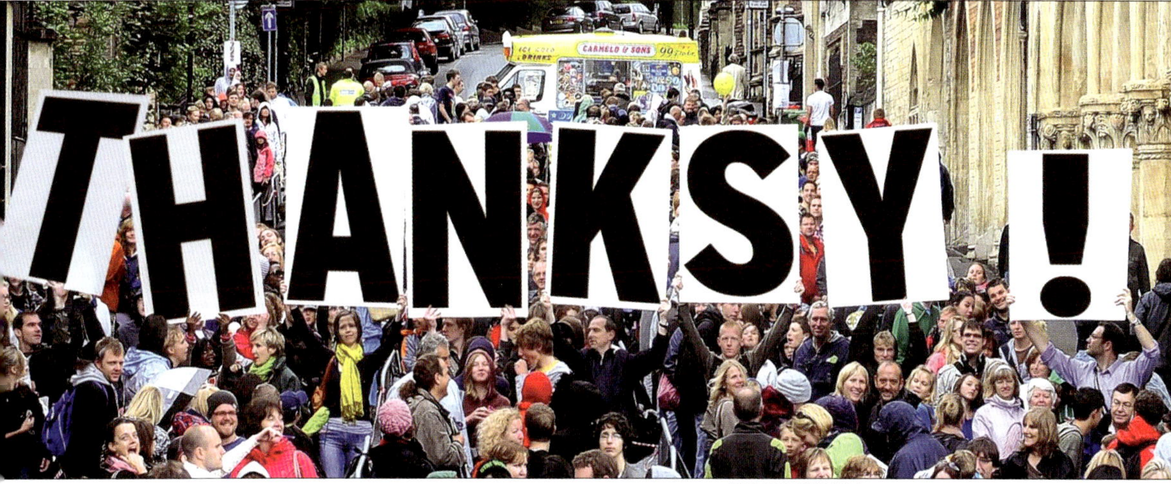

ng their appreciation: Thousands queued to see the Banksy exhibition at City of Bristol Museum

Photograph: Michael Lloyd
Image manipulation: Mike Chalmers

Banksy xhibition ings extra 0m into ty economy

● 4,000 people a day visit show – 300,000 in 12 weeks

● Donations top £45,000 – four times the normal annual figure

Jacqueline Steele & Julie Harding
epnews@bepp.co.uk

"Banksy Effect" has 10 million into the economy and doubled rnover of a number of businesses at the t of the recession.

the 12 weeks more than people, around 4,000 each ited the *Banksy vs Bristol* n exhibition matching useum's own annual r of visits.

rs queued come rain or shine for between two and six hours to see more than 100 works by the elusive artist in the exhibition, which closed yesterday.

In a statement sent by text message to the media, Banksy said: "It's nice to see it's been so popular but it makes me a bit suspicious.

"Throughout history all the great artists have been overlooked in their own lifetime and only appreciated once they've gone. I'm starting to worry I'm not one of the good guys."

In a separate message to the *Evening Post* he added: "In some ways I'm sorry it has to end but I promised my mum she could have her leopard-skin coat back."

The leopard-skin coat is part of an animatronic exhibit arranged in a tree to look like a real animal when viewed from one side, with the belt moving like a wagging tail.

Voluntary donations to the museum were also generous, reaching in excess of £45,000 – nearly four times the annual amount. Bristol Museum itself employed an extra 30 temporary staff to work over the three-month period.

And there have been 600,000 visits to YouTube's *Banksy vs Bristol Museum* video.

Economic experts say the interest generated by Banksy's work has had an unprecedented and unexpected effect on local businesses and other tourist attractions.

Hotel rooms, guesthouses and B&B bookings are up, takings by

● Turn to page 2

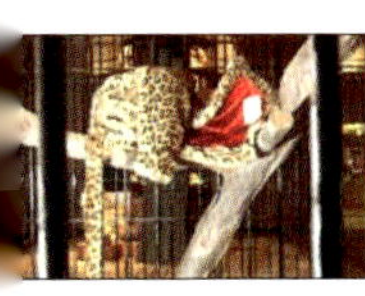

In some ways I'm sorry it has to end but I promised my mum she could have her leopard-skin coat back – Banksy

discarded pizza box is valuable: taken from a dumpster in Los Angeles and making $102 on eBay, the seller saying that the anchovies left there may have his DNA.[4]

I've been involved in Bristol's cultural development for 18 years and during much of this time Banksy has been present. It's only in recent years that he has become so prominent, however, culminating in the exhibition and the remarkable response this generated in the city. He's unquestionably a Bristol artist, but one, like many a Bristol innovator, who deserved official acclaim in the city well before he achieved it.

This is not surprising. Until recently, Bristol has had an ambivalent relationship with its artists. Street art and graffiti have been even harder to accept, as civic leaders struggle with celebrating heritage and trying to be modern, and radical underground art can be either an act of vandalism or a work of genius, depending on who is talking about it. The council had to hedge their bets with the exhibition: whilst it was a celebration of transgression, there were signs dotted about saying that Bristol City Council did not endorse graffiti.

We tried to cope with these tensions, even celebrate them, when we were asked to summarise Bristol in our bid to be '2008 European Capital of Culture'. Defining the essence of a city, especially one as complex as Bristol, is a pretty hopeless task, but we did our best. We put forward Bristol as 'a city of paradoxes: parochial and international; conservative and radical; maverick and traditional; old and modern; laid-back and ambitious; independent and collaborative; comfortable and restless.' We added: 'Bristol's maritime and engineering achievements - water, docks, bridges, ships and planes - the city's topography, green and urban spaces, myths and mysteries, and traditional and modern architecture promote a sense of place.' And concluded:

Our diverse population, the influence of outsiders, and our 'city villages' make Bristol a thrusting business centre, an intellectual hotbed, a cosmopolitan community, a home for alternative life styles, a centre for contemporary music, arts and media, and a model for urban living, playing and learning. Though it has a long history, Bristol is a young city, represented by a strong youth culture, with a young spirit willing to try the new.

Our bid didn't win, though much good came from the work that went into developing it. What is interesting for this book is to find that Banksy is mentioned once in the bid document and then only as one of many visual artists associated with the city. Graffiti is also mentioned once, in the same sentence; street art not mentioned at all. Though not as famous as he is now, Banksy was certainly well known in the city in 2003 when the bid was submitted: he had started his work in 1993 and his first exhibition (which I remember now) took place three years before the bid went in. Like many, we were late in appreciating his importance, but then that lack of recognition was shared by much of the city. If the bid had been submitted four years later, he would have been centre stage. It would have been nice, if that were the case, to have got his endorsement, but as with the Bristol musicians we tried to get to support our bid, we would have failed.[5]

I like much of what Banksy does. The 2009 exhibition was one of the best I have seen in Bristol. I like his rats, the gorilla in pink glasses, his House of Commons made up of apes, his Guantanamo prisoner placed on the Big Thunder Mountain ride at Disneyland, his Brunel, the Mona Lisa with a yellow smiley face, the security fence on the West Bank, the naked man committing adultery, and the ice cream van. I like his wit and the subterfuge. I like his cynicism too. How could you not like someone who said about his exhibition:

> *The people of Bristol have always been very good to me – I decided the best way to show my appreciation was by putting a bunch of old toilets and some live chicken nuggets in their museum. I could have taken the show to a lot of places, but they do a very nice cup of tea in the museum.*[6]

I like it that, as quoted in *The New Yorker*, one of his staff told a journalist trying to get an interview, that 'Mr Banks is away polishing one of his yachts'.

I like the fact that I know people who went to the exhibition, intrigued by the hype (even wanting to appear cool) but who would hate having a Banksy on their wall. And that's one of the interesting things about Banksy: the reaction of official, government and business Bristol. Just as there are many paradoxes about Bristol so there are paradoxes about Banksy, his relationship to art, and how as a city we see and try to use his work. There's no question that he wants to be noticed, but that he lives off anonymity, though there's good reason for this given that a prison sentence is likely for some of the work he has done. *The New Yorker* article on his work said that Banksy tries to flip 'off the art world… [and begs] it to notice him at the same time.'[7]

He must be a wealthy man, as the likes of Brad Pitt and Angelina Jolie buy his work, yet much of it is given away free. He clearly likes animals: significant parts of the exhibition were devoted to them, perhaps as a reaction to a former time when the museum's rear ground floor was reserved for a grotesque display of stuffed dead creatures, yet he painted a live elephant for the opening of his Los Angeles exhibition and was rightly criticised for this.[8] He is lauded for his anti-establishment stance, but almost at the same time is condemned for seemingly condoning violence in his

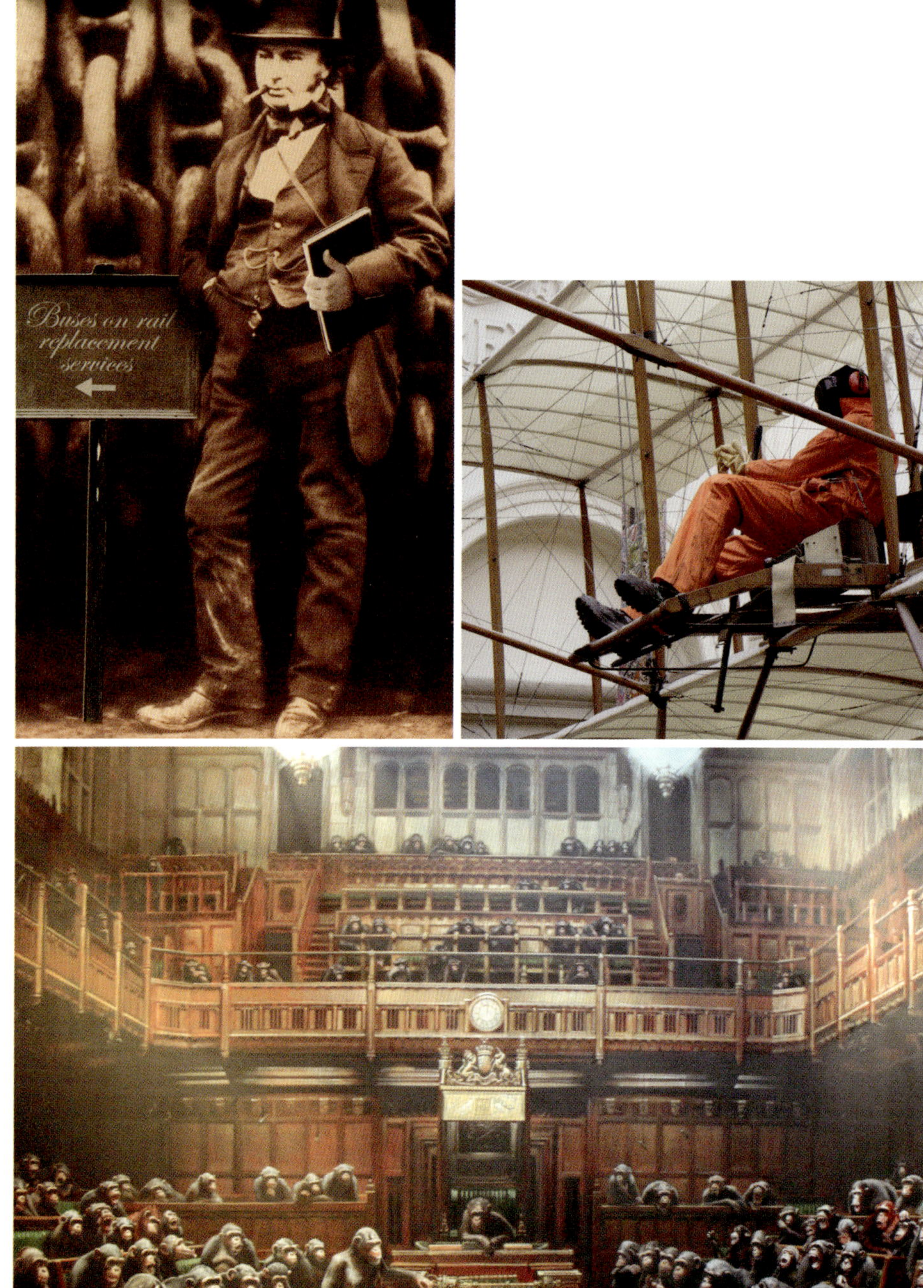

Three exhibits from the Banksy show. (photographs: Bristol Museum & Art Gallery)

 Banksy, The Bristol Legacy

response to the Stokes Croft riots. He's the best known street artist in the city, but there are many others, some would say, better than him. Is he Left-wing, or is he commenting on the Left?

None of this matters – especially to someone like Banksy. He's made it clear how cynical he is of the art world, quoted in *The New Yorker* as describing it as 'the biggest joke going…a rest home for the overprivileged, the pretentious, and the weak'. He's a rebel, rebelling against many things, and it's in terms of rebellion that his work should be seen as it fits well in a place where rebellion has often been present, belying the perception, not totally undeserved until recently, of a city characterised by lethargy and conservatism (that famous graveyard of ambition, again), at least in the areas of local government and business.

It's easy to romanticise rebellion, especially with regard to Bristol and its many riots, but there's something about the city where, on occasion, rebellion is important. Bristol can make claim to the beginning of the English Romantic poetry movement, with the publication of Wordsworth and Coleridge's *Lyrical Ballads*; Bristol was where Coleridge gave his famous lectures on religion and where he and Southey planned the utopian Pantisocratic Society in the US; it may have been home to the slave trade, but it was also the home of a significant abolitionist movement. Brunel was a rebel, challenging the Corporation and the Merchant Venturers to back his plans to modernise the city and to transform the world; it's where local MP Tony Benn launched his campaign to relinquish his peerage; and where bands like Portishead and Massive Attack have transformed the music scene. It's also the hidebound place the exasperated Chatterton escaped from to London, and which Richard Savage, the impecunious poet, described as a city of:

> *Upstarts and mushrooms, proud relentless hearts,*
> *Thou blank of Sciences, thou dearth of Arts!*

Banksy fits well in this tradition. An artist who breaks the rules. Who moves his art forward – the art of the street – and who has a genuine mystery about him which is both alluring and frustrating. It's what attracts people to him and what puts some off. He's independent. He's an outsider that many people would like to have on their side.

Official Bristol – at least government and business leadership – would dearly like to appropriate Banksy and have tried to do so. The fact that he comes from Bristol and has an international reputation, enhanced by the secrecy of his identity, would do much for the image of the place if it could be harnessed more than it is currently. Some could imagine him in corporate advertising, being an official spokesman for the city, appearing on stage in a national tour. He's already used as a tourist attraction: the *Visit Bristol* website includes four Banksy locations in its sightseeing section ('From Brunel to Banksy, Bristol has some of England's most recognisable landmarks as well as plenty of hidden gems') and he is listed among Bristol's famous people. But this is but a fraction of what could be possible with his cooperation.

It hasn't stopped people trying, wanting to be associated with him, though there's danger in this - praising someone one day can come back to bite you on another, especially if that someone is a rebel, radical and underground. It did not take long to move from the exhibition being the 'Best pound the council ever spent', according to Cllr Simon Cook, to Banksy facing the opprobrium of the political establishment. As others have commented in this book, the turning point was the 2011 Stokes Croft 'Tesco riots'. His picture of a Molotov cocktail in a Tesco bottle, sold at the Bristol Anarchist Bookfair allegedly to provide aid to those arrested, saw parts of official Bristol reject their adopted son. Local MP Stephen Williams said Banksy was 'completely outrageous'. Barbara Janke, Liberal Democrat leader of the Council, said:

> *What a sad, sordid way to thank Bristol for providing this talented, privileged but misguided young man with a springboard for his career as a graffiti artist. This city has long been proud of his work, but the decent citizens of Bristol who have been disgusted by the violence and intimidatory tactics of the recent rioters will be rightly appalled by Banksy's apparent willingness not only to identify himself with their cause but to aid them in their cowardly attempts to evade justice.*

I doubt he cared very much about this. It was a misguided gesture, however, complicated by confusion about where the money raised was to go.[9] And, as Katy Bauer explores elsewhere in this book, even some admirers saw the fickle nature of his fame and reputation when they condemned the Tesco poster sales on eBay (at the time of writing there were 15 still on sale at an average price of £150).

What all this shows, though, is that Banksy has an impact on people, the city and the arts, and for museums and cultural organisations demonstrating impact has been a key part of our work for the past 20 years: funders and sponsors require some evidence that their investment will do, or has done, some good; many of those running projects like justification that they have made a difference. Taking their cue from the McKinsey maxim 'What you can measure you can manage' (or perhaps better, what can't be measured doesn't count), consultants have come up with ways of demonstrating impact for arts activity. It used to be in solely economic terms - jobs created, wealth generated, money-spending tourists encouraged to visit - which came from the pioneering work of John Myerscough.[10] Consultants came up with more sophisticated measurements – of social impact (arts projects reducing crime, for example, or enhancing social cohesion); educational impact (encouraging better exam results); impact on urban regeneration – a popular one when it came to major grants – and others.

We've not been immune to this in our work, though in recent years have become disenchanted with both the methodologies used and the results generated – and you get the feeling that funders have begun, in a small way, to move away, too. Concentrating on financial spend often fails to acknowledge that people have not spent on something else; saying the arts create jobs invites comparison that investment elsewhere might create even more jobs. But for now it remains essential and, in the case of 'Banksy vs Bristol Museum', it was a key part of what followed.

So how do you measure the impact of the Banksy show and what does this mean? For that matter, how do you measure the impact of a piece of graffiti, a work admired as it is by some, feared and loathed by others? How do you measure the impact of Banksy on Bristol and on Bristol's image elsewhere? That the exhibition had an impact in terms of visitors is without doubt. I had to walk past the queues many times, and was always astonished by the numbers of people prepared to wait for hours to get in. That Banksy is associated with Bristol is generally a good thing (when he behaves himself). This temporary exhibition was unquestionably a catalyst for people to come to the museum and to the city. In its annual survey of exhibition visitors, the *Art Newspaper* ranked it in the world's top 30 (at number 30) and said it was the first time the Bristol museum had made the list. It was ranked second out of the UK venues. This is a major achievement. It was not the first exhibition about graffiti in the city – Banksy himself had previously done a much smaller one and, as Kath Cockshaw discusses in this book, the Royal West of England Academy had hosted its own (popular) show, but this was the most significant by far and is likely to remain so.

But it's the smaller things I remember: my colleague rushing to queue early; my brother insisting on getting a photograph of the adultery picture on Park Street (I'd not known him to have an interest in art before); the excited couple I saw, who must have been in their seventies, getting on the Park & Ride bus at Brislington and telling the driver that they were 'going to see the Banksys'. In fact, I thought that the best measure of impact should have been the figures for sales to queuers from the ice cream van, parked outside for the duration: presumably the owner has retired on the proceeds.

Both King Sturge, a local property agent, and Destination Bristol, responsible for tourism in the city, carried out research on the economic impact. According to Destination Bristol 308,719 people visited the show with seven out of ten people coming from outside the city specifically to see it.[11] About 55,000 extra hotel and bed and breakfast rooms were occupied by Banksy fans staying in the city. Visitors who came to the city solely to view the exhibition were estimated to have spent £10.3m in local businesses (though as some of these are national chains, the income may not have all stayed in the city). Bristolians themselves also contributed to the local economy, spending an additional £4.3m in shops, pubs and restaurants while on a day out to see the exhibition. Just over one in three exhibition-goers lived within 25 miles of the museum. Thirty temporary staff members were appointed. There were a reported 600,000 visits to YouTube's 'Banksy vs Bristol Museum' video, and the museum was delighted to have received £45,000 – nearly four times the annual amount received – in voluntary donations. Why such pleasure at such a small amount (for both this exhibition and annually) is bizarre, however: a paltry average of 0.14p for each visitor.[12]

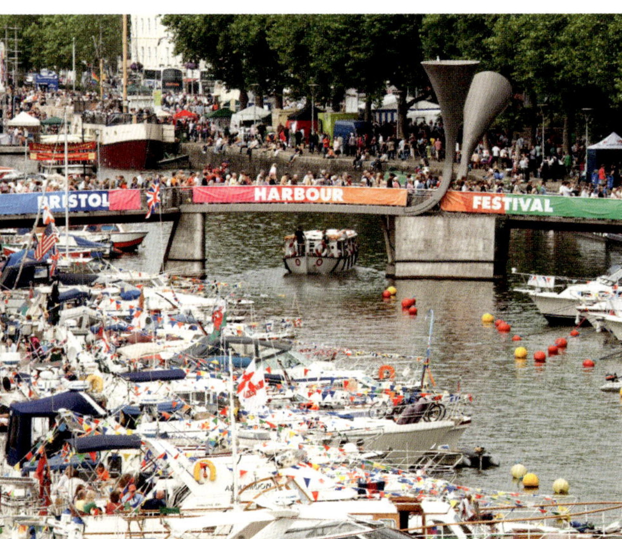
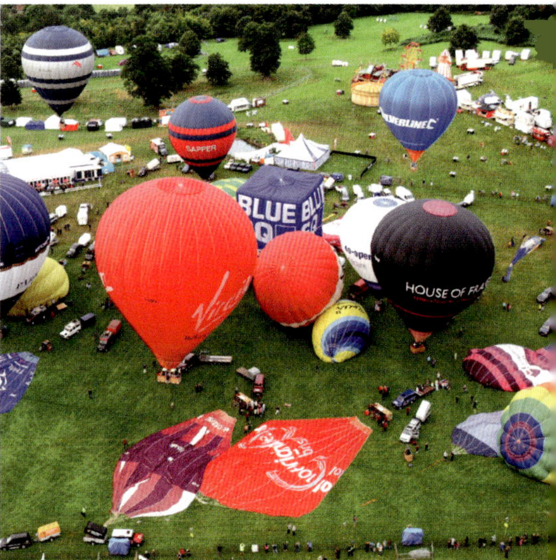

Neither of the two great annual crowd-pullers, in the city docks and at Ashton Court, could begin to match the appeal of the Banksy exhibition. (photographs: courtesy *Bristol Evening Post*)

When the research results were published, John Hallett from Destination Bristol said:

We can't think of a similar event which has come close in terms of revenue. Things such as the Harbour Festival, or the Bristol Balloon Fiesta each bring in about £5m to the local economy but nothing like the £15m we saw with Banksy.

Ned Cussen from King Sturge commented:

It is a fantastic example of what can be achieved by an exhibition such

*as this. It developed an immense sense of civic pride and was a welcome
boost for businesses who have been finding it tough in this current
climate.*

And Simon Cook, deputy leader of Bristol City Council said:

*We are absolutely delighted to hear the figure of £15m. I've always
believed that culture pumps the economy. We were told by Banksy's PR
people that we would get 100,000 people to the exhibition - in fact we got
more than 300,000. I think there is a great feeling of warmth towards
Banksy with his legacy of artwork around Bristol and beyond.*[13]

Elsewhere in this book Anthony Plumridge and UWE colleagues have
assessed the economic impact of the exhibition: demonstrating cultural and
artistic impact is much more difficult. While one person loves a Banksy work
- and there is much to admire and love about him - another person derides
it as tagging, the type of graffiti that ruins many an urban landscape. Keep
Britain Tidy are no fans: 'Banksy's street art glorifies what is essentially
vandalism', they say. Some do not see it as art at all - though satisfactorily
defining what art is is difficult to achieve. John Carey, in his book *What
Good are the Arts?* said this assessment should not just be left to the art
world to decide: 'A work of art is anything that anyone has ever considered
a work of art, though it may be a work of art only for that person' (it's a
good definition but it does mean that any person daubing a wall can claim
to be Michelangelo).[14]

Jonathan Jones of *The Guardian* said: 'there's some wit in Banksy's work,
some cleverness - and a massive bucket of hot steaming hype.' In reviewing
the exhibition Waldemar Januszczak in the *Sunday Times* saw it as a loss of
innocence and wished he had not done it. He said:

*Banksy the rebel was an artist you could trust, a free creative voice
that owed nothing to anybody. Banksy the respectable museum artist
is something else. What is being destroyed here is not the anonymity of
Bristol City Museum, it's Banksy's raison d'être.*[15]

Famously, Brian Sewell said about Banksy: 'The two words "graffiti" and "art"
should never be put together'. He called Bristol City Council 'bonkers' for
saving Banksy's work, accused the public of 'not knowing good from bad'
and feared that 'buildings of fine quality, and there are many in Bristol, will
be defaced. The architecture must take primacy over whatever street artists
may want to do.'[16] One who had a damascene conversion was Mike Norton,
editor of the *Bristol Evening Post*, who is generally against graffiti. As Eugene
Byrne also notes, Norton wrote, in response to criticism that he was guilty of
selling out his principles as Banksy's work was taken up by celebrities:

I am no street-art devotee. But this exhibition has made me realise there is a huge difference between intelligent, thought-provoking art and the mindless daub of a graffiti tag. So, just as Banksy's exhibition has brought the world to Bristol Museum, it has also brought this 45-year-old 'art traditionalist' to an appreciation of street art.

Banksy is no doubt famous and cool and all the other things that could be said by his supporters. He is admired by many in Bristol, regarded as the pre-eminent street artist of his generation, and those who know him (or profess to know him – there is no way of being certain) express warmth towards him. As I said earlier, I like his wit – in his art and his statements – and there is a great energy to the work. He's not consistent, but then which artist is?

Banksy is admired greatly by many people. Denise James of Bristol Clean & Green, who, while having a regard for Banksy, is not a fan of graffiti – unsurprisingly given the amount of money it costs to clear up each year in the city – told *The New Yorker*: 'All these little lads look at Banksy the way the youngsters who are into football look at Beckham – he's their hero'. He was among the figures voted by the public for inclusion in a new version of the painting *Some Who Have Made Bristol Famous* as part of the '2008 Great Reading Adventure: *The Bristol Story*' (though, for obvious reasons, only an image from his work could be included - see page 84 for illustration). Also as part of *The Bristol Story* project, the Banksy gorilla featured in the work on Bristol identity created by Year 3/4 pupils at Hillfields Primary which included the following short story using the butterfly theme – All The Same, All Different – adopted by the class.

One day, a butterfly set off for his holiday. His name was Joe!
'I'm going on holiday,' he would say, so he spread his wings and lifted into the air. He was a well travelled butterfly and this latest holiday would take him far from America – his home and his heritage. Lately he had been getting bored so he knew it was time to go.

It took him a long time to fly across the world, but he was looking for a landmark – the gorilla with the pink glasses that Banksy had created. He stopped on a wall on Fishponds Road and rested. He looked below and there it was the graffiti of a gorilla in pink glasses. Now he knew he was in Bristol!

He loved Bristol and decided not to leave. He wanted to enjoy his short life.

The gorilla later featured as one of the famous local 'people' depicted by the pupils when they represented the city at the national Portrait of a Nation celebrations in Liverpool in December 2008. Others included Brunel, Beryl

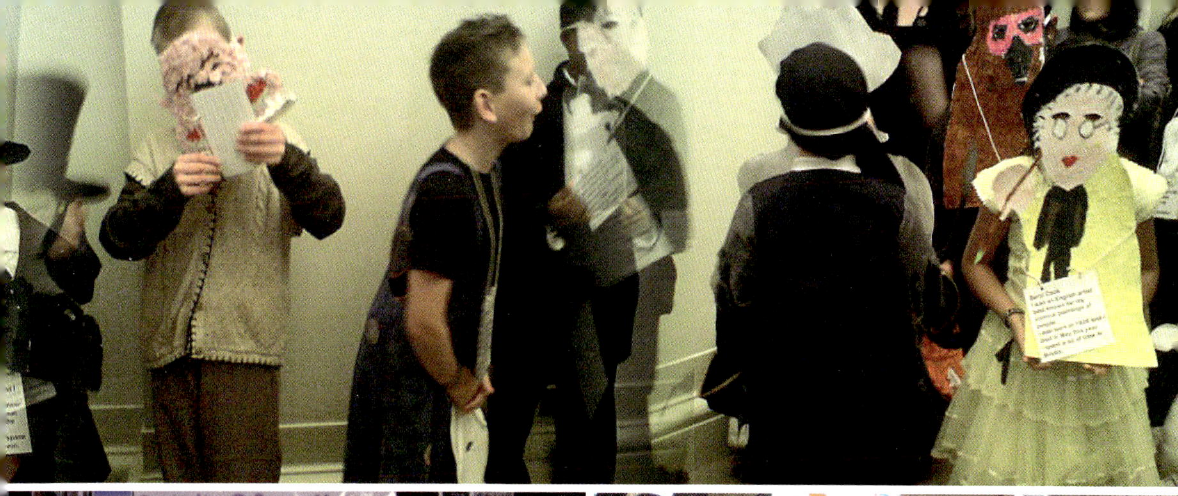

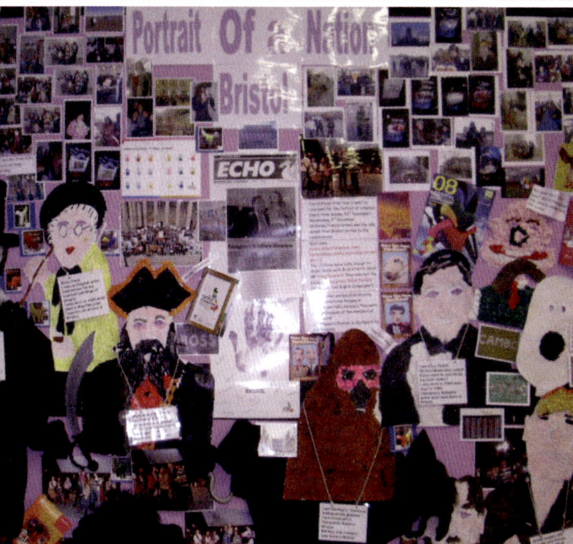

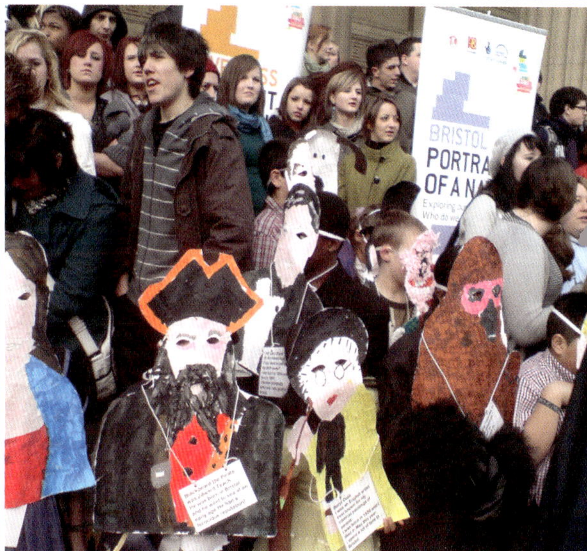

Banksy's gorilla was one of the city's iconic figures which Bristol schoolchildren showed at the Portrait of a Nation celebrations in Liverpool in December 2008.

Cook, Blackbeard, and Wallace and Gromit. On their tour of Liverpool, they were delighted to have seen a Banksy rat.[17] And in a visioning exercise Banksy was chosen by a group of fifty 13 to 14-year-olds representing five Bristol secondary schools at a Leaders of the Future Workshop in 2010 as among the things that made their city unique – others included Brunel (specifically the Clifton Suspension Bridge and the *SS Great Britain*), TV and media production, Cabot Circus, Concorde and aviation, architecture and the Bristolian accent.

Not all were so impressed by Banksy, even after the publicity and adulation that accompanied the exhibition. In 2011, *The Gorilla in Pink Glasses* on Fishponds Road, the same image that had inspired the pupils at Hillfields, was whitewashed, along with other graffiti and tagging, when the building was turned into a Muslim cultural centre. 'I thought it was worthless. I didn't know it was valuable. That's why I painted over it. I really am sorry if people are upset' said the building's owner. Though the painting was restored soon after, there are clearly some who have not been as charmed as the local children.[18]

That was an exception, however. Few people now can be unaware of Banksy and his work. He may be full of contradictions, some of his art may be hyped, too much made of the mystery, and graffiti, in the main, is a form of vandalism. Banksy may have an ambivalent relationship with official Bristol: he's a paradoxical artist in a paradoxical city now trying to celebrate art and take it seriously. But far better this, than a city that does not generate artists and art. He's also fun and makes you think. We should have more blockbuster exhibitions like 'Banksy vs Bristol Museum' about all types of art. I long for the day when I can see those queues again.

Andrew Kelly is Director, Bristol Cultural Development Partnership, the Great Reading Adventure and the Festival of Ideas. He was director of Bristol 2008 and Brunel 200. He is the author of 12 books including *Cinema and the Great War* (1997); *Filming All Quiet on the Western Front* (2001); *Managing Partnerships* (2002); *Brunel: in Love with the Impossible* (2006); *Darwin: For The Love of Science* (2009) and *Take Flight: 100 Years of the Bristol Aeroplane Company* (2010).

Notes

1. There's an obsession with suggesting statues to celebrate people who have done great work. As with Brunel and Sir George White – two other projects I have worked on and where there have been campaigns for statues – the tribute is in the recognition and celebration of their work. There is in fact a grotesque statue of Brunel which we would dearly like Banksy to do something with.

2. The latest, at the time of writing, was identified by Sam Downie, see: www.twitpic.com/5xc7a2/ accessed 7 August 2011.

3. The flat comprises lounge/dining room, kitchen, master bedroom with ensuite, a further bedroom and bathroom. Nothing Banksy about it. Another is called *The Hirst.*

4. Collins, Lauren, 'Banksy Was Here: The invisible man of graffiti art', *The New Yorker*, 14 May 2007.

5. We tried to get two of Bristol's well-known current musicians to endorse our plans and they said they would; a few days later I read in the local newspaper that they would not.

6. Banksy's statement was widely used in the national and international press. Even the *Daily Mail* ran it in full on 12 June 2009. www.dailymail.co.uk/news/article-1192595/Banksy-pulls-audacious-stunt-secret-exhibition-Bristol-museum.html

7. *New Yorker*, Collins article page 2 of the online version.

8. 'Ed Boks, Los Angeles's general manager of animal services, said he regretted that his office had issued a permit and, after visiting the show, wrote on his blog that looking into the elephant's eyes "nearly brought me to tears." He eventually ordered the animal hosed down.' Quoted in *New Yorker* article. Some contemporary graffiti artists thought this a stunt too far. A large painting at the 2011 UPFest (Urban Paint Festival) in South Bristol depicted a painted elephant with the tag line 'Serious artists don't paint elephants.' See page 14.

9. The Bookfair website claimed the money raised was going to 'local groups in the Stokes Croft/Bristol area who support local art, squatting and those arrested and harassed as a result of the recent Stokes Croft disturbances' but a spokesman for Banksy said money would go towards the People's Republic of Stokes Croft and other local community groups. PRSC chairman Chris Chalkley stressed his organisation did not believe violence was the way forward and that the money would go towards 'repairing the damage that has been done in our community and those directly affected by the recent violence'. Katy Bauer explores this issue in her chapter on the incident and the resultant artwork.

10. Myerscough, John *The Economic Importance of the Arts in Britain* (London: Policy Studies Institution, 1988).

11. It would have been nice to know approximately how many women and men came and also some assessment of whether the exhibition attracted members of Bristol's ethnic minority communities.

12. The exhibition fee paid by the museum to Banksy was £1.00 so in terms of cost it is immaterial. And he apparently did not want a charge for entry to be made. But there is an issue here about future exhibitions. One good result of 'Banksy vs Bristol Museum' is that there is more ambition now for similar scale exhibitions in the city. To have one that would have similar impact would cost hundreds of thousands of pounds – it is unlikely that other artists or lenders would be as generous as Banksy – at a time when there is no funding at this level available so the issue of charging for exhibitions has once again been raised. I have no problem with this: when I go to London I pay £12 for an exhibition. Most visitors would have been happy to pay for the Banksy exhibition.

13. Not all were impressed with these figures. One person wrote on the *Bristol Evening Post* website: 'Seriously though, this report is pure speculation. Are you trying to tell me that each member of the queue was timed, asked where they had come from, where they spent their money etc etc. True, it's called an "estimate" – but you can't help wondering how much this report cost to produce. I say it's cobblers – all numbers plucked from the air. No one I know who went to the exhibition was asked where they were from, how long they queued, how much they spent, where they stayed etc etc.' Another wrote, in a different vein, 'The man's an inspiration and myself and my family have come away from a couple of days at the Filton Holiday Inn (£370 for the local economy) totally recharged and brimming with ideas for creating our own art. Surely this is the sign of a true artist – someone who inspires others. We will be returning to Bristol because of Banksy and just hope attitudes to this great man will have changed a bit by then. The ballerina in the gas mask was my favourite but all the exhibits were brilliant.' That one was fine. I've had to read a lot of other, less thoughtful, readers' comments for this essay.

14. Carey, John, *What Good are the Arts?* (London: Faber, 2005) p.29.

15. www.entertainment.timesonline.co.uk/tol/arts_and_entertainment/visual_arts/article6530036.ece June 21, 2009, accessed 7 August 2011.

16. www.guardian.co.uk/artanddesign/2009/aug/31/graffiti-art-bristol-public-vote/ Monday 31 August 2009, accessed 7 August 2011.

17. The Bristol pupils can be rightly proud of their choice of icons. A colleague who attended a meeting about this project came back to tell me that some young people had chosen as one of their city's icons the clothes store Topshop and this was welcomed by organisers.

18. www.thisisbristol.co.uk/Whitewash-Banksy-erased/story-12946703-detail/story.html/ accessed 7 August 2011. In addition to comments you would expect on this piece, it also generated, sadly, anti-Muslim and anti-cultural centre comments.

Banksy vs Bristol Museum: Bristol Museum vs Banksy: Who Won? Anna Farthing

Anna Farthing considers who won in the mock battle of 'Banksy vs Bristol Museum'. She tries to find the heart of the matter and assess what impact it had on those concerned. This chapter contextualises the event of the exhibition among developments in museum practice locally and nationally, and discusses the different conceptions of knowledge, learning and visitor experience currently exerting an influence on those working in the heritage industry.

The Banksy exhibition in Bristol City Museum and Art Gallery was without doubt a blockbuster major event, but it occurred in a wider context as part of a continuum of change and development in museum practice both in Bristol and in the wider sector.

Bristol Museums Galleries and Archives is a local authority service. It has a number of sites, all of which are free to enter, and are run from the centre by a core team of specialist staff. While the Banksy exhibition was installed in the Bristol City Museum and Art Gallery in June 2009, members of the permanent staff team were simultaneously keeping open several other sites. These included Blaise Castle House Museum, The Red Lodge, The Georgian House, Bristol Record Office and Kings Weston Roman Villa. A major focus at the time was the planning and preparation of the content for M Shed, the new Bristol history museum which opened in June 2011. The team coped admirably with the various pressures of maintaining levels of service while planning ahead, but suffice to say, 'Banksy' was not the first thing on most of their minds, especially as only very few staff knew it was coming.

Although the title of the exhibition was 'Banksy vs Bristol Museum', I would

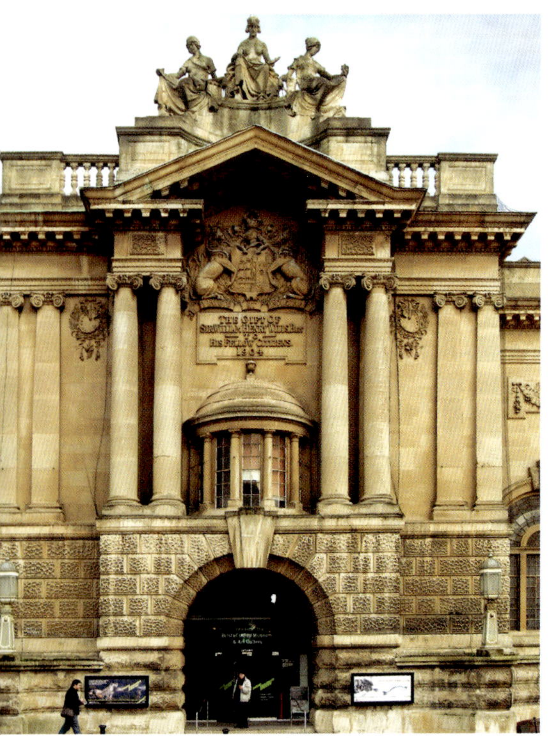

The 'Edwardian Baroque' Bristol Museum was opened as the city's art gallery, following in the nineteenth-century tradition of grand, awe-inspiring public institutions funded by wealthy businessmen. (photograph: Stephen Morris)

suggest that this oppositional stance, the 'versus', was not merely part of the headline, but was essentially performative; it was part of a continuous act that drew artists, fabricators, staff and visitors into a playful and fluid set of relationships and interactions. The role-players in this performance were both those senior museum staff who accepted the artist in, and the artist who, while enacting the persona of 'international man of mystery', demonstrated a domestic, intimate, almost familial understanding of the visitor's experience of Bristol Museum. This hybrid identity, the performative double-consciousness of Banksy both as a Bristolian and an outsider, one of the family but also the licensed *provocateur*, evokes the spirit of the court fool during a period of festivity or carnival. But like all carnivals, the period of reversal was time delineated. 'Banksy v Bristol Museum' was a performance in which the players colluded to inhabit their temporary roles. The Museum was not subjected to a riot, staff continued their roles, and there was no permanent revolution.[1]

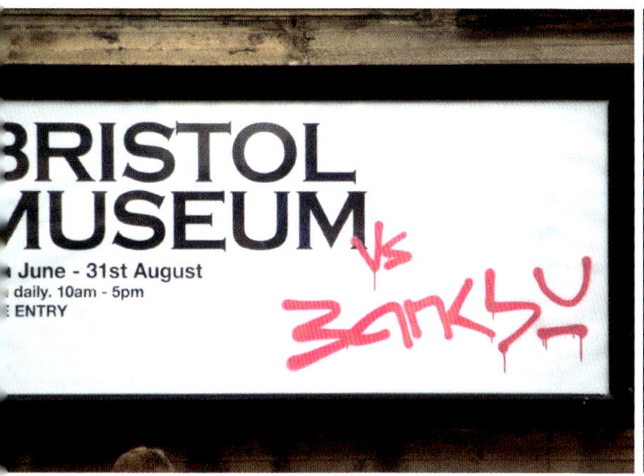
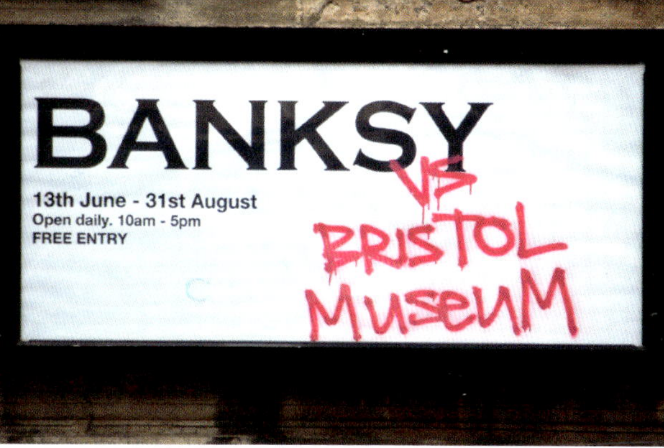

Banksy's interventions in Bristol Museum were very different to those single installations that were carried out with subterfuge in New York galleries in 2005, and in the British Museum the same year.[2] Although the set up was similarly secretive, the work shifted visitor perceptions of the museum as much as of the artist. It is significant that the exhibition was not confined to the temporary exhibition space, but compelled visitors to explore every remote gallery, peering into every case and gazing at the detail of every painting. Visitors may have been looking for Banksy's work, or evidence of where Banksy had left a trace, however tiny, but in doing so they were guided to see and appreciate much more of the permanent collections in the Bristol Museum than on an ordinary visit. I myself spent half an hour gazing at brightly coloured stuffed birds, questioning whether they had always seemed so vibrant, whether they had been re-stained by the Banksy team, or whether my perception was just heightened by the playful atmosphere. The engagement of visitors in the game of search and seek, comment and compare, while using their own digital tools to photograph

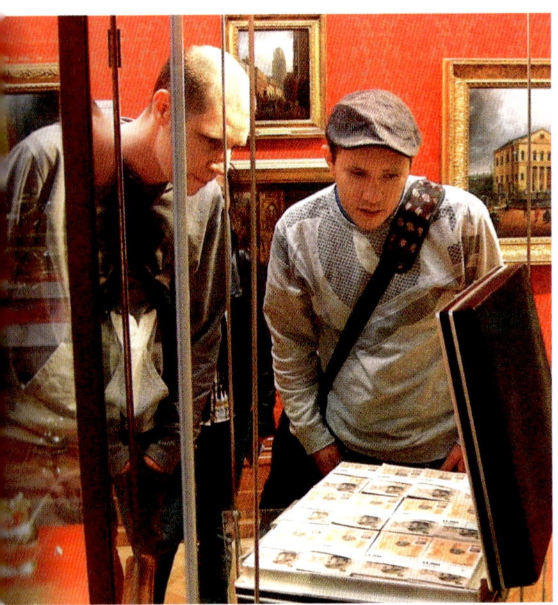

Visitors to the Banksy exhibition playing the game of 'search and seek'.

and upload to the web, enabled them to play with concepts of plurality and meta-cognition in a highly accessible and creative way that burst the walls of the museum building and spilled out into the web.

The title of the exhibition might therefore more accurately have been Banksy ♥s Bristol Museum; although such a display of affection, rather than of conflict, might not have attracted the crowds in such vast numbers. A fight will always draw a larger crowd than the sight of a group hug, even if it is a carefully staged mock battle in which, ultimately, no-one is hurt.

Banksy's developing career as an artist during the 1990s, and his spectacular homecoming in 2009, can be aligned with a period of rapid development in museum practice that has encouraged visitors to do more than come, look and see. For despite modern Western culture being 'a culture of the eye', Constance Classen asserts that 'sensory restraint is not intrinsic to the museum' and that there have in the past been many other sensory and aesthetic ways of engaging with museum artefacts besides looking[3]. The often eccentric private collectors of the seventeenth and eighteenth centuries, who exhibited their wondrous discoveries in 'cabinets of curiosity', invited selected guests to engage with artefacts through a range of intimate and domestic social rituals. Collectors impressed and entertained their visitors by inviting them to touch, smell, listen and taste as well as look. It was quite a performance.

Although Elias Ashmole's donation of his cabinet of curiosities to Oxford University in 1677 is regarded as the foundation of public museums, it was the nineteenth-century movement of bringing together private collections, augmented with philanthropic purchases, that created the network of public museums that still form the bedrock in British regional cities. This shift from private to public encounters with art and artefacts coincided with a rejection of individual, multi-sensory and hands-on interaction and the adoption of a strictly positivist way of considering knowledge, with its accompanying aura of the rational, authoritative and academic. Notions of class, learning, national identity and colonial superiority were developed through the processes of collecting, exhibiting and visiting.[4] Museums became serious, separated learning from entertainment, and lost their sense of humour.

During the museum building boom of the mid- to late nineteenth century, architects designed Palladian palaces devoted to public improvement so that the awe-inspired visitor would remain hushed and undisturbed by individual staff members, whose daily tasks were deliberately concealed in corridors and basements during opening hours.[5] Although coming some decades after most of the great provincial museum buildings, Bristol Museum follows this architectural plan of public and private spaces. Beyond the galleries there is a warren of basement store-rooms, concealed corridors, and hidden staircases leading to garret studios.

Much of what happens in museums remains hidden or out of bounds, despite recent attempts to expose the processes of collection, conservation and curation through public engagement programmes and museum studies courses. The introduction of glass walls into conservation studios in new museums such as The People's History Museum in Manchester and video surveillance into laboratories at the Natural History Museum in London enable visitors to see specialists at work, and in several National Trust properties volunteers can help 'put the house to bed' for the winter. Nonetheless, working with collections is seen as a specialist skill, and

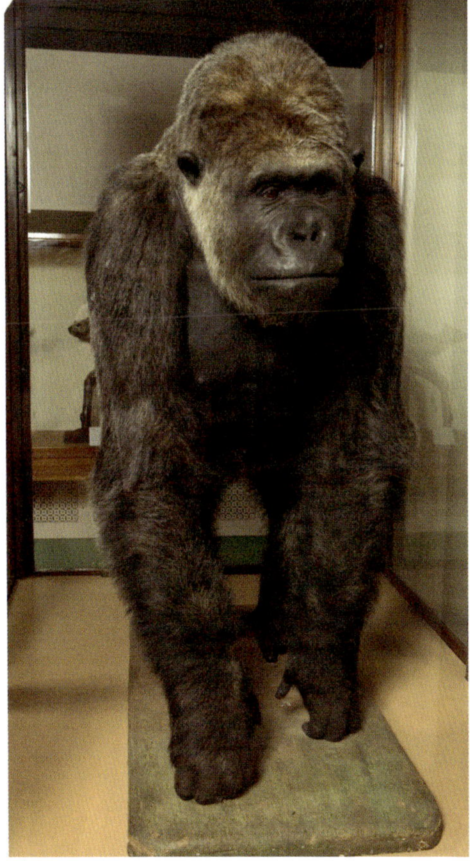
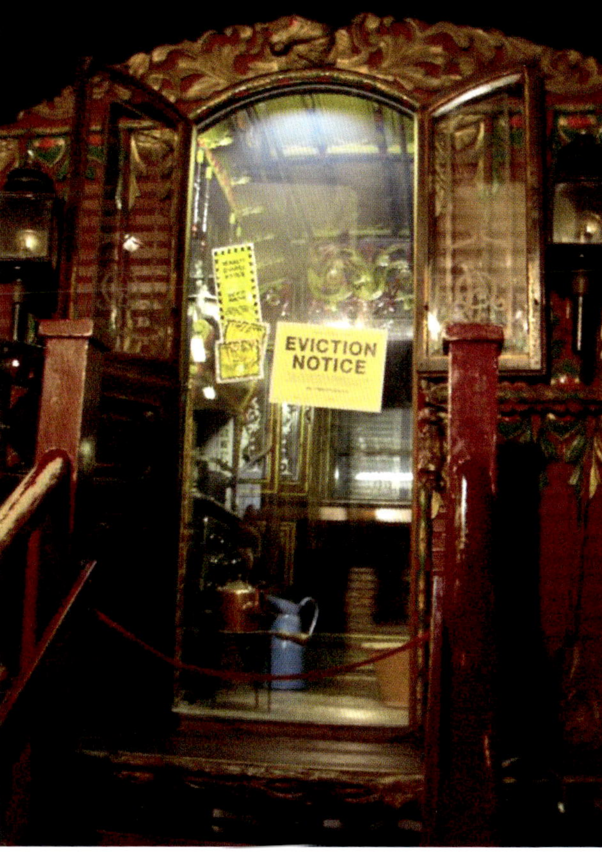

Iconic items in the Queen's Road collection: Alfred the Gorilla and the much-loved Gypsy Caravan, after a Banksy intervention. (photographs in this chapter: Bristol Museum & Art Gallery).

only a fraction of museums' vast collections can at any one time be on display. Furthermore, and somewhat bucking the trend, the curators and interpreters at Bristol Museum have remained largely anonymous. They display and interpret, but do not claim authorship of work that is often done by fluid teams.

However, in Bristol Museum's more traditional galleries, it was the simplicity of the interpretive concept, and the lack of touch screens and audio guides, that ensured there was a space for Banksy to develop the kind of interpretation that can 'provoke, relate and reveal' contemporary concerns.[6] Although the Egypt and Curiosity galleries have been redisplayed with the modern panoply of multi-media interactives, popular demand ensures that the objects that have become iconic over several generations of family visiting, such as Alfred the Gorilla and The Gypsy Caravan, remain *in situ*.[7] I would argue that it is the slightly old-fashioned mystery of the more traditional galleries, and the familiarity of some of the permanent exhibits, that lends Bristol Museum much of its popular charm, and secures its potential for future, flexible, creative interpretation.

The traditional gallery environments, rather than the more recent ones, play out the archetype of what a museum is expected to be, and build on the visitor's desire for mystery, adventure and suspense in museum settings, those very archetypical narratives that have been harnessed by popular storytellers from Alfred Hitchcock to Stephen Spielberg. Boundaries enable visitors to feel the thrill of occasional transgression. There is always exceptional demand for behind-the-scenes tours, and children love to hide and squeal in the darker recesses of some of the dimly lit galleries.[8] These reference points lent the experience of visiting the Banksy exhibition a spirit of quest. And an atmosphere of adventure and mystery obviously provides an ideal setting for an artist who chooses to subvert authority and yet remain anonymous.

Although Bristol Museum may appear traditional, and some of the galleries have remained unchanged for many years, the principles applied for public engagement are less conservative. As part of the preparations for M Shed, which is a social history museum incorporating the multiple perspectives of diverse Bristolians past and present, staff consulted widely among the general community, and applied research about visitor and learner behaviours at the leading edge of constructivist understanding.

Constructivism, which entered museum practice during the 1990s, led to a major re-assessment of the place and ownership of knowledge in museums. Constructivism proposes that knowledge is personal and provisional and that an individual makes new meanings for him or herself by combining new experience with previous understandings. 'Generic

Learning Outcomes'[9] were sought as best practice was identified in the cusp between education, interpretation and communication.[10] As a consequence, museums became noisier, busier, and messier. Visitors were encouraged to construct their own narratives rather than absorb the grand narratives of the past.[11] Discussion was encouraged rather than shushed[12] and interactivity was provided through computer screens as well as human interpreters.[13] According to this principle it is learning experience, rather than knowledge, that is provided by the museum.[14] The Museums, Libraries and Archives (MLA) Vision Statement exemplifies this objective:

> *To enable museums, libraries and archives to provide more and more people in England with high quality experiences that enrich their lives.*[15]

Some commentators have protested against the constructivist approach, preferring that museums remain aloof. As James Delingpole argued:

> *...the harder they try to make themselves more user friendly and socially relevant, the less they fulfil their purpose as wholly distinctive institutions which provide a refuge from the mundane cares and concerns of ordinary life.*[16]

Constructivism, in allowing for individual irony, has encouraged some museums to regain their sense of humour along with their sense of purpose.

Moreover, I would argue that it was this constructivist, post-modern and ironic sensibility that enabled Bristol Museum to allow its own practice to be satirized by the Banksy exhibition, for example by printing maps that indicated where the 'boring old plates' could be found. Visitors knew that Banksy the Bristol-born artist was reframing their looking, and guiding their responses, rather than an anonymous corporate graphic designer, thus increasing their enjoyment of the experience.

Visitors knew that Banksy the Bristol-born artist was reframing their looking, and guiding their responses

However, an increase in humour does not indicate a lack of seriousness. Banksy's more politicially provocative works can be seen as part of a movement towards using the museum as a forum for debating those very cares and concerns that Delingpole seeks to avoid. The particular museum of which Delingpole complains, National Museums Liverpool, is led by director Dr David Fleming OBE. He believes that museums should respond to contemporary events, such as race-hate crimes, by providing space for dialogue and debate in addition to exhibiting historical context.

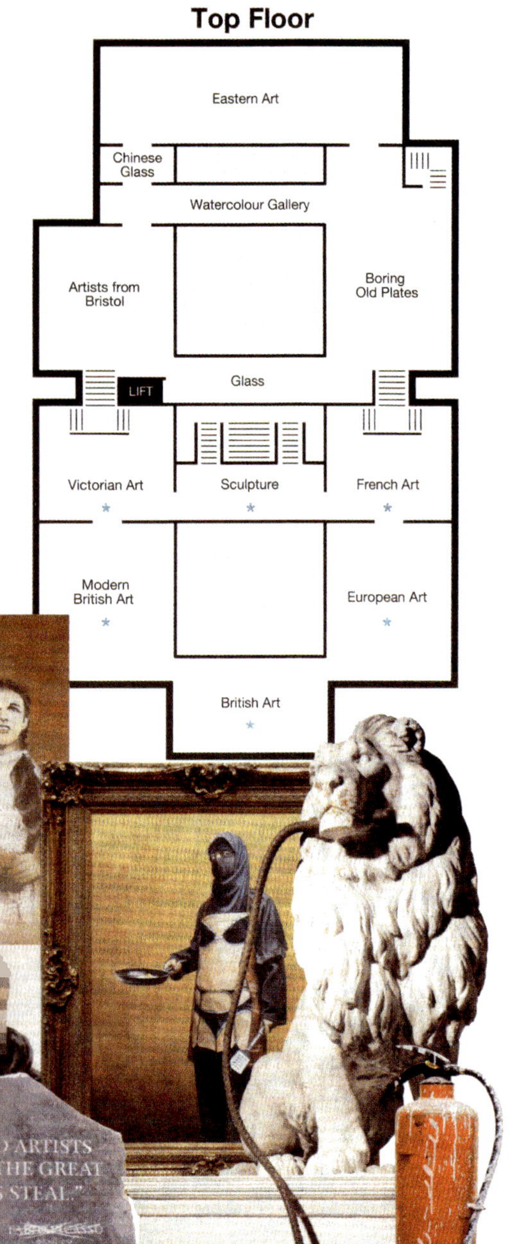

The Anthony Walker Education Room at The International Slavery Museum, part of National Museums Liverpool, is dedicated to the memory of a black British teenager who, while crossing a park with a white female friend in July 2005, was brutally murdered in a racist attack. His remarkably forgiving family subsequently set up a charity to promote racial harmony among young people. The room memorialises both his death and their benevolence. Activities are programmed in this room to stimulate dialogue on the links between the past, present and future. On the eve of the opening of The International Slavery Museum, David Fleming set out his vision, making explicit the museum's contemporary social agenda:

Make no mistake, this is a museum with a mission. We wish to help counter the disease of racism, and at the heart of the museum is a rage which will not be quieted while racists walk the streets of our cities, and while many people in Africa, the Caribbean, and elsewhere, continue to subsist in a state of chronic poverty. This is not a museum that could be described as a 'neutral space' - it is a place of commitment, controversy, honesty, and campaigning.[17]

Banksy's political and social commentary on diverse topics from war to fast food, and the move of his provocative work indoors into museums and galleries, can be seen in the light of this movement.

Following the periods of positivism and constructivism previously outlined, this reintroduction of personal passion introduces activism to the museological mix.

M Shed, the museum of Bristol life opened in 2011, is a brave new museum of multiple perspectives, multiple viewpoints and multiple voices, and the latest in the service's portfolio. It is intended to enable visitors to shape the future as well as comprehend the past. Visitors can engage their imaginations to envision the future of Bristol, and pledge to change personal behaviours as a contribution towards progress. The museum is arranged thematically rather than chronologically and makes extensive use of media, interactive displays, comment cards and explanatory text panels. Objects are chosen and arranged in ways that are illustrative of selected themes. One theme traces Bristol's history of radicalism, non-conformism and unorthodoxy, particularly focusing on key figures who have effected change in the areas of race relations, politics, education, religion and environmentalism.

Yet the display of one highly relevant object risked causing much controversy. Just before M Shed opened there were riots in the Stoke's Croft area of Bristol. As Eugene Byrne notes in this volume, the initial disturbance was prompted by an eviction, related to opposition to the opening of a new Tesco store in one of the few remaining areas of independent shops. Police suspected that petrol bombs were being prepared in a house that was being used as a squat. They raided the house and evicted the occupants, but the situation escalated and a street riot ensued. This became national news and the subject of much media debate. Although a reproduction of Banksy's famous Tesco-branded petrol bomb had been donated to the museum's collections, destined for the MShed walls, there were concerns over whether to install it.[18] Would exhibiting it fuel an already incendiary situation? Might the image receive disproportionate media attention during the museum's launch period, unbalancing the multi-faceted history of Bristol being exhibited? Although museums have customarily presented, interpreted and re-interpreted objects representing the past, and are engaging with envisioning the future, their place in responding to current events was under scrutiny.

After careful consideration, the piece was installed on 4th July 2011, taking its place in the context of the city's long history of non-conformism and dissent and bringing that history bang up to date.

So in retrospect, in the mock battle of 'Banksy v Bristol Museum', who won? Did this subversive street artist actually contest Bristol Museum's practice? Perhaps it was the equivalent of a teenager's party; the parents go away for the weekend, trust the kids with the keys, and hope that the house can be returned to 'normal' afterwards.

Allowing Banksy to exhibit both new work and to playfully comment on the old school displays of objects in the permanent collections put Bristol Museum firmly on the cultural map, and garnered more press and media coverage than the opening of the new M Shed museum. The secrecy and surprise around the event may have temporarily damaged internal relationships between those who knew and those who did not, but externally it redefined the service as one that was courageous and decisive.

As a gift from the artist, it famously cost the museum next to nothing financially, and also contributed to changing the perception of the local authority towards the political value of popular culture and the economic and social value of the creative and cultural industries.

'Banksy v Bristol Museum' was therefore a success on many counts, but it relied heavily on the contribution of a visiting mystery catalyst who, who knows, may have had a particular inside knowledge from a childhood of visiting what was his local museum. The potential impact and legacy of his playful approach to the museum's practice may actually have been diminished by the independence of the artist and the secrecy surrounding the exhibition. The museum provided space and resources in the galleries for the artist to communicate with the public, and hired temporary staff to ensure the visitor experience was supported, but the majority of the staff got on with their other tasks in the corridors, basements and garret studios.

Owing to financial considerations, including changes to museum funding and cuts in local authority spending, the future of museum development may well be in re-interpretation rather than re-display. However, current fashions in gallery design may make it much more difficult for anyone, whether internal or external, to playfully re-interpret or publicly comment upon what is displayed. Despite the provision of comment cards and touch-screen feedback opportunities, new galleries typically provide very little space in which to congregate, annotate, or create. Moreover, if genuine dialogue and debate is to take place across the museum service, it will need to be initiated, programmed and facilitated on a regular basis by those on the inside, who feel sufficiently supported to respond to events on the outside, and are resourced to make use of all of the various venues and their collections.

Those taking creative interpretive risks in the future may not have the benefit of anonymity, but they will hopefully be equally ambitious for challenging visitor perceptions, and will regard the collections of the Bristol Museums Galleries and Archives service with the same affection.
Banksy ♥s Bristol Museum.

Dr Anna Farthing is a writer, director and producer, founder of Harvest Heritage Arts and Media, and Chair of The International Museum Theatre Alliance. Her PhD concerns engaging the public with sensitive histories and her clients span museums, theatres, broadcasters and universities. She has devised and produced launch activities for The Tobacco Factory Theatre, The International Slavery Museum, The Institute for Cultural Practices, The National Museum of the Royal Navy and most recently for M Shed, the new museum of Bristol.

Notes

1. For a similar time-limited intervention by artists, see 'The Enchanted Palace' project curated and produced by Wildworks at Kensington Palace. www.hrp.org.uk/KensingtonPalace

2. Banksy left artwork at several museums in New York including the Museum of Modern Art (MoMA), The Brooklyn Museum and the American Museum of Natural History. The fake prehistoric rock stuck to a wall at the British Museum, which went unnoticed for several days, depicted a 'caveman with a shopping trolley'. Its caption read: 'The artist responsible is known to have created a substantial body of work across South East of England under the moniker Banksymus Maximus but little else is known about him. Most art of this type has unfortunately not survived. The majority is destroyed by zealous municipal officials who fail to recognise the artistic merit and historical value of daubing on walls.'

3. Classen, Constance (2007), 'Museum Manners: The Sensory Life of the Early Museum', *Journal of Social History,* 40 (4), 895-914.

4. See: Anderson, Gail, *Reinventing the museum: historical and contemporary perspectives on the paradigm shift* (Walnut Creek, Ca.: AltaMira Press, 2004) and Impey, O. R. and MacGregor, Arthur, *The origins of museums: the cabinet of curiosities in sixteenth- and seventeenth-century Europe* (London: House of Stratus, 2001).

5. Alberti, Samuel J. M. M., *Nature and culture: objects, disciplines and the Manchester Museum* (Manchester: Manchester University Press, 2009).

6. Tilden, Freeman, *Interpreting Our Heritage, fourth ed. expanded and updated*, ed. R. Bruce Craig (Chapel Hill: University of North Carolina Press, 2007).

7. Other galleries will be changed when the project to install a lift is completed in 2011/12.

8. Sleep-overs are not offered at Bristol Museum, but they are very popular in other cities, and are often accompanied by a suitable film screening such as *Night at the Museum.*

9. In 2004, the Museums Libraries and Archives funding council (MLA) introduced the 'Inspiring Learning for All' programme which applied constructivist learning theory to gallery settings. This 'self-help improvement' programme was designed to 'develop more effective learning opportunities and create learning environments'. The accompanying Generic Learning Outcomes (GLOs) framework required museums to evaluate learning experiences in a number of categories. In addition to 'Knowledge and Understanding', 'Activity, Behaviour, Progression', and 'Skills', there were categories for 'Attitudes and Values'. There is also a category for 'Enjoyment, Inspiration, Creativity'. See also: George E. Hein, *Learning in the Museum* ([S.l.]: Taylor & Francis, 2001), Mla, 'Inspiring Learning for All', in Museums Libraries and Archives (ed.), (2004).

10. Hooper-Greenhill, Eilean (ed.), *The Educational Role of the Museum* (2nd edition edn., Leicester Readers in Museum Studies, London: Routledge,1999).

11. Roberts, Lisa C. and Smithsonian, Institution, *From knowledge to narrative : educators in the changing museum* (Washington, D.C. ; London: Smithsonian Institution Press, 1997).

12. See Leinhardt, Gaea and Knutson, Karen, *Listening in on museum conversations* (Walnut Creek, Calif.: Altamira Press, 2004) and Falk, John H. and Dierking, Lynn D., *Learning from museums : visitor experiences and the making of meaning* (American Association for State and Local History book series; Walnut Creek, CA ; Oxford: AltaMira Press, 2000).

13. Caulton, Tim, *Hands-on Exhibitions: managing interactive museums and Science Centres* (London: Routledge, 1998).

14. Hein, George E., *Learning in the museum* ([S.l.]: Taylor & Francis, 2001).

15. MLA (2004), 'Inspiring Learning for All', in Museums Libraries and Archives. See also MLA (2010), 'Three Year Plan', www.mla.gov.uk/about/three_year_plan, accessed 1 February 2010.

16. Delingpole, James, 'What are Museums for?', *The Times Online,* 17 March 2006 www.timesonline.co.uk/tol/comment/article742307.ece accessed 6 August 2011.

17. Fleming, David, 'Transcript of the speech given by David Fleming, director of National Museums Liverpool, at the gala dinner to celebrate the opening of the International Slavery Museum on 22 August 2007'.

18. As Katy Bauer explains elsewhere in this volume, a similar image, unconnected with the museum but with Banksy's encouragement, was sold in the form of a poster to raise funds for the legal fees of those arrested, with a portion donated to the People's Republic of Stokes Croft Museum.

Banksy: the economic impact

Anthony Plumridge and Andrew Mearman

The economic impact of the Banksy exhibition was immediately apparent: queues and crowds around the top of Park Street gave a boost to local businesses, especially those in the food and beverage sector. Many visitors came from outside the city attracted predominantly by the exhibition. This resulted in a short-term boost to the local economy. Like a pebble thrown into a pond, ripples from this impact spread out through the economy but very soon become dissipated and disappear. The pond returns to its previous relatively tranquil state. Is this all?

Almost certainly there are longer lasting, more enduring effects. Perceptions of Bristol may have changed in ways that incrementally change economic decision-making. Further, the economic value of Banksy's artwork and of Banksy himself as a productive asset have been spectacularly revealed.

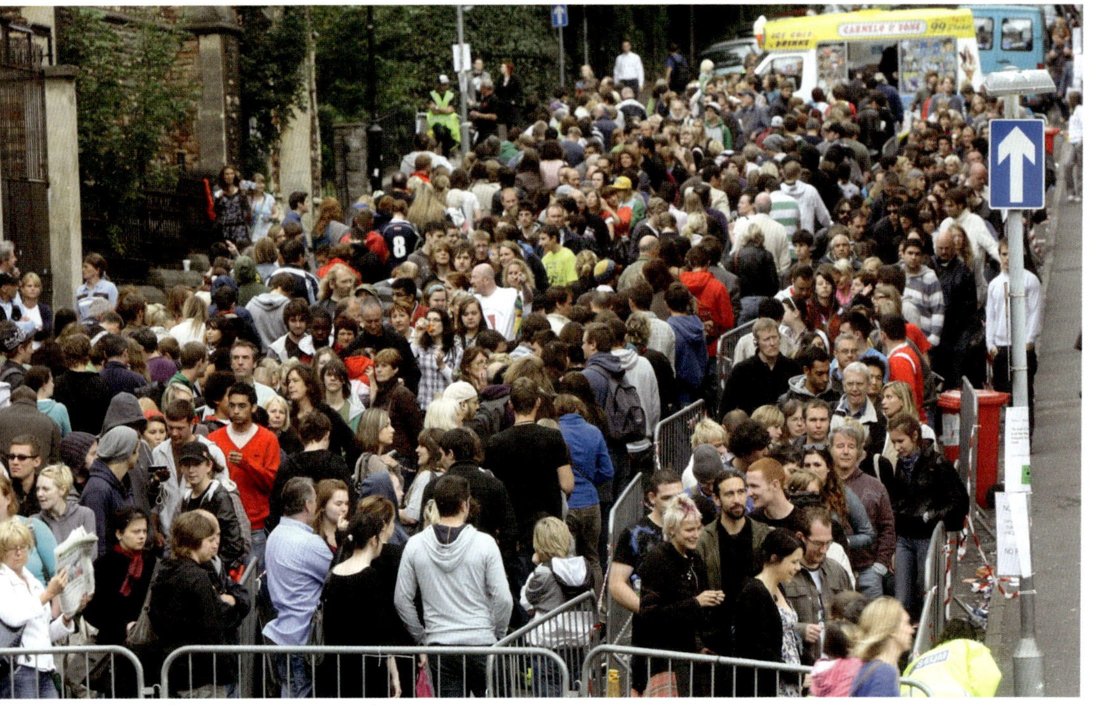

(photograph: *Bristol Evening Post*)

The short-term boost to the economy

There is a well-established methodology to determine the overall effect of an increase in expenditure on a local economy.[1] This approach is generally known as the multiplier method. In the case of the Banksy exhibition, the key characteristics of the economic impact are as follows:

Spending generated by non-local visitors whose trips were solely motivated by the exhibition was estimated as £6,169,610 by staying visitors; with a further £4,238,736 spent by day visitors.[2]

No detailed breakdown of this expenditure is available, but anecdotal evidence supports the assumption that it would fall within the 'general tourism' category, including money spent on hotels, catering, transport and other entertainment. In addition, there would have been some additional general retail spending. As in the 'pebble in the pond' metaphor, waves of this expenditure flow through (and out of) the local economy. This process can be simulated by using econ-i software[3] which incorporates the multiplier method.

Expenditure is received first by businesses such as restaurants, bars, cafés, hotels and taxis. This is termed 'direct expenditure'. From the data gathered, we know that there was a total £10,408,346 (£6,169,610 + £4,238,736) of direct expenditure – the first wave in the pond. However, that is not the end of the story. The money received by these businesses is used to pay staff, suppliers and overheads such as rent and rates. Staff receiving a portion of this expenditure as pay spend it on a wide range of goods and services and may also use it to pay regular bills such as loan interest and insurance premiums. This expenditure by staff is known as 'induced expenditure'. Some of this will be spent with local businesses and thus stay within the local economy. Some will be spent with businesses or organisations outside the local economy or overseas and thus 'escape' the pond. Some will not be spent at all but either be saved for future use or paid in taxes. Money which escapes in this way or is saved or taxed is known as leakages. However, a portion of the original additional income paid to staff will be spent with local businesses and a portion of this will also be paid to the staff of those businesses. This process continues round after round until leakages absorb most of the additional pay and the residual becomes negligible. To pursue the pond analogy, these diminishing rounds are the waves spreading out but becoming weaker over time. Econ-i suggests that the accumulative impact of these rounds of induced expenditure would add a further £1.5m of expenditure in the Bristol area.

As we have indicated, some of the additional visitor expenditure received by local businesses will be paid to suppliers and used to pay overheads such as rent and rates. This is known as 'indirect' expenditure. If the recipients of this expenditure are within the local economy then this part of the money flow will remain in the local economy and be used to pay the staff of these local businesses, their suppliers and overheads. As with induced expenditure, some of the money flow will also escape as leakages. Once again rounds of indirect expenditure will spread out across the local economy pond becoming weaker over time owing to leakages.

Econ-i suggests that the accumulative impact of these rounds of indirect expenditure would add a further £0.75m of expenditure in the Bristol area. Overall, the total direct, induced and indirect expenditure might amount to some £12.5m. This represents some 0.1% of the expenditure in the area. Most of the additional spending would occur just before, during and over a few weeks after the exhibition. This impact is not great. Using econ-i to translate the additional expenditure into jobs created, perhaps some 200 additional full-time jobs might result. Again, as a proportion of employment in the Bristol area, this is a mere 0.1%.

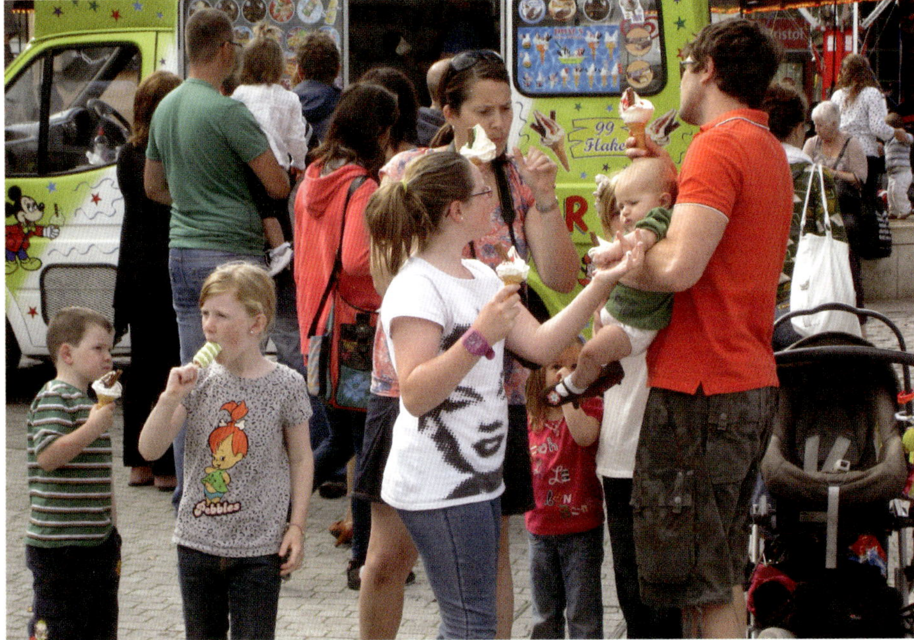

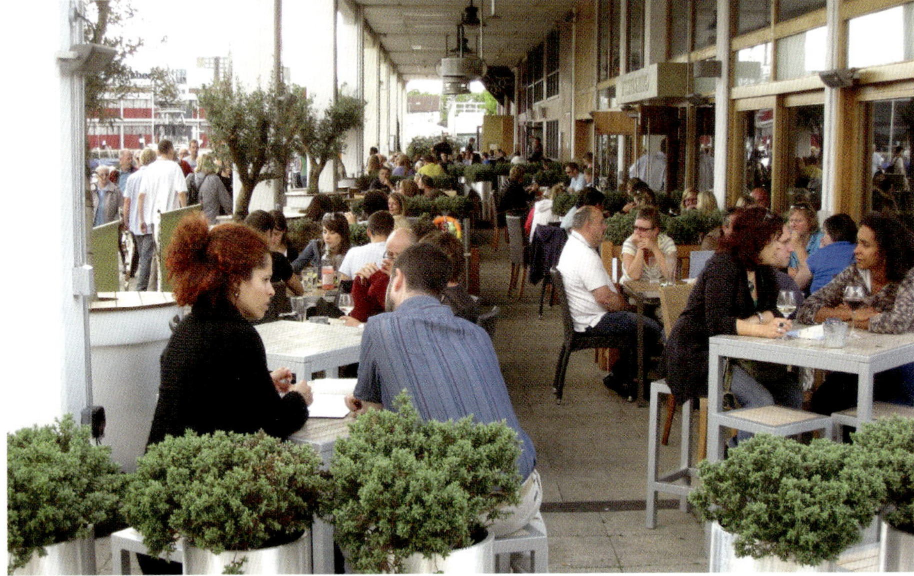

Among the first businesses to benefit from tourist expenditure are food outlets. (photographs: Paul Gough)

  Banksy, The Bristol Legacy

Even the modest employment impact that we have identified may overstate the increase in jobs. There is anecdotal evidence that local businesses responded to a sharp increase in demand by simply absorbing it, asking permanent staff to work overtime and by employing temporary staff. Thus little permanent increase in employment is likely to have occurred. In spite of this, there may well be a longer term impact of the exhibition that will be greater and more enduring than conventional economic analysis suggests.

The long term impact on the economy

After the crowds, the queues and the hype have gone, the ripples in the pond have dissipated, what remains? It is arguable that there has been an enduring shift in the awareness and perception of Bristol. The association of Banksy with Bristol is likely to be positive for young entrepreneurs and the creative industries. The city is on the radar of more people than previously, both in the UK and overseas. It is possibly seen as more vibrant and might be perceived as a city that embraces the unconventional and edgy. It is not difficult to see how the image shift might have a beneficial effect on the development of the local economy. Clearly the city appears a more relevant location for creative industry business start-ups and re-locations. But the positive impact may actually be wider than just the creative industries. It is often stated that lifestyle factors are behind the decision to re-locate to or set up a business in a new location. Many entrepreneurs and drivers of innovation and change are likely to want to work and live in a city that reflects and responds to the latest social and cultural phenomena, is buzzing with ideas and embraces the new. Certainly the Banksy exhibition reinforces such perceptions of Bristol and adds to a reputation for a rich diversity in the city's cultural life, a point stressed by many other contributors to this book.

The value of the Banksy versus Bristol Museum exhibition

The multiplier method (combined with a kind of input-output approach) offers one way to value the economic impact of the Banksy exhibition on Bristol. However, we can also provide a valuation of the event itself. Normally we would say that the entrance fee paid by people was an indicator of the value they placed on the event. An interesting feature of the exhibition was that entry to it was free. However, to say visitors did not value it would be absurd. A similar problem emerges in valuing national parks and the like. Their value can be assessed in numerous ways. One might ask people to offer their intrinsic valuations of the object. Another option is to pose hypothetical questions about how much compensation they would need if the object were not there. The data available to us did not ask these questions, so we cannot employ those methods. A further method is to value a place or event via the cost of travelling to it. Cost can be direct, such as fuel; and indirect, as in the time sacrificed to attend the event. Again, we do not have definite information on these questions. However, we can offer some informed estimates of them.

We know that 201,975 people attended from outside the local area, and of these some 140,170 were motivated primarily by the exhibition in making the trip. We will assume that on average these people lived 50 miles away. Thus they travel 100 miles to see the exhibition. We will assume that each person-mile costs 20p - based on mileage allowances for cars, advanced train fares, etc. - although that assumption is rather arbitrary. At that rate, the direct travel cost associated with coming to the exhibition is £20 per person, or £2,814,000 in total. However, these visitors also gave up their time to attend. We will assume that travel time was on average 2.5 hours, and queuing and exhibition visit time was on average 4 hours - although again these are arbitrary. That is 6.5 hours per person. We must multiply this by some value of time. This would usually be based on wage rate, on the assumption that people sacrifice work time to take leisure. Based on median weekly earnings of approximately £500; taking into account the fact that some of the visitors were children, and bearing in mind that visitors to art exhibits are usually wealthier than the average and in the case of this exhibition, older, we will assume an hourly rate of £14 per hour. At this rate, 140,700 visitors spending 6.5 hours represents a value of £91 per person, or £12,803,700.

In addition to that, local visitors also incur costs to attend the exhibition. We will assume that travel costs to locals is a notional £2 per head. Also, these local visitors sacrifice their time to attend the event. Again, we assume that they spent on average 4 hours queuing and visiting the exhibition; and that each hour is valued at £14 per hour. So, the 106,744 visitors living within 25 miles spent £213,488 travelling to the event; and another £5,977,664 attending it. To calculate the total value of the exhibition, we must add up the additional travel costs by locals and non-locals plus the value of the time spent at the exhibition. That is, then: £2,814,000 + £213,488 + £5,977,664 + £12,803,700. Thus, the grand total valuation of the Banksy exhibition is estimated at £21,808,852.

Some caveats

We have already admitted that many of our calculations are based on rather bold assumptions. That is partly a reflection of the data we were working with, which did not provide detail on exactly how people spent their money. However, we also must confess that our estimates of the multiplier effect are also rather blunt. One of the limitations of multiplier analysis is that it can omit important factors which would reduce the economic impact of the event. For this reason, alternative ways of calculating impact have been developed, which try to take into account the wider economic and non-economic effects of events. These models attempt to capture the interconnectedness of the complex local economy. Thus, we ought to consider congestion. In this case, congestion has two meanings. One is inside the exhibition; the other is outside. Some exhibitions can be too popular: too many people there can reduce the quality of the visitor's experience and thus the value of it. In the case of the Banksy exhibition – with some 310,000 visitors, many queuing for several hours – this is a distinct possibility. Related to that, there may be people who wanted to visit the event but could not, because of the lengthy queues (for example, one of these authors!). These people would also have spent time and money getting to the event, which was not captured in the visitor data. Outside the event, the extra visitors coming to Bristol could potentially have created disruption to traffic (both vehicular and pedestrian). This disruption would reduce the economic benefit of the exhibition. If local people decide not to spend money in the area because it is swarming with tourists, economic activity is reduced. It is also possible that other tourists who were considering coming to Bristol decided against it because of the large number of Banksy-related visitors. Again, some of the visitors were planning to come to Bristol anyway but re-scheduled their visit to coincide with the exhibition. The value of the exhibition is overstated by allocating all the travel cost of these visitors to the value of the exhibition. Further, some of the expenditure reported by these visitors would have taken place anyway, albeit over a different time period. There might also be events which would have happened, which could not because of the presence of the event: another reduction in activity. Though we do not have data on this, the large visitor numbers could have required considerable extra security, perhaps involving the police. Any such activity distracts police from their usual activities and this could have knock-on effects. Similarly, normal council services may have been displaced by the extra burden created by the large number of additional Freedom of Information requests they had to process.

Conclusion

We have considered the impact of the Banksy exhibition from a number of perspectives. In terms of the boost to jobs and expenditure in the local economy, the scale of the impact is relatively insignificant. In terms of the long-term effects on decisions by entrepreneurs and innovators to set up in Bristol, the exhibition and the publicity surrounding it may well tip marginal decisions in favour of the city. In terms of the absolute value of the experience of the exhibition to those who attended it, we suggest a total value of around £22m and a value per visitor in excess of £60 per head. However it is valued in strictly economic terms, it was, as many others have noted, an event of undoubted significance for the city, the region and indeed the UK creative economy.

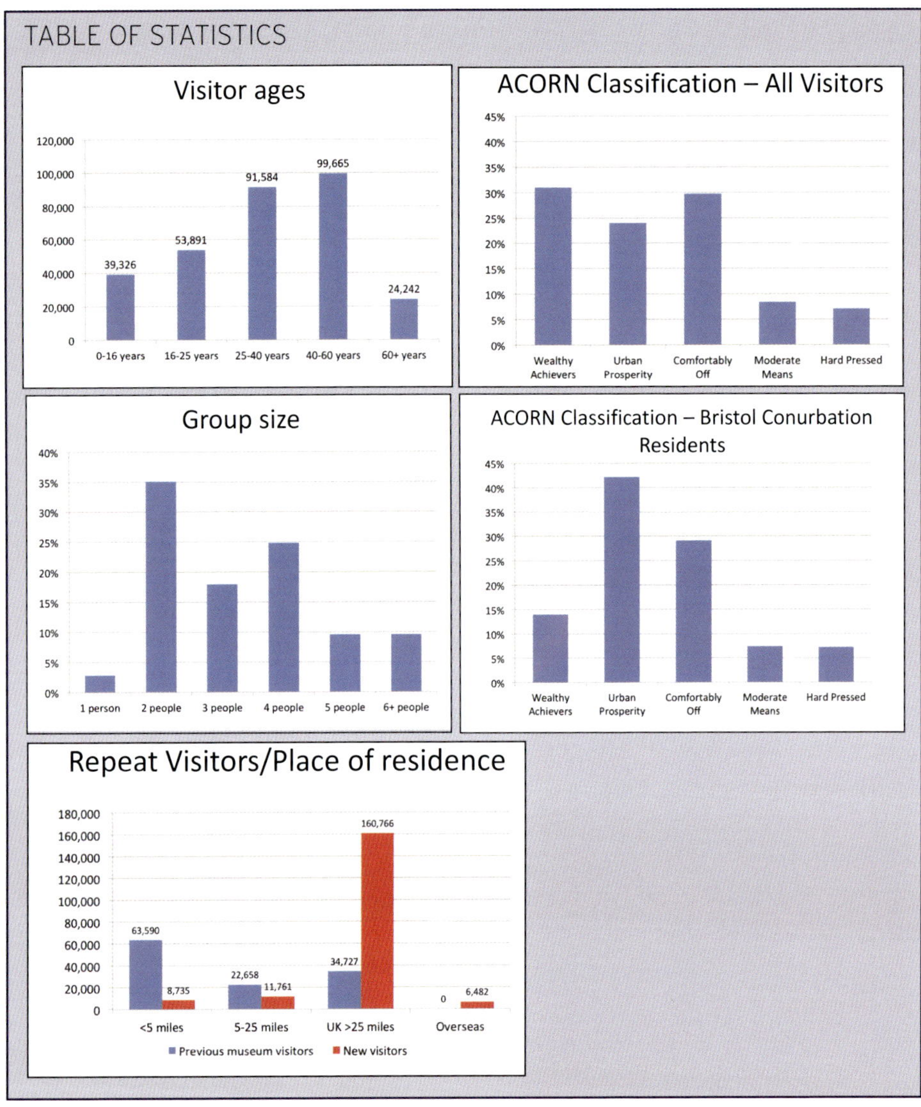

Andrew Mearman is subject leader for Economics at the University of the West of England, Bristol. He has published widely on the design of the economics curriculum, sustainability, and how economists think and work. He has worked to advocate pluralism and the cause of 'heterodox economics', whilst being fundamentally sceptical about the meaning of each.

Anthony Plumridge is an economist who has also worked as an architect and product designer. He teaches Sustainable Business at Bristol Business School, the University of the West of England and is currently working with Arup, Cardiff on the economic impact of the Severn Bridge tolls for the Government of Wales. Anthony lives in the foothills of the Black Mountains tending 12 acres of woodland, orchards and meadows.

Notes

1. We are defining 'the local economy' as within 25 miles of Bristol.

2. This information was calculated from the responses to a survey of exhibition visitors conducted by staff from King Sturge, a local property agent, and Destination Bristol, responsible for tourism in the city. As is revealed elsewhere in this volume, exactly 308,719 people visited the show with 70% coming from outside the city to see it. Some 55,000 extra hotel and bed and breakfast rooms were estimated to be used by visitors to the show. Visitors were estimated to have spent £10.3m in local businesses. Bristolians contributed an additional £4.3m in shops, pubs and restaurants. Just over one in three exhibition-goers lived within 25 miles of the museum. There were a reported 600,000 visits to YouTube's Banksy vs Bristol Museum video, and the museum received £45,000 in voluntary donations.

3. Econ-i was made available by the South West Regional Development Agency (SW-RDA) and is based on an input-output model provided by the University of Plymouth. It can be used to provide an indication of the final economic impact of an initial stimulus. However, it only provides results for the South West UK region as a whole. We have defined the local economy as within 25 miles of Bristol. We have made adjustments to the model parameters to give some approximate impact figures for this smaller area.

The Nelson Street transformation:
Bristol street art reaches new heights. Or does it?

John Sansom

The most dramatic and obvious legacy of the Banksy show was the descent of graffitists from around the world into the drab canyons of Nelson Street in Bristol's central area. The people of Bristol came out in their thousands, loved it, and gave the city council a big 'thumbs up' for allowing the invasion. But once the artists, the scaffolding, the entertainers, the food and drink and the crowds had gone, one had to look at the art itself. After spending a quiet hour or so there, John Sansom had his reservations.

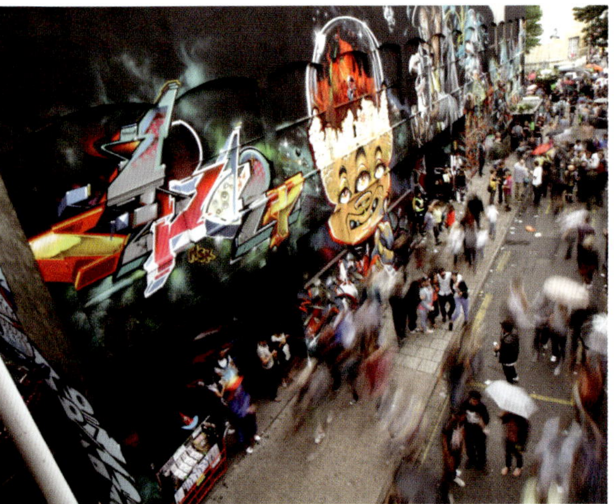

For several days towards the end of August, 2011 a slice of Bristol adjoining the ancient heart of the city was thronged with sightseers. They had turned out to watch more than 60 spray painters transforming a street of dire post-war office buildings into a sea of graffiti. Some of the buildings, including the former magistrates' court, are due for demolition. Events organisers are notorious for hyping numbers, but newspaper reports put the number of sightseers at 16,000 for the first day alone. Photographs in Bristol's *Evening Post* of the milling crowds speak for themselves. Ultra-favourable comparisons were made with the attendances, earlier in the summer, at Bristol's new harbourside museum of local life.

'See No Evil', claimed to be Europe's biggest street art project, cost the city council £80,000 to set up, half of which was reported as being met from the salary of Mike Bennett, appointed in 2010 as Bristol City Council's 'place-making' director.   The trail-blazing

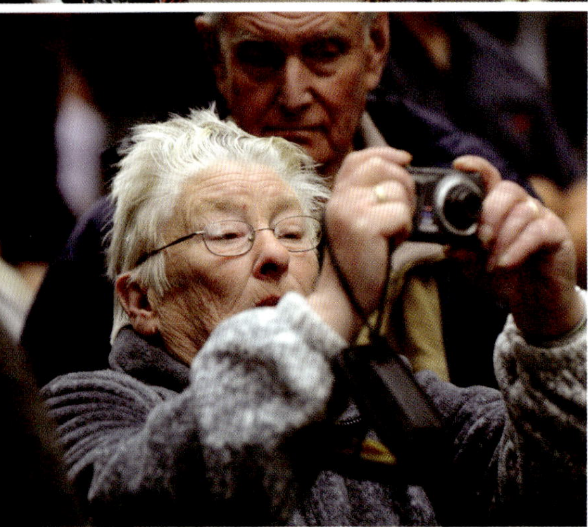

The crowds flocked to see the Nelson Street murals.

project, organised for the city by Bristol street artist Tom 'Inkie' Bingle and Cheba and Sam Brandt from the Weapon of Choice gallery, aimed to attract hundreds of thousands of visitors a year. A similar project in Melbourne, Australia was now a top attraction with getting on for half a million visitors annually.

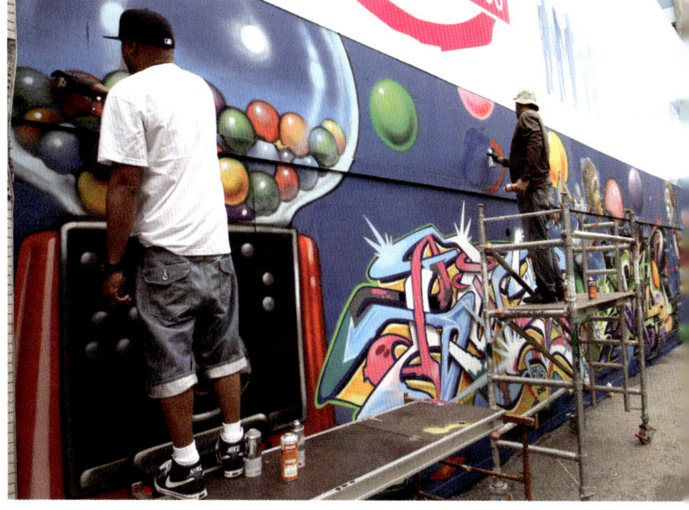

As to the significance of the crowds, we all see what we want to see. In *The Banksy Q*, her ambitious visual record of the 2009 exhibition, Katy Bauer clearly wanted the patient queues to reflect a political bonding with The Outsider challenging The Establishment. To most observers, the crowds at both events spoke of no more than curiosity and folk of all ages and backgrounds enjoying a day out.

The artworks are concentrated in and around Nelson Street, which runs outside the line of the old city wall and indeed one piece abuts onto a window of the ancient city church, St John's on the Wall. A stone's throw or so away are some of the city's finest buildings and streetscapes.

During the event, which included music and other attractions, the air was full of superlatives and self-congratulation. A relieved Mike Bennett, who had been appointed to raise the city's profile and attract more investment into the city, said: 'It's looking fantastic. I've been blown away, shell-shocked by the footfall. It has massively exceeded my expectations. We've had people asking if this is going to be one-off or an annual event.

It seems to have genuinely captured people's imagination. I think what we've got here is a real "Team Bristol" story – one which a lot of people have bought into to make it work.' Organiser Inkie weighed in with: 'It's made the drabbest street in Bristol into the coolest place on the planet for the weekend. It's going to cement Bristol's reputation as a world-wide centre of excellence for street art.'

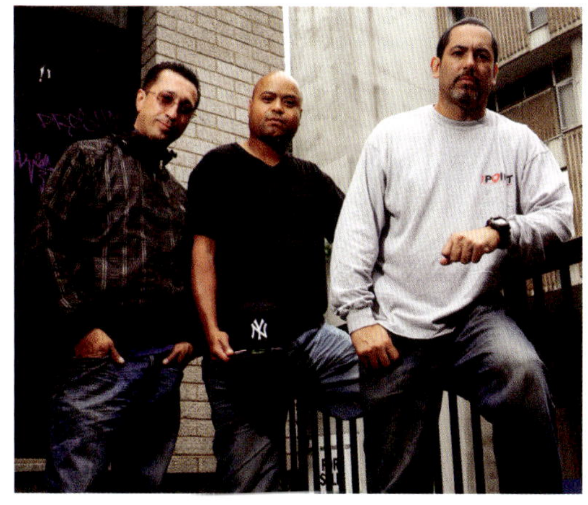

The Tats Cru from New York.

Not to be outdone, Simon Cook, the city council's cabinet member for culture, thought this 'one of the most exciting things that's happened in Bristol for a long time. Basically, we've got some of the best street artists in the world to turn one of the crappest streets in the city into an international destination.'
The *Evening Post's* editor, Mike Norton, added his early praises:

It's art, but not necessarily as we know it. Bristol's innovative project is officially up and running with ambitious works of street art already transforming Nelson Street. Not only will this extraordinary exhibition confirm Bristol's reputation in the alternative art world, it could also attract many visitors to the city.

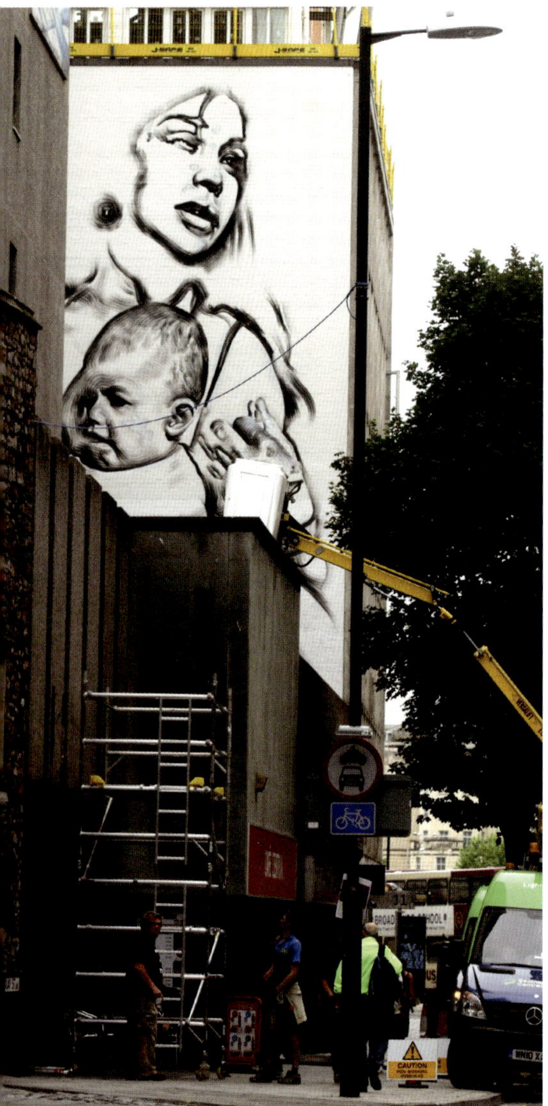
Artist El Mac in a cherry-picker working on his *Mother and Child* above the Blue Arrow building

There are those who cannot see street art as anything other than graffiti. They should join the crowds watching the artists at work. They will quickly learn that this fine, intricate artwork is a million miles from the prehistoric daubs of a tagger.

And anything that makes Nelson Street look better is to be welcomed.

These were early days before a proper assessment of the project could be made, but some *Evening Post* readers were quick to express their doubts. This, from M.T. of Redland:

Who condoned the appalling display of 'art' on the end of Broadmead? Being big does not make it art. Calling it urban something or other doesn't make it art. Being colourful doesn't make it art either – but most of all, real art doesn't look like it was done by a 10-year old with issues.

If what's being done was meant to make the area look better it's failed badly. Is this how Bristolians want their city to be seen?

It would be all-too-easy to dismiss this as a typical knee-jerk reaction, but we would do well to remember that M.T., and others who reacted in similar vein, represent a

largely unarticulated groundswell of popular
scepticism, if not antagonism. Street artists
cherish the thought of Bristol becoming a
leader in their field, but by its nature, street
art is intrusive, 'in-your-face', anti-democratic
and aesthetically unappealing to many. In
their rush to be cutting-edge, the city's
leaders shouldn't forget the hundreds of
thousands who didn't turn out to welcome
the Nelson Street transformation.

As a spectacle, as an enormous street party,
'See No Evil' has demonstrably been an
enormous success. It may achieve what its
funders want: to attract visitors to the city.
And by any definition, the work on display is
'art', but is it *good* art?

This is where the reservations start to creep
in. Overall, there seems little coherence
in the scheme of things. How rigid was
the selection process? One or two of the
works on display are, by any standards,
embarrassingly poor; others, mawkish,
some gratuitously ugly, some chaotic. Not
surprisingly, perhaps, El Mac's gigantic
Mother and Child towering above the Blue
Arrow building, was the favourite among the
people I spoke to.

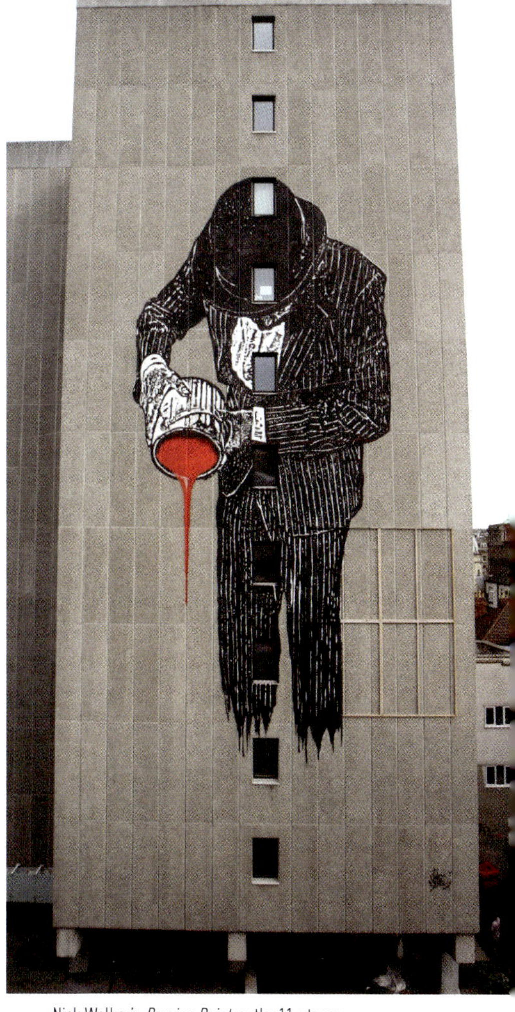

Nick Walker's *Pouring Paint* on the 11-storey
Lawrence House office block.

But there were several impressive pieces. For me, some of the best work
was by Bristol artists, especially Nick Walker's superb *Pouring Paint*,
depicting a bowler-hatted businessman pouring paint down the 11-storey
Lawrence House. I liked also the witty elegance of China Mike's *Birdcage
Man* on Christmas Street.

Where 'See No Evil' perhaps disappoints is in its lack of focus. Was
it intended primarily to promote street art, to boost Bristol's tourist
industry or to provide some remedial attention to a visually ailing corner
of the city? Clearly the first two, but if the latter was a serious aim –
rather than a justification for bringing a massive amount of graffiti into
the city centre – I'm not sure it worked. There is an almost palpable
absence of common artistic integrity. It doesn't take much thought to
suggest alternatives.[1]

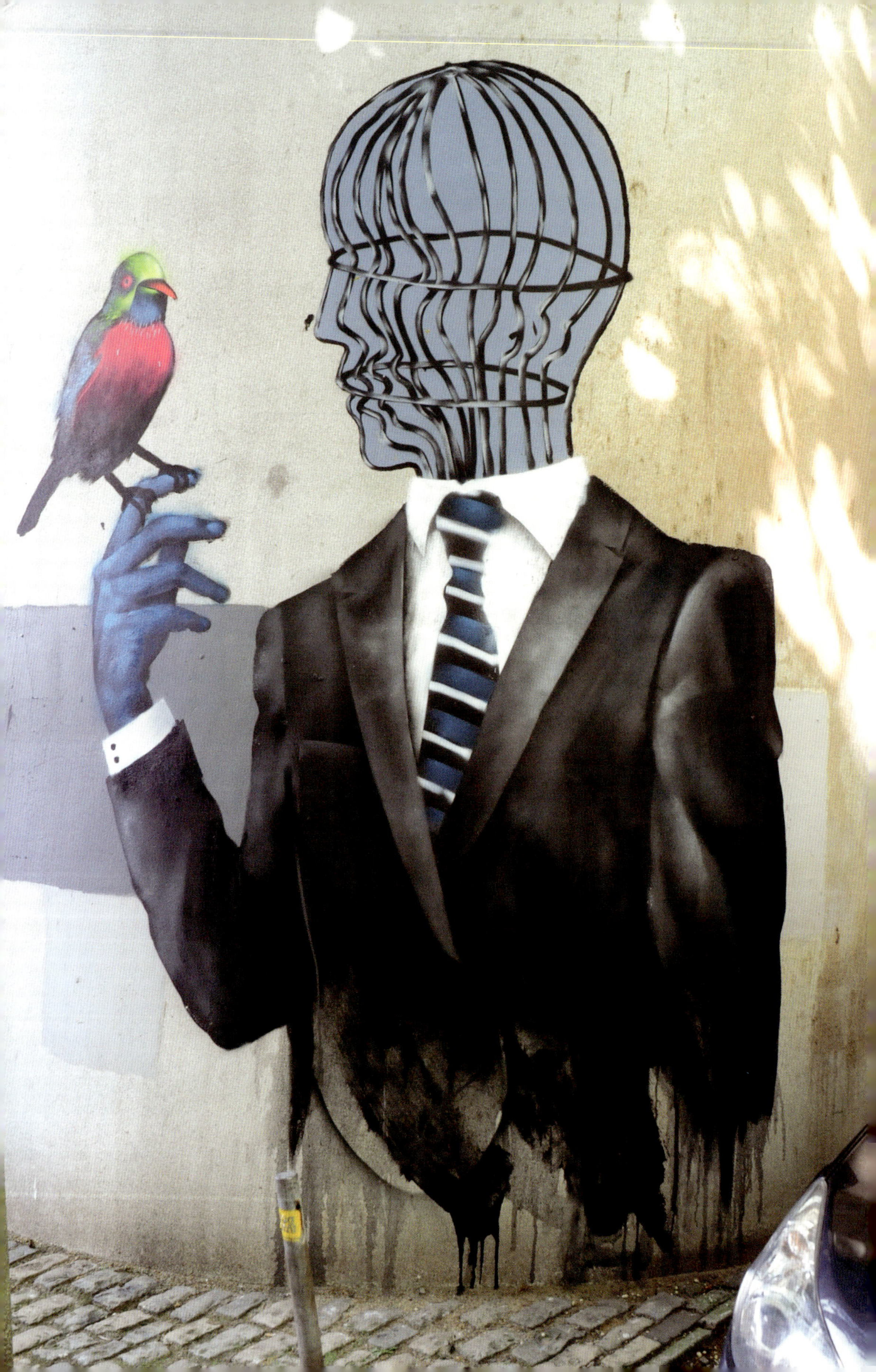

As it is, Nelson Street remains a mess. It is an important route from the
City Centre to Broadmead and Cabot Circus. In a well-ordered world
it would be rased to the ground, or at least its buildings refaced, and
imaginative architects commissioned, perhaps to work with artists – street
or otherwise – to create a truly impressive streetscape. Meanwhile, an
international tourist attraction? As it stands, that's an open question.

John Sansom publishes books about Bristol [now more than 230] and British art from
the nineteenth century to the present day. He has received a number of awards for
services to publishing and to the city of Bristol.   A moderate Banksy fan-cum-sceptic,
he commissioned this much-needed book: a balanced assessment of the Banksy
phenomenon and the impact of the groundbreaking Bristol Museum exhibition.

Notes

1. For example, a judicious number of well placed, discrete [not to be confused with discreet] artefacts of the quality and wit
of the two Bristol artists mentioned in the article, along with large areas of solid colour washes covering individual buildings,
could have worked well: striking, colourful and yet integrated.

(All photographs in this chapter are courtesy of *Bristol Evening Post*)

Birdcage Man, on Christmas Street,
by Bristol artist China Mike.

'Endearing enough,
but it's not art'

David Lee

Performing stunts and living in the public eye are poor substitutes for lasting accomplishment. David Lee argues that being an eyecatching entertainer, who is not really that serious about either dissent or art, is only enough to command interest and respect from the less bright. Even so, the success of the Banksy Bristol exhibition may prove to be a watershed in the State's reaction to popular art.

Don't get me wrong, it's agreeable enough glancing at Banksy's mural as I pedal past on my way up west. There's no faulting its immediacy: two seconds and you have it all. A supermarket chain as God and Authority. Shopping and capitalism as the opium of the masses. How on earth does he think of them? This daub on the side of a chemist (now protected by perspex presumably to preserve its increasing value as a capital asset for the freehold owner) is a diverting addition to the street, a decorative improvement to an otherwise unsightly expanse of flaking plaster. Yes, I'd rather it was there than not.

Encountered accidentally Banksy's little narratives represent clean fun and will, among those who are biddable and whose laughter is cheaply bought, perhaps even raise a chuckle of approval. For these are the interventions of that fondly regarded folklore character, the harmless renegade. If he were too much of a rebel – if he were actually dangerous, for example – we wouldn't indulge Banksy at all. Instead of leaving him alone to continue his serial misdemeanours, the police, who are always supposed to be tracking him down, would have crushed him.

As the fleeting backdrop to pedestrian business Banksy is tolerable enough. But travelling to an exhibition in Bristol, or anywhere else, to see his works *en masse* is another matter. I wouldn't walk a hundred yards, let alone journey a hundred miles, to see a whole show of Banksy because his is not the kind of stuff one needs to see in the original. There is no point in being there. Nothing of the original is missed in newspaper reproduction or when seen on a television screen. The message only, such as it is, is the medium. Attending an exhibition is, therefore, unnecessary unless you wish to use it as a social event, or can think of nothing better to do.

The main reason I didn't visit the Bristol exhibition is that I'm interested in art and when visiting an art gallery this is what I expect to see. It

sounds snobbish, and is intended to be, but I'm too discriminating, far
too knowledgeable in the history of art and its highpoints, to bother with
a show of such facile glibness and perfunctory execution. I need more
than that. Banksy is endearing enough, a hard-working entertainer with a
winning, streetwise attitude and the odd clever quip up his sleeve, but he's
no artist. No art worth anything is a mere gag, a point scored.

I am, however, genuinely curious when informed about Banksy's latest
exploits – his stealing into museums and wrong-footing of the fuzz, and
giving generously to causes good and bad – and relish it like everyone else
when he puts one over on officialdom, or when the public defend his work
against jobsworths whose heads are busy with by-laws. It is fascinating to
watch his carefully stage-managed career unfold – in this respect he has
learned much from his buddy Damien Hirst: the
paintings might be crap but the husbanding of the
reputation is pure genius.

'...a show of facile glibness and perfunctory execution.'

What Banksy does has nothing more to do with art
than the quickly jotted lyrics of a pop ditty relate
to literature. Banksy is not the sort of painter who
would arouse feelings and sympathies because of any special vision he
owns. And his treatment is more or less lifeless and perfunctory, repetitive
even, though undeniably recognisable as his own style. No work he's ever
produced requires more than a moment to take in. And this for me runs
up against the very essence of fine art: namely, something that is new,
different and uniquely stimulating and refreshing every time it is looked
at. The best art is never tired or merely solved. Art is never exhausted,
but Banksy's is out of petrol before reaching the first corner. No one
concerned with art would return for a second glimpse of a work by Banksy,
because there's neither stamina nor depth to them as images, thoughts or
interpretations. Neither love nor refinement informs the execution, but only
functionalism. If what he does is art then it represents a new (and lesser)
species for a generation who can't concentrate on anything for more than
the blink of an eye or the press of a button. His limited technical abilities
are, however, perfectly adequate for what he does, and, apparently, for
his undemanding audience. But – and I repeat – what he does has nothing
whatsoever to do with art. Blanket television coverage of the Bristol event,
no doubt organised by his slickly efficient PR machine, didn't suggest that
he was doing anything more in the museum than he had done a hundred
times before outside it; and by this I mean an illustration with a visual pun
or written punchline. Such material is unworthy of more than a moment of
any serious person's time.

His trite, anti-capitalist messages are little above the level of the greenhorn
undergraduate who has suddenly realised the vile imperfections of the

world he inhabits to which everyone else, he believes, is blind. Thus does Banksy operate at the basement level of Lefty sloganising. His dissent is so harmless it's institutionalised. His posturing is no different to other anti-establishment rebels who eventually come on side and find their natural resting place hung in the museums they purported to despise: and then worst of all, following a polite elapse of time, they accept medals from the Queen. In the end artistic outlaws like Banksy can't resist complacency, the lure of position and official acclaim. Usually they begin their passage to conformity by invoking the legal system, which they began by opposing, to defend their brand, their copyright and by extension their stash. Like Banksy, Marcel Duchamp also denounced museums and art as merchandise, but he didn't loathe their bourgeois connotations and audiences sufficient to resist capitalising on his own fame as the most influential artist of the twentieth century. Eventually he editioned his readymades for ready money because no museum of modern art worth the name could be without its 'found object'. In 1999 the Tate paid over a million for its fake urinal. If there isn't already there'll soon be limited editions of Banksy's best gags in a range of sizes and colour combinations to suit every home. Museums will exhibit his excised walls like holy relics.

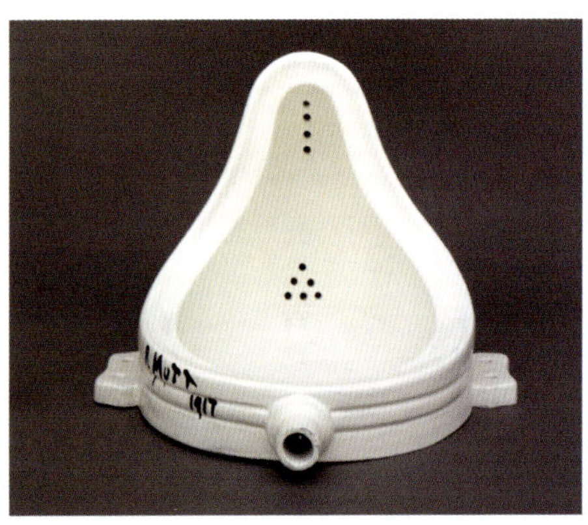

Anticipating Banksy? In 1997 the Tate paid over a million pounds for a Marcel Duchamp 'ready made' urinal. [*Fountain*. Digital image © Tate 2011. © Succession Marcel Duchamp/ADAGP, Paris and DACS, London 2011]

The Bristol exhibition didn't need my attendance. Plenty of youngsters consider Banksy to be a pop star. We are told 300,000 over a period of twelve weeks queued for up to five hours in order to see his Parliament of monkeys, the Madonna and Child draped in ipods and a car wreck in a Claudean landscape. And then there was that classical statue with its designer accessories, sunglasses and bags. Not to mention the circus lion who has eaten his tamer: echoes of Stanley Holloway and Mr and Mrs Ramsbottom there. What sedition! By the way, I never believe attendance figures put about by museums because lying about their popularity is in their interests and has become their deceitful habit. But you can't argue with photos of long queues, which were indeed impressive. Sir Nicholas Serota, whose Turner Prize exhibitions are empty, must have been green with envy. The pious among us will doubtless be delighted at the turn-out for Banksy and point to the possible spin-off that these apparent neophytes, brought in by such catchpenny dross, may decide museums are a good thing after all and return for more demanding sustenance. This is not likely because Banksy's audience has already demonstrated its lack of interest in art by turning out for Banksy.

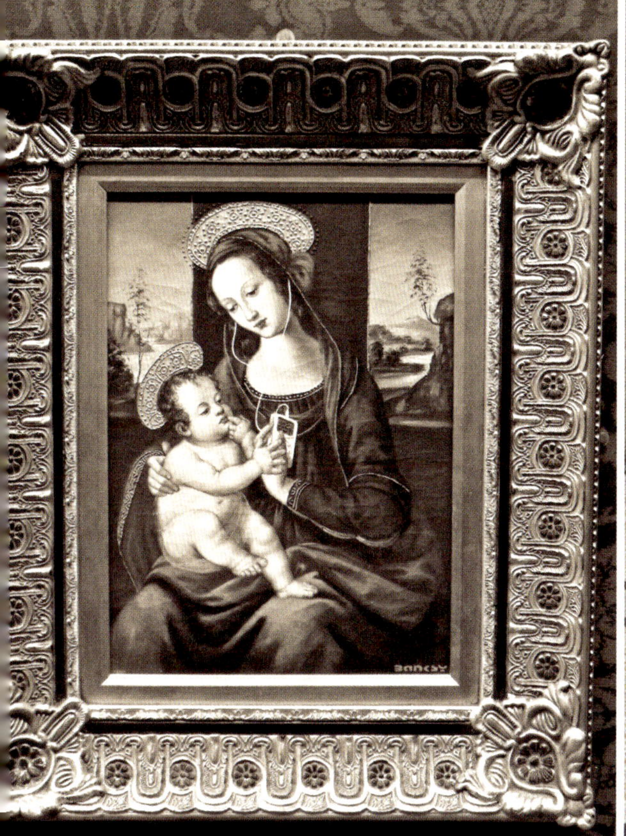

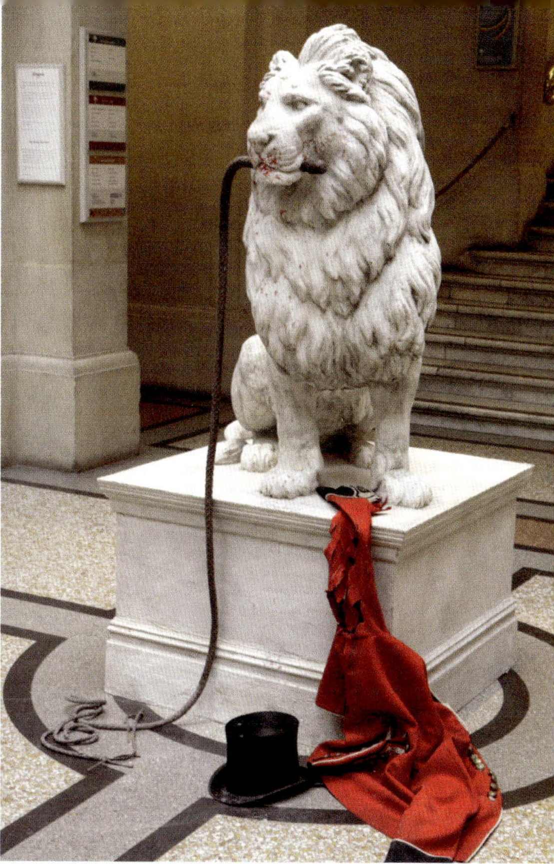

Madonna and Child with ipod: a Banksy intervention which 300,000 queued for hours to see. (These two photographs: Bristol Museum & Art Gallery)

Echoes of Stanley Holloway: Banksy's lion with deceased lion tamer.

The legacy of Banksy's exhibition lies not in his non-existent contribution to art, but in his lesson to the narrowly orthodox art establishment about the power of popular culture which is unpretentious, honest, accessible and free of written gibberish. Banksy exposed the conspicuous lack of appeal in official contemporary art. He proved that if you want to attract hordes to art galleries you have to give them the kind of entertainment they like, the sort they can understand and, in some cases, don't even have to think about; in short, the type where they don't have to be told what they are looking at. Not everyone wants to stare at blank white canvases, or blue ones, or 'significant' scribbles and skidmarks dispersed across half an acre. They don't want to be told that this pile of dust is more meaningful than that one because this special one was put here deliberately by an artist. Who cares if it was? An infant wouldn't be deceived by such casuistry and charlatanism. Despite establishment lies to the contrary, hardly anyone but art students and socialite investors are interested in such things, nevertheless the rest of us have such material shoved down our throats to the exclusion of everything else. Banksy has unwittingly done a great service by proving that the spectrum of art which is admired, and which people are willing to support, is appreciably wider than the 'challenging contemporary art' promoted by the establishment. The Arts Council should also take note. Banksy has informed them that they have a responsibility to all of us not just a few shopkeepers with fashionable artists to market.

Holing the State Art vessel below the water line, Banksy demonstrated that everything that is the best of its type should be shown by an art establishment which too often feeds us a prison diet of trash. The only similarity between Banksy and the young British artists worshipped by contemporary art's influential apostles is that he has learned from them the power of self-promotion and has developed a worrying eagerness for regular doses of recognition. He is eager to catch the public's eye and exhibits dangerous signs of addiction to self-advertisement. Indeed the more one penetrates the phenomenon that is Banksy the less appealing he becomes and the more he appears to be indistinguishable from that common fixture of contemporary art: the self-promoting artist with nothing original to say but a career to advance and money to make whilst the going is good. He is undoubtedly representative of an entrenched process by which the talentless have taken a cruel revenge on serious art.

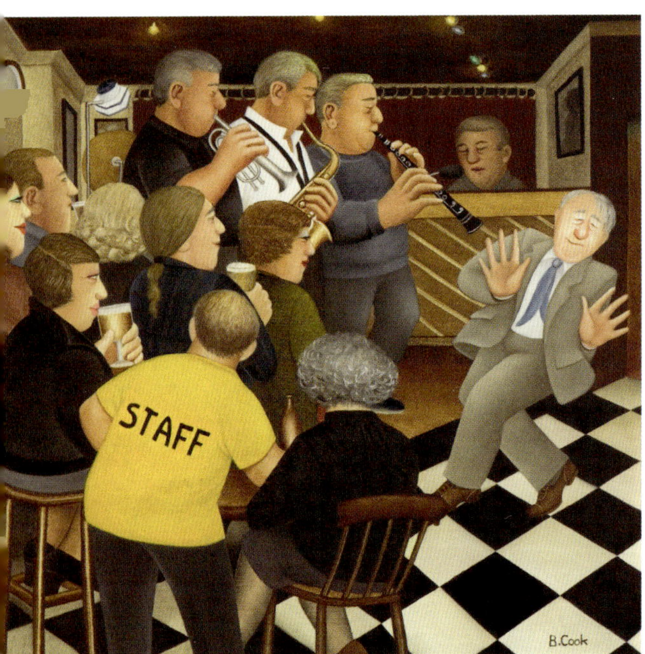

Another Bristol Art Gallery concession to popular taste: Beryl Cook's *Jazz in the Winter.* [courtesy: Bristol Museum & Art Gallery]

Like him or not, the effect of Banksy's Bristol exhibition has been remarkable, if only so far in Bristol. In raising the profile of the museum concerned, the Banksy effect has unleashed a surge of populism. Other museums are envious of the footfall achieved in Bristol – and it has claims to have been the most attended regional art exhibition since 1945. In 2011 Bristol Art Gallery staged a show of another popular artist, Beryl Cook. Just as the Tate won't show any of their 20 pieces by Lowry because, they say, of his popularity, few galleries collect or exhibit works by Beryl Cook and her ilk. At the same moment Cook was showing, the Royal West of England Academy, just up the road, and no doubt envious of the public's response to Banksy, mounted an exhibition of Jack Vettriano, a Scottish artist of undoubted popularity whose work is unrepresented in any museum in the British isles, apart from that in Kirkcaldy, the artist's home town. The problem for Cook and Vettriano is that they don't have the media profile built up so relentlessly by Banksy's promoters. The dealers of popular artists are amateurs compared to those handling Banksy. Only time will demonstrate if there is more public support for the likes of Cook and Vettriano than there is for other kinds of art, conceptual or conventional. It is conceivable that Banksy is unique in his appeal to less discerning audiences.

As museums need to attract more visitors in order to generate income, the example of Banksy will be looked upon as an opportunity to cash in. And it is, intriguingly, only a short step from museums showing popular work to actually collecting it. His exhibition may yet be seen to have marked a watershed in the State's reaction to popular art.

David Lee studied art history and is a former editor of *Art Review*. He is currently publisher of *The Jackdaw*, an independent, mildly scurrilous and occasionally childish art paper, which he founded eleven years ago. In a previous, decent life he worked for *The Times* and was a tutor in photography at the Royal College of Art.

Vox Pop: Thank you, Mr Banksy

Maria Bowers

2pm and the last day of the Banksy exhibition and I'm in the now dwindling queue. I'm reading my John Simpson book and trying to ignore the slightly patronising middle-aged media couple behind me, one of whose brother worked with John and 'didn't like him' much. Thanks. In front I'm quizzical about the three girls in what look like 4-inch stilettoes and incredibly short party dresses, what did they think they were going to see?

 I had been adamant I wasn't going to see the Banksy, hype and all, but it was only on the last day that someone – my 84-year Clifton father-in-law who'd smugly visited twice and 'really enjoyed it' – pointed out that everyone would be talking about it for years to come and that I wouldn't be able to join in the conversations. Good point I suppose, hence a last-minute saunter to Queen's Road, Bristol.

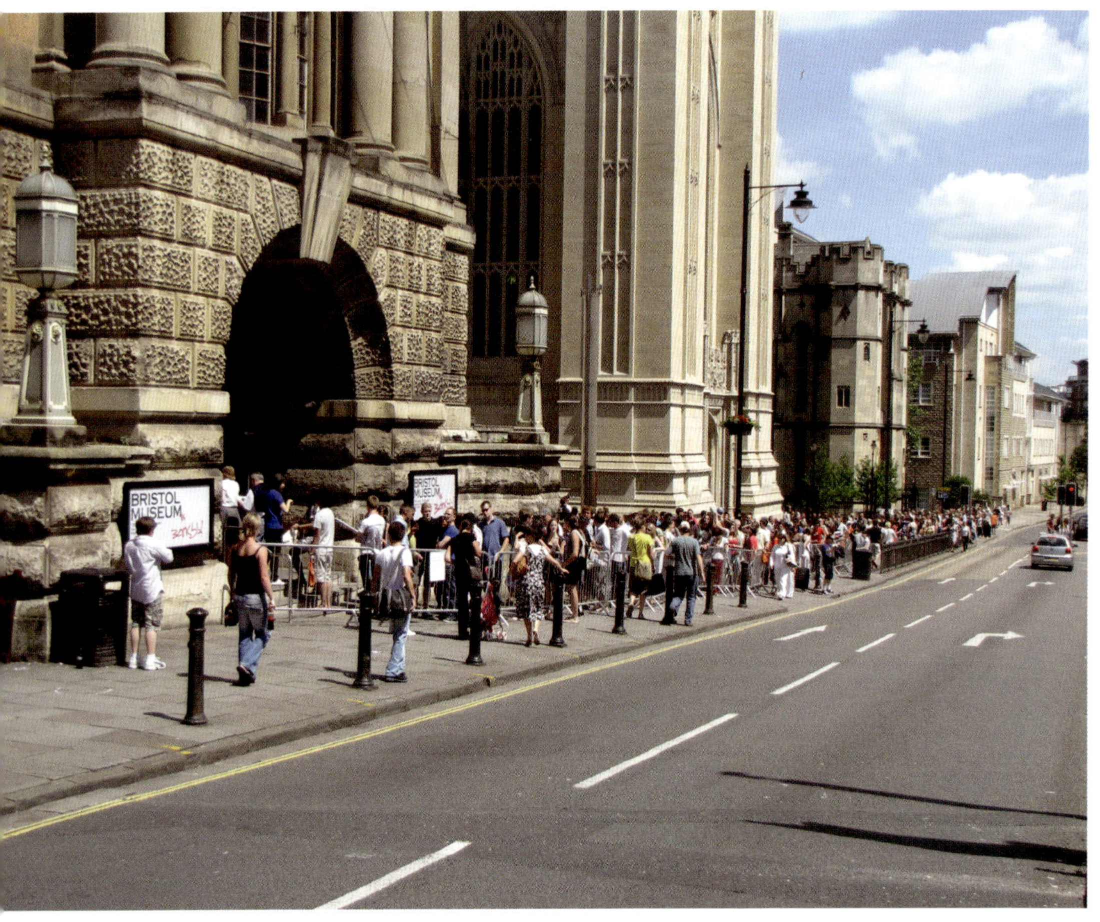

Once in, the ground floor was interesting, the animatronics would have amused my two-year-old but no question of queuing with her as well. The well-known pieces on display were nothing more than I expected and nothing really gave much away that we didn't already suppose. I enjoyed the idea that Banksy himself might be lurking in the darkened room, a social outcast, in his Primark jeans giddy with power watching his awestruck audience in secret before hopping into his Vauxhall Zafira to get back in time for his kids' bath-time and the X-factor.

So I moved on quickly to get away from the crowds and headed for the top floor to work my way around the rest of the museum and spot the pieces hidden amongst the permanent museum collection.

The penis-shaped form nestled amongst the stalagmite collection was fun, as was the brief-case of money in the glass case, but it was only when I got to the rarely visited oriental ceramics section that a new theory dawned on me. Maybe Banksy Bristol Boy was really clever and that this was his way of giving something to his home town. Aside from offering free entertainment to the crowds, and bringing tourism to Bristol, actually getting people to look beyond their noses to explore the amazing collection of permanent artefacts in the museum…? Just to say to people … Look at what is already around you.

I'm probably way off but I'd like to imagine that, as Mr Banksy is now probably in his mid-to-late forties and like me trying to get his kids interested in 'boring' places like museums, maybe that was where the idea first started.

Maria Bowers took a Masters degree in Multi-Disciplinary print making at UWE Bristol, graduating in 2011. Her work has been exhibited in the UK and overseas and she is a member of Spike Print Studio based at Spike Island, Bristol.

Protecting Banksy's Legacy:
a lawyer's view
John Webster

It can be argued that Banksy's work, owing to its artistic qualities, and its political and social statements, carries a cultural significance in modern society. An application for listing under the Listed Building Acts could ensure that the work is preserved for future generations and actions could be taken to preserve landmark street art. Here, John Webster, a Bristol-based specialist planning solicitor, considers the legal position for protecting Banksy's public art as a cultural asset.

It is no castle or cathedral but, thanks to The Beatles and a ten-minute photo-shoot one August morning in 1969, it has just as strong a claim as any to be seen as part of our heritage and as such it merits the extra protection that Grade II listing provides.

Besides being an early Christmas present for Beatles fans, these words, spoken by none other than John Penrose, Secretary of State for Culture, Media and Sport on 22 December 2010, explained why the Government had taken the unusual step of adding the Abbey Road zebra crossing to the statutory list of British buildings of special architectural or historic interest.

Although there are nearly half a million listed buildings nationwide, being granted an entry on this list is far from an easy task. English Heritage (as the Government's advisor) stated that whilst the architectural or structural interest of the crossing was low, the historic interest was so significant that it outweighed the lesser interest of the fabric. The principal reasons given for the designation were the crossing's historical value and the fact that it was made internationally famous by the Abbey Road album. It also had group value alongside the Grade II listed Abbey Road Studios, listed earlier that year, following a vocal campaign to protect the studios from being renovated into luxury flats.

One reason why the historic interest was so vital in achieving listing was because the crossing had been moved several times over the last forty years. Thousands of people from all over the world visit Abbey Road each year to pay homage and have their photograph taken on the crossing, usually in an attempt to 'recreate' the album cover. Given the importance of the setting, it would be reasonable to assume that they would have preferred to have seen and stood on the real thing.

The listing of the Abbey Road crossing is interesting as it raises two key points: firstly, the power of popular cultural appeal in preserving what the public cares about (and perhaps also the political capital carried with it); secondly, it highlights the great flaw in trying to preserve our heritage, in that it is only what stands the test of time which eventually gets protection and unfortunately in the case of the crossing, this is not even what was there originally.

The power of overwhelming public support has also been seen in the 'saving' of the Park Street Banksy. When the work first appeared in 2006, Bristol City Council held an online poll seeking the public's views. Over 90% of voting respondents felt that the work should be saved from removal. A subsequent Council resolution actually prevented the Street Cleaning Team from taking any action to remove the work, as they would have diligently done in the past. As others have commented in this book, this decision caused considerable tension in the Council, but it responded to public sentiment.

In 2009, at the time of the 'Banksy versus Bristol Museum' exhibition, the Council also took the step of carefully removing the results of an overnight paintball attack on the Park Street Banksy, reported locally (somewhat strangely) as 'removing the graffiti from the graffiti'. Some of the blue paint still remains on the work itself today. Bristol City Council clearly saw its duty was to preserve the Park Street work, now that it was in the public interest to do so.

Today, nearly five years after first appearing, it is arguably one of the more famous alternative landmarks in Bristol, with canvas prints (using images taken before the attack) even being sold in English Heritage's online shop.

The approach taken by Bristol City Council was at the time highly unorthodox. Graffiti has traditionally been seen as a menace by local authorities and also by central government. When it appears it is seen as an indicator of decline in amenity or evidence of criminality and therefore something that should be painted over or scrubbed away. Nearly all the laws on the statute books are (not surprisingly) aimed at the entire removal of graffiti and street art, rather than making any allowance for the preservation of it.

It is important to note that some of these legal powers can override the intentions of the property's owner. Even if the owner of a wall wishes graffiti to stay, a local authority can serve a notice under Town and Country Planning legislation which will require them to take steps to remediate the 'decline in amenity'. Failure to respond and carry out steps as instructed can lead to further enforcement action, which includes criminal prosecution or the local authority carrying out 'remediation works' themselves.

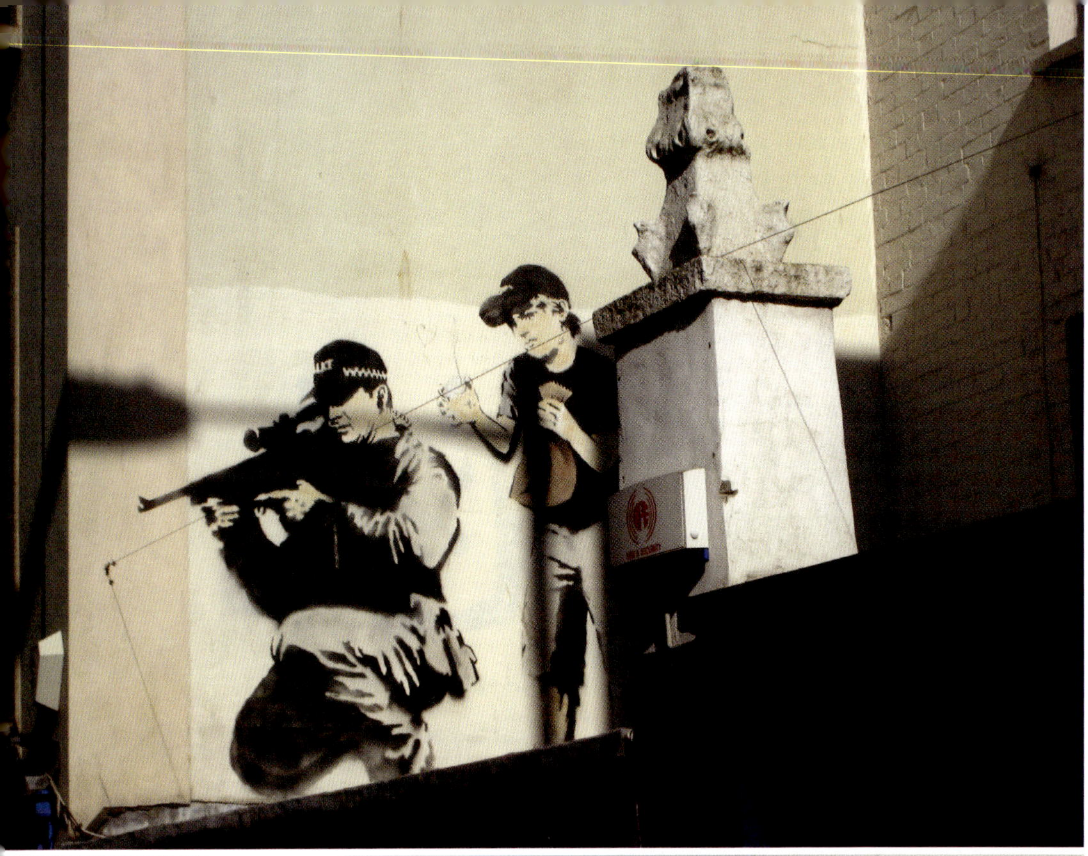

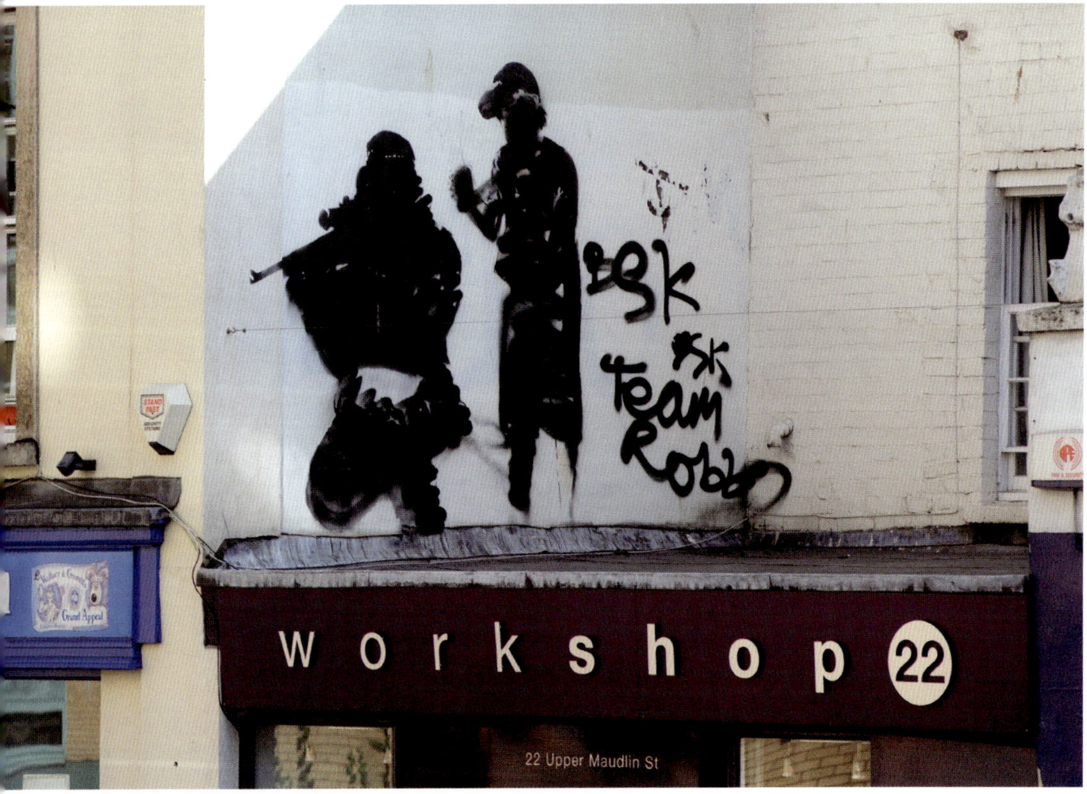

Banksy's Sniper in Upper Maudlin Street, before and after being blacked out by a rival. Listed building protection in itself cannot prevent attacks such as this. [photographs: Paul Gough]

Although a Council could withhold its powers to scrub graffiti or serve statutory notices, the retention of Banksy's work on private property depends on the owner wishing it to remain. The current owners of the Park Street Clinic may be succeeded by a new owner who may wish to paint over the work and have a uniformly coloured wall. This very situation occurred when a ten-year old Banksy stencil, known as the 'Gorilla in the Pink Mask' was accidentally whitewashed over by the building's new owner in July 2011.

It is clear that an original Banksy or other piece of prominent street art cannot be easily replaced if lost. If the Park Street Banksy were allowed to deteriorate further, or the building was demolished at a point in the future, it could even be considered to be a loss within its setting.

The danger of loss creates a serious concern if the public have stated *en masse* that they wish to retain a wanted or cherished part of their environment. A community may wish to preserve landmark or prominent pieces of work for the next generation; indeed, grants could be applied for to preserve the work.

If a community feels strongly about the preservation of a prominent piece of street art, there is a method by which they can secure protection in law. An application for listing under the Listed Building Acts could ensure that the work is preserved for future generations and that actions could be taken to preserve landmark street art.

Bestowing a building listed status is not only a recognition of cultural value, it is also affords considerable protection under the law. However, the effect of listing is serious. Those who visit the Abbey Road crossing commonly sign their names on the Belisha beacons at either end; they also 'mark' or sign the Abbey Road sign itself and the walls alongside Abbey Road Studios. For any part of those buildings which are listed, it means that those who do 'make their mark' could be committing a criminal offence in damaging a listed building. A decision to make an application should not be taken lightly. There is certainly a difference between stating that something may be informally kept on the wall and giving it the benefit of legal protection.

It is open for any individual or group to submit an application for listing the Park Street Banksy. By construction of case law it could be possible to list a 'Banksy' work spray-painted to a wall. It can arguably satisfy the physical legal tests of annexation. The comparative youth (in heritage asset terms) of a 'Banksy' work must also be outweighed by the fact that the work is under real threat. The argument rests then on Government policy and the willingness of the property owner and a community to strongly support such an application. A listing application relies heavily on the historic interest argument that is being advanced, and upon the existence of significant social and cultural importance.

If statutory listing is a step too far, it may be worthwhile to take advantage of the shift in thinking of some local authorities, which is leading away from the idea that all graffiti should be considered the same. A community-led agenda could be promoted to introduce a 'Street Art Policy' to preserve and maintain what is considered to be high quality, prominent or landmark graffiti. Such a policy could set out further provisions for retention or removal of graffiti and a mechanism for public consultation. A Street Art Policy indicating that a local community wishes an approved piece of graffiti to be considered for preservation could be used as part of the justification for a future listing application.

Thus street art could find a policy footing within strategic planning, through local plans. In fact, Bristol City Council is considering bringing forward a Street Art Policy which will encourage neighbourhood groups to identify pieces of street art of significance for inclusion within a local list. This will not just include graffiti-based street art. The effect of such a 'local listing' is twofold: firstly, it will recognise the value which the community places on the street art and secondly, it will help prevent accidental damage by the property's owner or agents.

Although the Listed Building Planning System gives the greatest protection, it is not designed for the purpose of preserving graffiti and it would require both a policy and legal argument to justify a listing. Any action would be a test case. However; it is unclear who would actually object to the listing if the owner is complicit and if there is overwhelming community support for such an application.

It is clear (as many contributors have stated in this book) that when a 'Banksy' appears it will be appreciated by some and hated by others. There are, therefore, valid arguments against proceeding with statutory protection. Many people believe street art should remain a transitory art form and that permanence, especially if secured by legal protection, will fundamentally change its nature and should out of principle be resisted. There is also understandable resistance to the idea of singling out one particular artist, who holds mainstream recognition, as being more worthy of protection.

Those taking such polarised views will either seek to preserve and cherish, as was the case with Bristol City Council's protection of the Park Street Banksy, or attempt to destroy, by either paintball attacks or some other form of deliberate removal. As was proved in autumn 2011 by the despoliation of the 'sniper' stencil opposite the Bristol Royal Infirmary, even the most prominent of Banksy's street paintings can be vandalised by rivals.

The only tool presently available to those who want to take a further preservation step is using legal protection. In the case of street art, this should be instigated by a community that has decided what they wish to keep, through a locally-owned process instead of imposition from above. Making decisions at a local level, on local issues, is the reverse of the 'establishment' deciding what has merit and what hasn't. The overriding concern, however, is not about who the artist is, or what he has done in the past, but what a community wishes to preserve in their own surroundings.

John Webster is a solicitor specialising in Town and Country Planning Law, with a particular interest in listed buildings and conservation. He currently practises and lives in Bristol.

This chapter is taken from John Webster's Master's dissertation, a portion of which was published in the *Journal of Planning & Environment Law* entitled 'Should the work of Banksy be listed?'

The article in the *Journal of Planning and Environment Law* received considerable national press attention. However, correspondents to the on-line web page 'The Lawyer', which ran a long piece on 13 October 2011, were more divided. One reader 'Alex' answered the question 'Should the work of Banksy be listed?'

'The answer is no because there are far more important things to be discussing than Bristol's tourism opportunities. It is articles like this that have created such a ridiculous hype surrounding the so-called 'Banksy effect' and turned him from a bloke who liked to paint walls into some kind of folk hero legend who has somehow done a great service to the city. Has he supported local causes? Has he helped sort out the city's social problems? No, the only people who have benefited are poncey [sic] art collectors and the Council who are selling him off as a tourist attraction.'

Banksy: the urban calligrapher

Paul Gough

In the closing pages of _Wall and Piece_, Banksy offers some helpful (if pretty idiosyncratic) advice on making stencils. Unfortunately, only two of the eleven tips actually refer to the precise process of designing, cutting, and spraying, namely:

· A regular 400 ml can of paint will give you up to 50 A4 sized stencils. This means you can become incredibly famous/unpopular in a small town overnight for approximately ten pounds.

· Spray the paint sparingly onto the stencil from a distance of 8 inches.

The other nine tips are provocative and caustic, quintessential Banksy-speak, amongst them:

· Mindless vandalism can take a bit of thought.

· The easiest way to become invisible is to wear a day-glo vest and carry a tiny transistor radio playing Heart FM very loudly. If questioned about the legitimacy of your painting simply complain about the hourly rate.

· Try to avoid painting in places where they still point at aeroplanes.

It's not that stencilling is technically easy, nor can it be reduced to a simple set of instructions. It's a precise art form that requires methodical processes and an eye for simplified two-dimension design. That much is clear from a photograph of Banksy's studio, its floor strewn with A1 stencils assembled into life-size figures. At a glance you can see the precision needed to conjure up a facial expression or the folds in clothing. Cutting out a single letter or a 'Nike tick' logo is pretty straightforward; 'drawing' the bling on the silhouette of a street rat takes an artistic eye and a steady hand.

The origins of Banky's interest in stencilling is well known. In a tract of autobiographical writing he relates how at the age of eighteen while trying to paint 'LATE AGAIN' in silver bubble lettering on the side of a passenger train in Bristol, he was chased by British Transport Police. Deserted by his mates (who had made it to their getaway car) Banksy spent over an hour hidden under a dumper truck with oil leaking over him:

As I lay there listening to the cops on the tracks I realised I had to cut my painting time in half or give up altogether. I was staring straight up at the

It was a creative breakthrough. Crawling home undetected, he later told
his girlfriend he'd had 'an epiphany' (to which she allegedly replied that he
ought to stop taking that drug as it was bad for his heart).

It is significant that Banksy's breakthrough occurred in a goods yard. Stencils
are essentially an industrial graphic – economic, spare, instructive. They have
their aesthetic root in utilitarian styles of signage used by the military, utility
companies and governments. Stencilled lettering and logos are found on
packaging, industrial goods, and temporary signs that must be obeyed, or
at least followed. A well-cut stencil will spell out a simple, bold message in
two-tone, with no grey scale, no in-between, no middle. They have the smack
of the military, the language of authority, they shun ambiguity, they are the
official calligraphy of mass production. Their adoption by graffiti artists is
a canny ironic twist in their customary use, 'mocking it by subverting its
meaning through the artful juxtaposition of image and text', or through the
witty remixing of familiar icons, symbols, phrases.

So what actually is a stencil? How do you make one? It's usually a thin
sheet of material, card, paper, plastic, or metal with letters, numbers or
a design taken out of it. Cutting the stencil requires a bit of forethought
and some dexterity with scissors or a blade. Working from a sketch or
a drawing, sections of the material are cut away to create the positive
forms of the design; every so often interior sections – 'islands', as they are
called – have to be connected by narrow 'bridges' of material that must be
left intact. It's these 'bridges' that lend traditional stencils their particular
graphic character, their taut economy of shape. They also help keep the

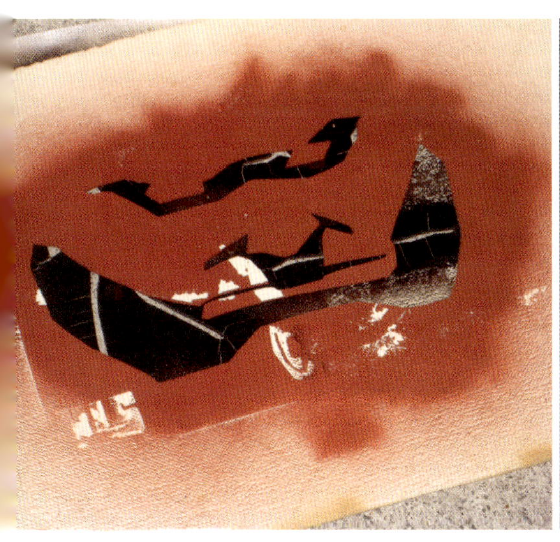
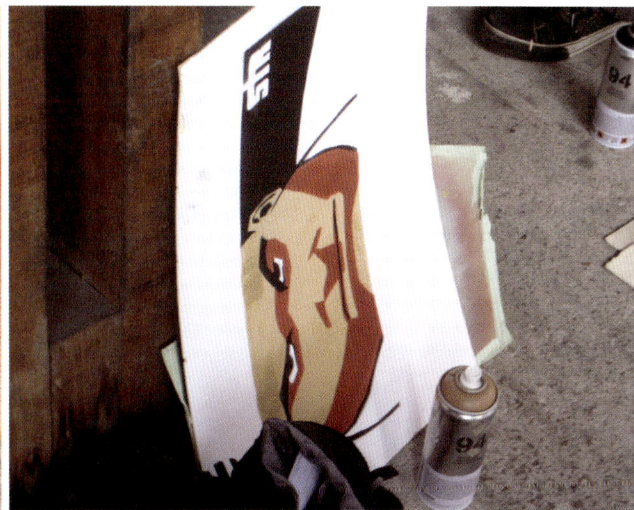

Stencil, Bristol, Bristol UPFest, June 2011. (photograph: Harry Gough)

stencil robust enough to be re-usable. Without them the template would lose its form, it would wilt at the intensity of the aerosol jet, would become floppy and difficult to hold in place – quite a liability for a clandestine street artist working at night, in fear of being spotted and caught.

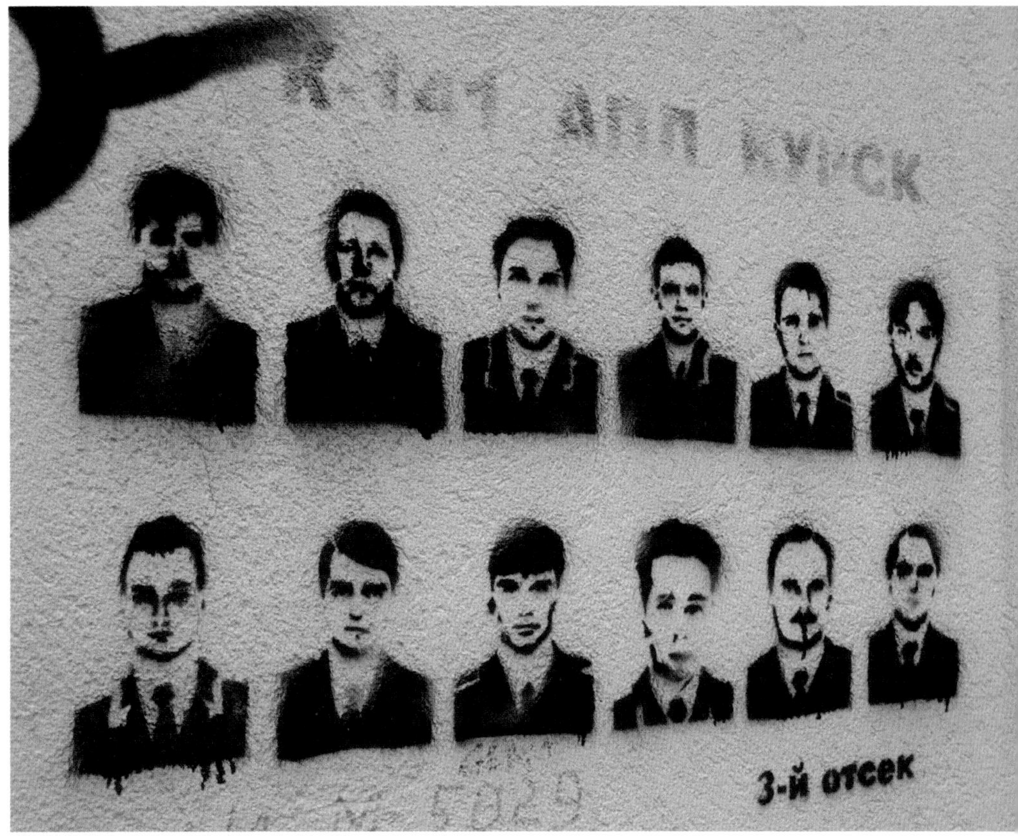

Stencil artwork, near Grand Canal, Venice, August 2011. (photograph: Paul Gough)

As well as its striking simplicity, the real advantage of the stencil is that it can be re-used to rapidly produce the same motif over and over again, a particular boon to the early graffiti artists such as Blek le Rat who is reputed to have created the first pre-stencilled poster in Paris in the early 1980s. Also credited with the invention of the life-sized stencil, Blek was one of the first to transform the basic letter stencil into a pictorial form capable of considerable sophistication.

Acknowledging Blek's influence on his own work, Banksy has written 'that every time I think I've painted something slightly original, I find out that Blek Le Rat has done it as well, only twenty years earlier.' In turn, Blek has taken issue with those who argue that the Bristol-based artist is little more than an imitation of the French master:

People say he copies me, but I don't think so. I'm the old man, he's the new kid, and if I'm an inspiration to an artist that good, I love it. I feel what

From his early, rather crude, stencils of chimpanzees adorned with slogan-stencilled tabards ('You're No Safer in First Class', District Line, London Underground, 2002) Banksy's stencils have become increasingly more sophisticated. He has progressed from the simple silhouette – Nipper the HMV Terrier pointing a Milan Missile Launcher at the Horn of the Record Player, or the Banksy 'ape' stencilled onto a yellow wheel clamp – to stencils that needed multiple templates. His striking image of a goggle-eyed dustbin on legs (painted in Brick Lane, east London in 2005) for example, clearly required an initial stencil of black body tone (for the trousers and the deep shade of the bin), a mid-grey for the shoes and the cylindrical surface of the metalwork, and a final addition of white paint to add an ironic punchline – the myopic peering eye poking with alarm from the lid. A final, fourth, stencil would have been needed to paint the solid black question mark hovering over this very strange assemblage.

However, as with all proficient painters, Banksy selects the method best suited to the motif, the message is strongly allied to the medium. He uses stencilled lettering where an icon will just not do – writing 'FAT LANE' on a sidewalk in Venice Beach, USA (2003), for example – and where he wants to mimic (and of course, mock) the conventional street lexicon, such as 'Cycle Lane', 'Mind the Step', and so on.

On occasion he will reverse the silhouette, painting white on black – such as the pale vertical ladder crawling up the face of the Peace Wall at Abu Dis, or the 'Grim Reaper' figure rowing alongside the *Thekla* in Bristol harbour. Compared to the economic simplicity of the small black silhouetted rats (which have become the painter's trademark) the larger ghostly white stencils are a little more painterly, the painter's approach is less mechanistic, possibly less rushed. There is a rather strange unevenness in the distribution of the white spray, which gives the figures a more haunted, elusive look. None more so than the stencilled white image of an angelic down-and-out in West London (2002) armed with wine bottle, cigarette and broken halo.

So, returning to Banksy's eleven (not especially relevant) tips for the stenciller. Are they useful? At street art displays or urban paint festivals you can freely watch graffitists at work. Whereas the freehand painters are rather relaxed about displaying their skills, happily showing off their dexterity with the spray can or the chunky felt pens, the stencillers are a little more reluctant to impart their secrets. Perhaps it's the industrial nature of the process, the methodical arrangements of one shape over another, the rather monotonous way they 'label' the wall rather than draw their images. If you watch closely, they're even a little furtive, taking their

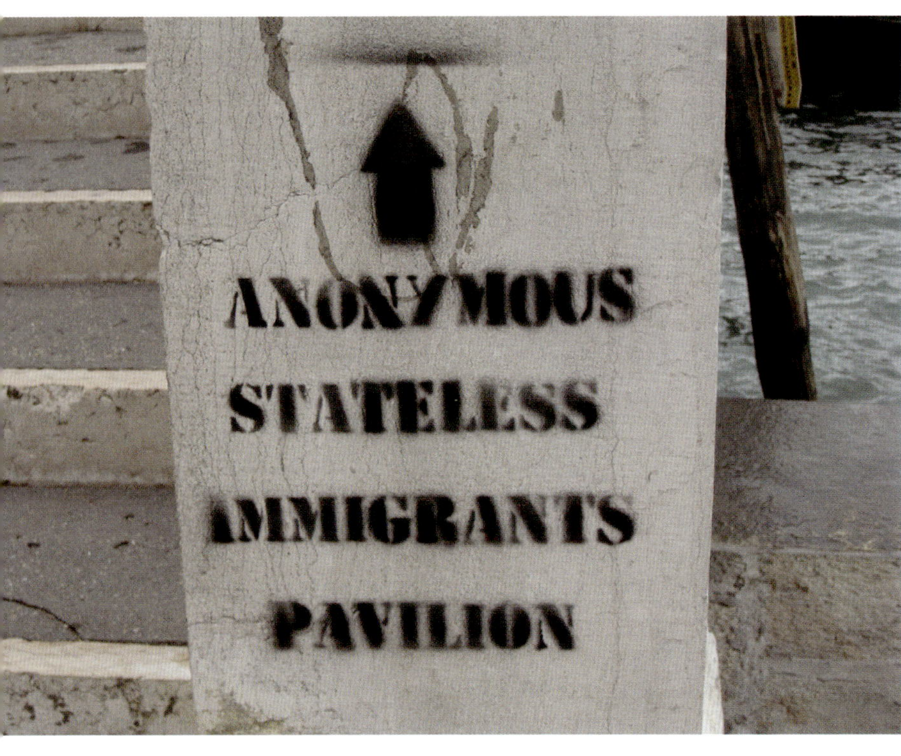

Anonymous Stateless Immigrants Pavilion stencil, Ponte della Paglia, Venice, August 2011. (photograph: Paul Gough)

precious card templates from their folios one at a time, making sure they don't share them with their rivals, sliding them back into the folio the moment they have used them.

Apart from the flick of a wrist as they direct the nozzle, there's little 'craft' involved. They don't cut the stencil there and then; it's all pre-fabricated. Are these the printmakers of the fine art world? A breed of technophiles capable of producing dazzling results but somewhat embarrassed that their work is reprographic not autographic; machined rather than wrought by hand, industrial rather than crafted.

That's a rather harsh judgment but you can tell that it rankles. It may be the reason why Banksy took to paint on canvas and gilt frames for his Bristol show in 2009; indeed it may be the presiding legacy of the show – that anyone can cut a shape out of a piece of card, hold it to a wall and liberally spray or paint the negative shape to produce a positive motif. It explains the rash of copycat and wannabee Banksys that litter our urban surfaces, but it doesn't explain the continuing popularity of a genuine Banksy.[3]

Notes:

1. Banksy, *Wall and Piece*, p.7.

2. Coan, Lee (13 June 2008). 'Breaking the Banksy: The first interview with the world's most elusive artist'. *Daily Mail* (London). www.dailymail.co.uk/moslive/article-1024130/Breaking-Banksy-The-interview-worlds-elusive-artist.html.

3. See for example the regular rash of 'Banksy sightings' such as 'Has Banksy been busy in Weston?' in *The Weston Mercury*, March 15, 2001. www.thewestonmercury.co.uk/news/has_banksy_been_busy_in_weston_1_829967

The Last Word

So, after all that, what has been the lasting impact, if any?
The tangibles are plain to see: Bristol has become an epicentre for festivals of street art; it is firmly on the global map, attracting artists from all over the world, only too happy to pitch themselves against 80-foot concrete walls, or to animate grim inner-city roadways with lurid designs the size of cinema screens. Despite being licensed by the city council, the artform still divides the public. There are those who flock in their tens of thousands to watch the spray-painters and hooded stencillers; others stay firmly indoors preferring to fume in the letters pages of the local newspapers. Others are indifferent. Yet, despite the fans and the festivals the art form might actually be dying – or at least mutating – precisely because it's being legitimised: many street artists have abandoned the alley for the gallery, creating multiples and prints that now adorn local and national collections. In London, the Victoria and Albert Museum began quietly collecting such work in 2004, five years before the blockbuster show in Bristol. Around the same time Banksy began inserting his own irreverent artefacts into museums in London and New York. Had he sensed the shifting times? Was he ahead of the curve? Was his Bristol show in 2009 actually an awkward attempt at institutional validation?

With a rather smaller budget than many national collections, Bristol Museum and Art Gallery saw an opportunity on the back of his show to become a centre for the display and temporary curation of street art (if that's not a contradiction in terms). Banksy's remix of the Bristol galleries and its collections threw down a quite radical challenge to the very institution that had invited him in: could one day the artists actually take control, devising their own programmes, implementing their own ideas rather than watch as others curated on their behalf? The discussion is still very much alive as Bristol asks 'Well, we did Banksy – what next?' Indeed, regional galleries and museums look with envy at what Bristol achieved, though they don't relish the risks they took in the run-up to the exhibition, nor the challenge of working with an artist, his crew and his PR machine notorious for insisting things are done strictly to their terms. One phrase that I heard over and over again during the creation of this book was that everything had to be done 'by his rules'.

However, as we have discovered in this book, the economic impact was short-lasting; the press coverage – despite its extraordinary global reach – was ephemeral, and the social legacy difficult to calibrate; nebulous at worst, anecdotal at best. And yet, as is clear from the hundreds of blog sites, the 'apps' and the vast photo-albums that can be browsed on-line, Bristol still buzzes audibly with the aftermath of the show. In any one week

there is a fresh Banksy story – whether it is the defacement of one of his
signature pieces, a new sales record set in some distant auction house, or a
spurious stencil found in Weston-super-Mare – and most visitors recall with
a mix of pride and bravado exactly how long they queued to see the show,
even those who actually sneaked in or left it too late.

Someone said recently that 'Blogging isn't writing. It's graffiti with
punctuation.' It's an accusation that could easily be aimed at Banksy –
stencils aren't proper painting, it's just tracing with a spray can. Yet the
Bristol exhibition showed an artist in the full flow of his creative powers, a
former 'tagger' now capable of working in multiple dimensions on a grand
scale; a group leader able to motivate and direct a large production team,
pulling off a brilliantly conceived stunt that would have been applauded (or
at least envied) by many of his artistic contemporaries and predecessors,
whether they be the Surrealists or the Situationists, Warhol or the YBAs.

So, there can be no last word. The project is still very much alive, wriggling
like one of those animatronic pork sausages in a fusty bap tucked away
in the dark recesses of the Bristol show. Banksy may have entered the
mainstream, stepping out of the shadows of urban Britain into the glitz of
Hollywood, but (with his anonymity intact) he still has an unerring ability to
pass penetrating comment on the hot issues of the day. His Tesco-labelled
Molotov cocktail print is a case in point; brilliantly timed to irritate those who
had cosied up to him, it was designed to offend and thrill in equal measure. It
was also a timely reminder of the power of the visual over the written word.
After all Banksy is an artist, a cocky one-liner perhaps, a filmmaker one day
possibly, a new category of painter definitely, but an artist all the same.

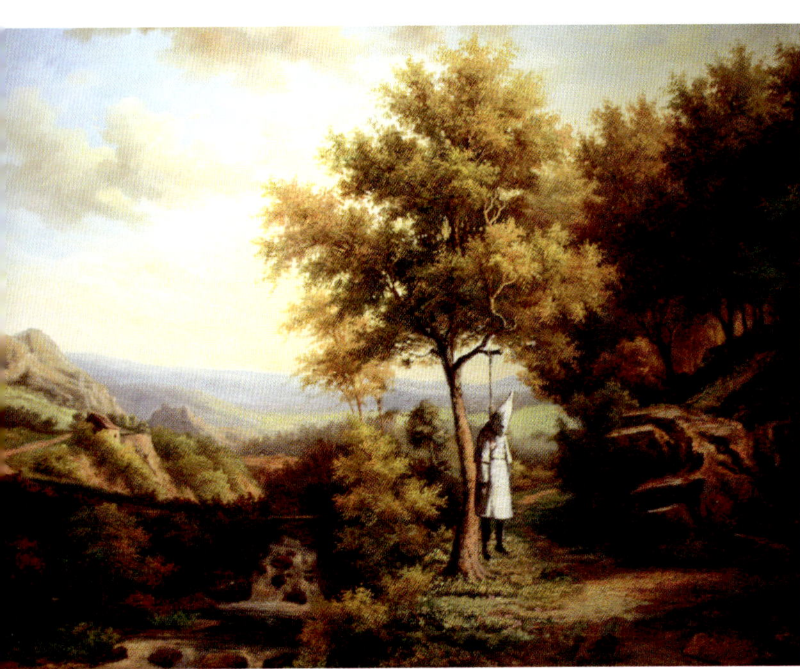

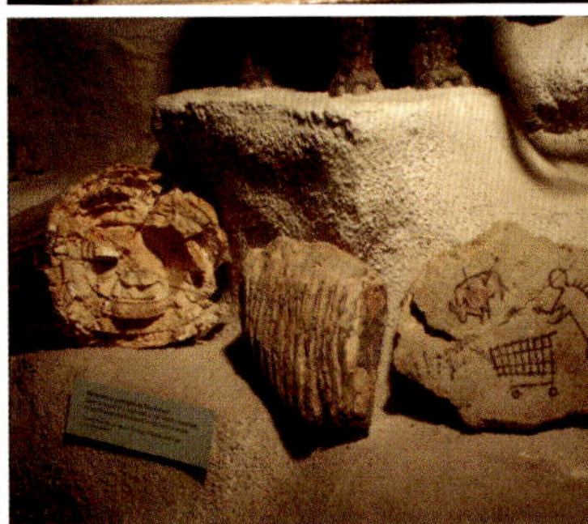
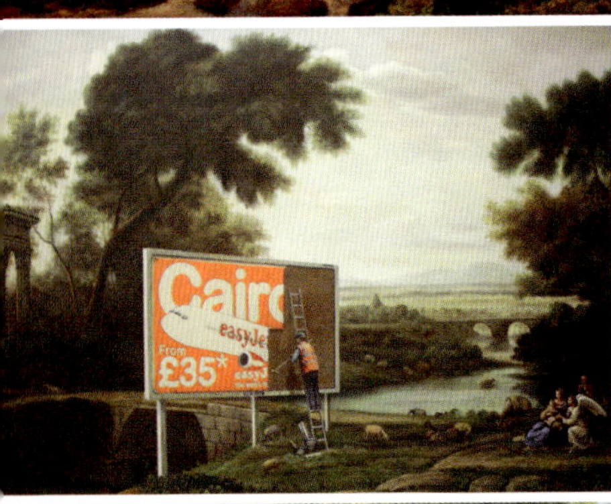

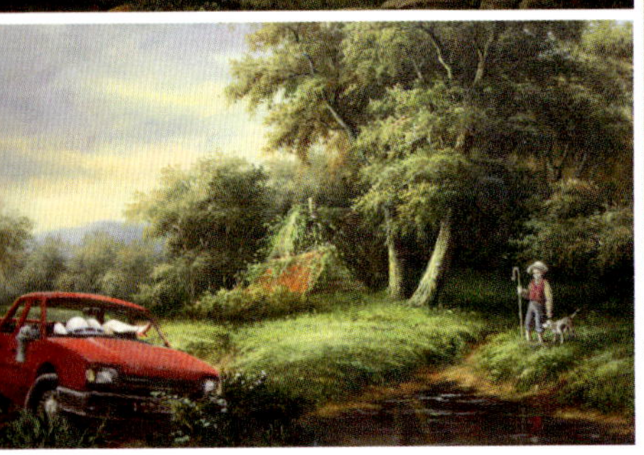
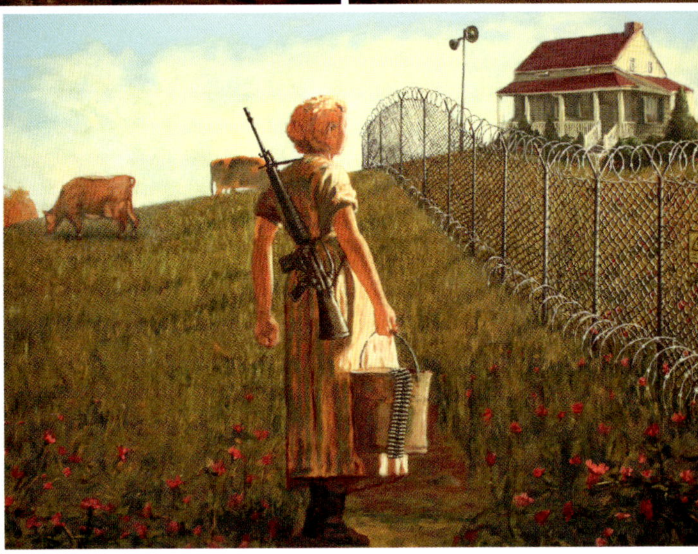

More images from the 'Banksy versus Bristol Museum' exhibition in 2009. [photographs: Dr Shawn Sobers and students from the BA Hons Photography course at UWE Bristol]

Further reading about Banksy, his art, and his milieu

This bibliography is set out in six sections

- Books by Banksy
- Books about Banksy
- Books with reference to Banksy
- Unpublished theses/dissertations
- Journal articles
- Recent newspaper articles, since 2009

1. Books by Banksy
Wall and Piece, Century: London, 2005.

Banksy. *Banging your Head against a Brick Wall*, self-published, 2001.

Banksy. *Cut it Out*, self-published, 2004.

Banksy. *Pictures of Walls* – Conceived and compiled by *Banksy*, Pictures of Walls Ltd, London, 2005.

Banksy. *Existencilism*, self-published, 2002.

2. Books about Banksy
Bauer, Katy and Chris Chalkley. *The Banksy Q*, Tangent Books: Bristol, 2010.

Blanché, U. *Something to s(pr)ay: Der Street Artivist Banksy. Eine kunstwissenschaftliche Untersuchung* 2010.

Bull, M. *Banksy Locations & Tours: A Collection of Graffiti Locations and Photographs in London*, Volume One, Shellshock: London 2006.

Bull, M. *Locations (and a Tour) Vol. 2. More Graffiti Locations from the UK*, Shellshock: London 2010.

Gough, P. (ed.) *Banksy: the Bristol Legacy*, Redcliffe Press: Bristol, 2012.

Wright, S. *Banksy's Bristol: Home Sweet Home*, ed. Richard Jones. Illustrators Mark Simmons and Trevor Wyatt, Tangent Books: Bristol, 2009.

3. Books with reference to Banksy
Alonzo, P. and Peter Doroshenko. Curators. *Spank the Monkey*, Saarbrücken: Verlag, 2006.

Catalogue of an exhibition held at BALTIC Centre for Contemporary Art (Gateshead), 27 September 2006-7 January 2007. Includes works by Aya Takano, Banksy, Barry McGee, Chiho Aoshima, Davis Shrigley, Dr. Lakra, Miss Van, Ryan McGinness, Shepard Fairey, Takashi Murakami, and other artists.

Fisk, P. *Creative Genius*, Chichester: Capstone. 2010. Contains a section on Banksy: 'When Graffiti becomes a work of art'.

Ganz, N. *Graffiti World: Street Art from Five Continents*. Abrams: London, 2006.

Gough, P. 'The 'versus' habit: Bristol, Banksy and the Barons'. In: Andrews, M., Bagot Jewitt, C. and Hunt, N., eds. *'Lest We Forget': Remembrance and Commemoration*, The History Press: London, 2011. pp. 128-132.

Hirst, Damien, and Hans-Ulrich Obrist. *In the Darkest Hour There May Be Light: [works from Damien Hirst's Murderme Collection: Francis Bacon, Banksy, Don Brown, Angela Bulloch…],* Serpentine Gallery: London, 2006.

Kuittinen, R. *Street art: Contemporary Prints,* V&A Publishing: London, 2010.

> Contains running references to Banksy and his contribution to street art, proclaiming him to have created a wholly new category of artist.

McCormick, C. Schiller, M. and Schiller, S. *Trespass: A History of Uncommissioned Urban Art.* Taschen: Coln, 2010.

> In addition to covering graffiti and unsanctioned work the book includes dozens of previously unpublished photographs of long-lost works and legendary, ephemeral urban artworks. A special feature is an exclusive preface by Banksy

MacPhee, Josh E. D. T. R. F. *Reproduce and Revolt,* Turnaround: London, 2008.

> Both a striking collection of images and a graphic toolbox for political activists this book suggests that there is a great deal more to the genre than Banksy, from eager 'politickers' to street art aficionados.

Mathieson, E. and Xavier A. Tàpies. *Street artists: The Complete Guide*. Graffito Books: London 2009.

Montague, B. *A Year on the Sauce.* O Books: Alresford, 2011. Print. Includes a section entitled 'Banksy Backlash: Is Bristol graffiti artist a public school toff?' (pp.148-151)

Morris, S. *Further off the Wall: Bristol Street Art*, Redcliffe: Bristol, 2011.
Morris, S. *Off the Wall: A book of Bristol Graffiti*, Redcliffe: Bristol 2007.
Morris, S. *See No Evil*, photographs of the Nelson Street graffiti project, Tangent Books: Bristol 2011

Parry, W. *Against the wall: The Art of Resistance in Palestine,* Pluto Press: London, 2010.

Peiter, Sebastian, and Goetz Werner. *Guerilla Art,* Laurence King: London, 2009.

Sartwell, C. *Political Aesthetics,* Cornell University Press: Ithaca, 2010.

*United Kingdom Graffiti Artists: M. I. A. , Banksy, Cartrain, Ben Eine, D*face, the Cans Festival, Charles Uzzell Edwards, Paul Insect, Moose,* General Books LLC: Memphis, 2010.

4. Unpublished theses and dissertations

Bengtsen, P. 'Faile Vs. Banksy: an Investigation of the Unsanctioned Urban Expression and Its Development in the Transition from the Street to the Gallery.' Dissertation, Lunds universitet/Avdelningen för konsthistoria och visuella studier, 2007.

Gilmour, A. 'A comparative study between site specific work in dance and site specific work in graffiti. using Trainstation by Seven Sisters Group and the work of Banksy as representations.' BA Hons dissertation, Dartington College of Art, 2007.

Mckaness, William; O'Connor, Liam 'Why Here and Not There? a Gis Approach to Graffiti.' MSc Dissertation, University of Edinburgh, 2010.

Parker, T. 'Intertextuality and dialogism in street art: D*Face, Swoon, Banksy' MA dissertation, Howard University, 2009.

Stephens, S. 'Fun with Vandalism: the Illegal Street Art of Shepard Fairey and Banksy'. Dissertation, University of Cincinnati, 2006.

Westendorf, E. J. 'Banksy as Trickster: The Rhetoric of Street Art, Public Identity, and Celebrity Brands', BSc dissertation, Ohio University Honors Tutorial College, 2010.

5. Journal articles
'Banksy Artwork Appears on London Pharmacy Wall', *Pharmaceutical Journal*. 280.7493 (2008): p.295.

Brassett, J. 'British irony, global justice: a pragmatic reading of Chris Brown, Banksy and Ricky Gervais', *Review of International Studies*, 2009 Volume 35.

Chung, Sheng Kuan 'An Art of Resistance: From the Street to the Classroom', *Art Education,* July 2009, Volume 62, Number 4, pp.25-32.

Dickens, L. 'Placing post-graffiti: the journey of the Peckham Rock', *Cultural Geographies,* Volume 15, Number 4 (October 2008), pp. 471-496.

Dickens, L. 'Pictures on walls? Producing, pricing and collecting the street art screen print', *City.* February 2010, Vol. 14 Issue number 1-2, pp. 63-81.

Edwards, I. 'Banksy's Graffiti: A Not-so-simple Case of Criminal Damage', *Journal of Criminal Law;* August 2009, Vol. 73 Issue: Number 4, pp.345-361,

Kennard, P. 'Art attack', *New Statesman,* Volume 137, Number 4880 (21 January 2008), p.38.

Mount, Nick. 'Searching for Banksy', *Queen's Quarterly* 117.2 (2010): pp.262-271.

Raychaudhuri, Anindya. "'Just as Good a Place to Publish'': Banksy, Graffiti and the Textualisation of the Wall', *Rupkatha: Journal of Interdisciplinary Studies in Humanities,* 2010. Volume 2 Number 1.

Slenske, M. 'The gangster.' *Modern Painters*, Volume 22 Number 7, 2010

Seifert, Lauren S and Roberts, Ian D. 'Strictly street art', *PsycCRITIQUES,* Volume 55, Number 42, 2010.

Truman, E.J. 'The (In)Visible Artist: Stencil Graffiti, Activist Art, and the Value of Visual Public Space'. SHIFT: *Queen's Journal of Visual & Material Culture.* Issue 3, 2010, pp.1-15.

Visconti, L.M. 'Street Art, Sweet Art? Reclaiming the "Public" in Public Places', *The Journal of Consumer Research,* Vol. 37, No. 3 (October 2010), pp. 511-529.

Webster, J. 'Should the Work of Banksy Be Listed?', *Journal of Planning* and Environment

Law. 4 (2011) pp.374-385.

'What We Can Learn from Banksy – Text in Landscape', *Green Places*. Issue 59 (2009): p.32.

6. Newspaper articles, selected from UK and US newspapers written since 2009
Adams, G. 'Did Banksy's latest work bring misery to a homeless man?', *The Independent* (19 March 2011).

Adams, G. 'Hacked Off: The art show that's driven Banksy up the wall', *The Independent* (3 September 2011).

Akbar, A. 'The story goes on, anon', *The Independent* (2 March 2011).

   The anonymous author of O: *A Presidential Novel*, which is a thinly disguised imagining of Barack Obama's 2012 campaign for re-election as President, has now been identified as Mark Salter. Discusses how the practice of anonymity is a powerful marketing tool, recalling the hunt for the author of *Primary Colors* in 1996, the intrigue and market value of Banksy's graffiti art, the excitement about Daft Punk, and the success of erotic blogger Belle de Jour.

Appelo, T. 'Banksy's Stealth Oscar Campaign', *Hollywood Reporter* (19 February 2011) p.16.

   This article reports on the so-called British graffiti artist 'Robert Banks' (sic) Oscar campaign under which he promoted documentary *Exit Through the Gift Shop* with a guerrilla paintings around Los Angeles.

Appelo, T. 'Banksy artwork pushes up bids on derelict pub'. *Estates Gazette* (27 February 2010) p.65.

   This article reports on the sale of the Grade II-listed former Whitehouse pub on Berry Street, Liverpool in England which featured the largest piece of authenticated graffiti by artist Banksy for £114,000, although (allegedly) the winners of the bid were not interested in the Banksy graffiti.

Bates, S. 'Banksy's gorilla in pink mask painted over', *The Guardian* (15 July 2010).

Battersby, M. 'Urban myths', *The Independent* (7 October 2010).

   A review of new exhibitions of street art at the V&A ('Street Art: Contemporary Prints from the V&A' and 'New Work by Fresh Paint' at the Herbert Art Gallery, Coventry). The shows featured work by Ben Wilson, Ben Eine, Paul Insect, Meggs, Banksy and others. Discusses whether such anarchic work really belongs in a gallery: V&A curator Gill Saunders believes that it is, though ephemeral, a type of performance art.

Battersby, M. 'The gloves are off', *The Independent* (21 April 2011).

Child, A. 'Urban renewal', *Financial Times* (28 January 2011).

   Child interviews London art gallerist and collector Steve Lazarides, who 'discovered' graffiti artist Banksy in 2001. In 2007 he was at the centre of the urban art boom, and continues to expand his street art empire, opening a new gallery in Newcastle and staging his largest US show yet in December 2011.

Daily Mail 'Reporter' 'Banksy's graffiti is part of the nation's heritage and deserves protection by law', *Daily Mail* (22 August 2011).

Dolan, Matthew. 'If You Take Street Art Off the Street, Is It Still Art?' (cover story). *Wall Street Journal* Eastern edition (9 March 2011).

   This article discusses controversy over a slab of cinder block removed from an abandoned factory in Detroit, Michigan containing graffiti that may have been drawn by Banksy. Members of the 555 Nonprofit Gallery and Studios removed the section of wall in an effort to preserve the art. The owner of the factory, Bioresource Inc., is suing to recover it.

Fairey, Shepard. 'Banksy', *Time* Magazine, Vol. 175, No. 18 (10 May 2010) p.96.

Gruber, Fiona. 'Banksy Versus the Bristol Museum (Bristol City Museum and Art Gallery).'TLS, *The Times Literary Supplement.* (31 July 2009).

Januszczak, W. 'Banksy goes home to shake-up Bristol: Elusive graffiti artists talks on eve of largest project to date, infiltrating the Bristol collections (with permission)', *The Sunday Times* (14 June 2009).

Januszczak, W. 'Banksy takes over the Bristol City Museum', *The Sunday Times* (21 June 2009).

   Review of exhibition, 'Banksy Versus Bristol Museum', at Bristol City Museum. Argues the critic: 'The show is great fun but far too respectable. Banksy is as witty as ever and every nook and cranny of the museum holds a fine one-liner, making an amusing commentary on the grubby little world in which we live. The big change is not in the artist but in the setting and the fact that the museum director was in on it from the start. What is being destroyed here is not just Bristol City Museum's anonymity but Banksy's 'raison d'etre'.'

Jones, A. 'Tunnel visions', *The Independent* (12 October 2010).

   Jones interviews artist Steve Lazarides, who is best known as Banksy's dealer and the 'godfather' of graffiti artists. He and fifteen of his protégés had produced an exhibition of street art and installations – 'Hell's Half Acre' – for Frieze Art Fair in London, sited in a dark and dank tunnel under Waterloo station.

Leopold, S. 'Banksy Revealed? The Zorro of street art talks about his new film, Los Angeles and, of course, Mr. Brainwash', *L.A. Weekly* (8 April 2010).

Mills, E. 'Banksy woz 'ere' *The Sunday Times* (28 February 2010).

Pacey, E. 'Bag a Banksy', *Design Week* (23 September 2010).

   The article provides an overview of the company 'Don't Panic', which is a distributor of club and arts flyers in Great Britain.

Potter, A. 'Where shock art is still dangerous', *Maclean's* (24 May 2011).

   This article presents the author's views on art as a form of dissent and people's growing inability to be shocked by it. The author discusses public attitudes towards art and general complacency, noting how it has changed artists' boundaries. Information is also provided on Chinese performance artist Cheng Li and artist Ai Weiwei, describing the arrests of artists in China for disturbing social order.

Relph-Knight, L. 'There's plenty of creative talent in the South West – but where are the writers?', *Design Week*, Volume 25, Issue 49 (12 September 2010).

In this article the author discusses the abundance of creative talent in the South West of England indicated by the integration of advertising and design in which there is a shortage of good writers across the South West.

Sawyer, M. 'Take a stuffy old institution. Remix. Add wit. It's Banksy v the museum', *The Guardian* (13 June 2009).

Sherry J. F. Jr, et al. 'Symbiotic postures of commercial advertising and street art', *Journal of Advertising*, Volume 39 Number 3 (2010): pp.113-126.

An ongoing tension between new ways of achieving novel, meaningful, and connected forms of expression is permeating the practice of advertising and igniting a lively academic debate. Novelty and social connection have long been preoccupations of art worlds. In this paper, we explore the creative tensions and synergies between countercultural and commercial communication forms of street art and advertising. Viewing each form as a species of rhetoric, we analyze a set of rhetorical practices employed by street artists that not only reflect, but might also be used to shape, commercial advertising in the near future.

Sandbrook, D. 'The art of outrage', *New Statesman* (2 August 2011).

Sharp, R. 'Meet the heirs to Banksy', *The Independent* (14 August 2009).

Topping, A. 'Banksy graffiti feud given a fresh coat: Banksy alters King Robbo "tag" on Regent's canal', *The Independent* (23 April 2010).

Tuckey, B. 'Warning: Graphic content', *The Independent* (16 May 2010).

The three books advertised on the following pages all relate to
the stories told in *Banksy: The Bristol Legacy.*

Further off the Wall is a collection of photographs by Stephen Morris of
street art in Bristol, including some by Banksy.

See No Evil is photographer Stephen Morris's take on the remarkable
street art project in a run-down area of central Bristol. The results of the
project are analysed in *Banksy: The Bristol Legacy* in John Sansom's article
'The Nelson Street Transformation'.

The Banksy Q sees Katy Bauer working the queues outside Bristol Museum
& Art Gallery to create a photographic record of the event and to canvas
members of the queue to offer their own drawings to illustrate her book.
She has contributed an article to *Banksy: The Bristol Legacy.*

FURTHER OFF THE WALL
BRISTOL STREET ART

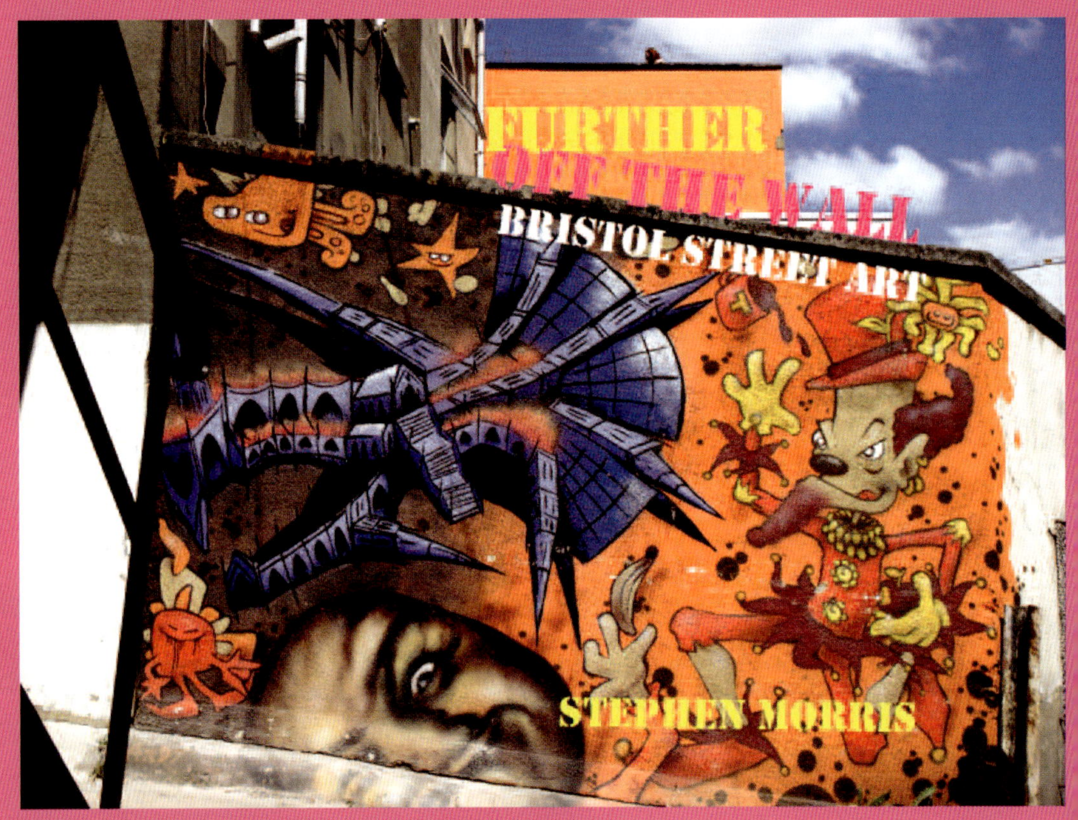

Stephen Morris

Published by Redcliffe Press Ltd ISBN 978 1 908326 02 7
64 pages with 80 illustrations softback £5.00

www.redcliffepress.co.uk

The Banksy Q

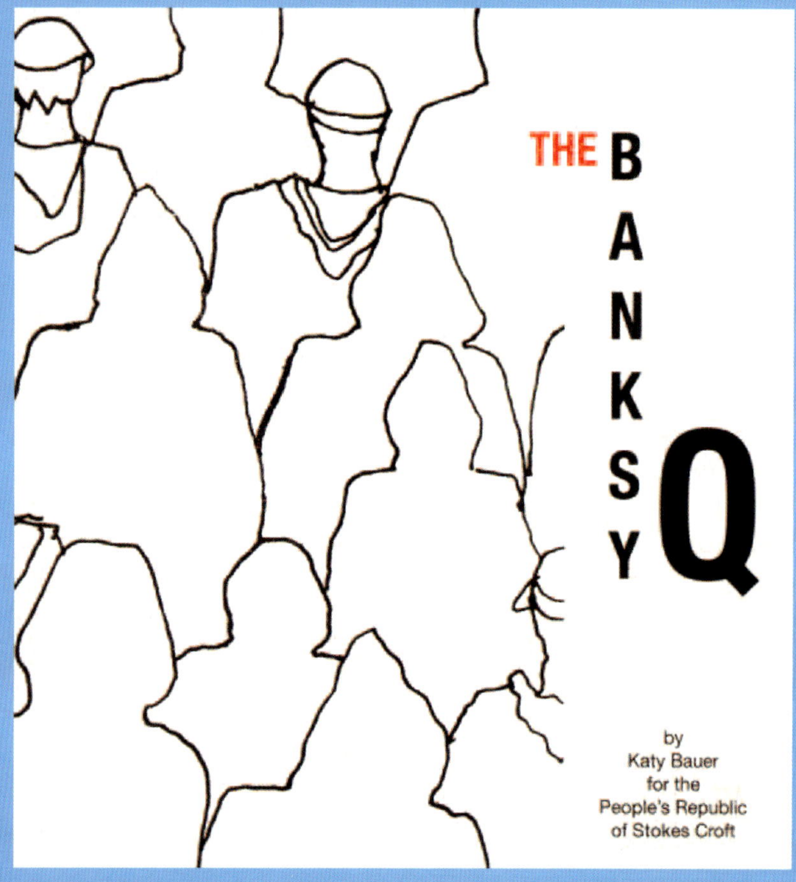

for the People's Republic of Stokes Croft

Published by Tangent Books ISBN 978 1 190647742 4   134 pages with almost 100 illustrations softback £12

www.tangentbooks.co.uk

About us

Redcliffe Press publishes a wide range of books from Bristol art and architecture to poetry and from biography to historic gardens.

An associated company, Sansom & Company publishes books on British art and artists, specialising in the twentieth century and contemporary. It has a growing sculpture list.

For more information, please see our websites:

www.redcliffepress.co.uk
www.sansomandcompany.co.uk

or for a 48-page catalogue of our current and forthcoming art titles email info@sansomandcompany.co.uk or write to:

Sales Department, Sansom & Company Ltd., 81g Pembroke Road, Bristol BS8 3EA

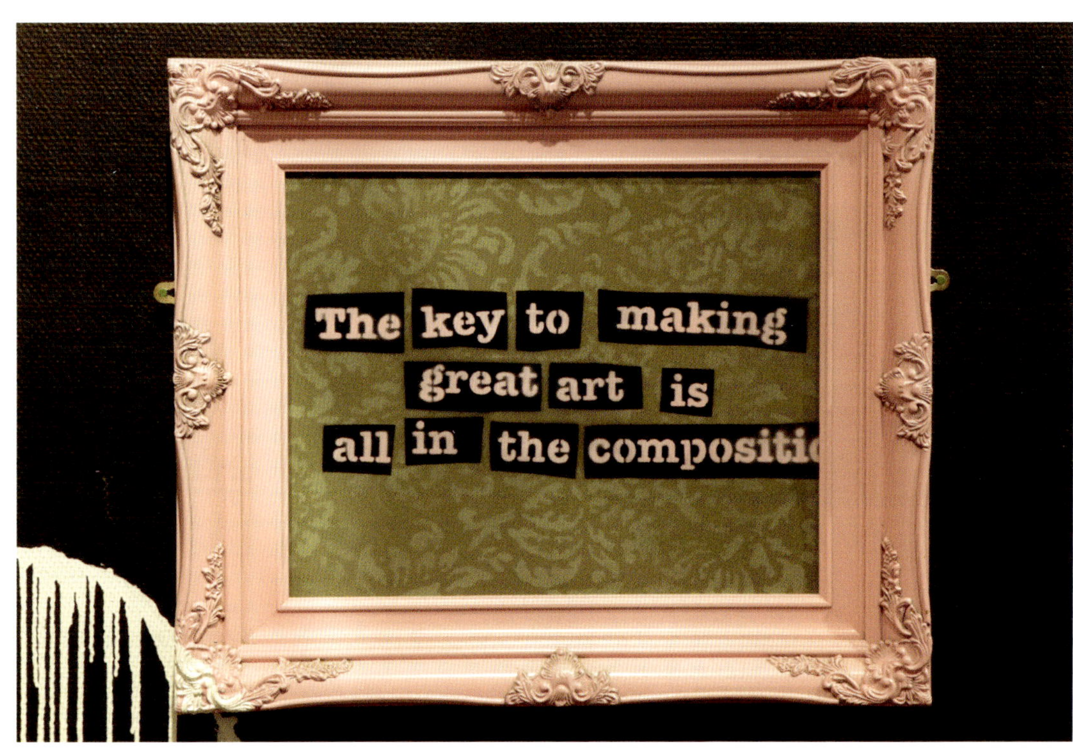
The key to making great art is all in the compositi